Leo XIII and the Modern World

LEO XIII and the MODERN WORLD

Edited by
EDWARD T. GARGAN
Loyola University

SHEED and WARD - NEW YORK

LIBRARY OF CONGRESS CATALOG CARD NUMBER 61–7288

This book is based upon a symposium held in Chicago, Ill., March 18, 1960, under the sponsorship of the Department of History of Loyola University, to commemorate the sesquicentennial of the birth of Leo XIII. All the papers in this volume were presented at the symposium with the exception of those by Raymond Schmandt and Eric McDermott, S.J.

NIHIL OBSTAT:
    JOHN R. READY
    CENSOR LIBRORUM
    JANUARY 28, 1961

IMPRIMATUR:
    †ROBERT F. JOYCE
    BISHOP OF BURLINGTON
    FEBRUARY 2, 1961

I WANT TO SEE THE CHURCH SO FAR FOR-
WARD THAT MY SUCCESSOR WILL NOT BE
ABLE TO TURN BACK

Leo XIII

Contents

INTRODUCTION   3
Edward T. Gargan

1. THE LIFE AND WORK OF LEO XIII   15
Raymond H. Schmandt

2. THE CHURCH AND THE WORLD IN THE NINETEENTH CENTURY   51
Kenneth Scott Latourette

3. LEO XIII AND THE SOCIAL CRISIS   65
Rt. Rev. Joseph N. Moody

4. LEO XIII AND THE PROBLEM OF HUMAN LIBERTY   89
Most Rev. Egidio Vagnozzi

5. LEO XIII AND THE ROMAN QUESTION   101
S. William Halperin

6. LEO XIII AND ENGLAND   127
Rev. Eric McDermott, S.J.

7. LEO XIII AND AMERICA   157
Rev. Thomas T. McAvoy, C.S.C.

8. LEO XIII AND THE PHILOSOPHICAL APPROACH TO MODERNITY   181
James Collins

9. LEO XIII AND CONTEMPORARY THEOLOGY   213
Rev. Gustave Weigel, S.J.

SELECTED BIBLIOGRAPHY   227
NOTES ON CONTRIBUTORS   243

Introduction

EDWARD T. GARGAN
Loyola University

IN A LETTER of September 1875, discussing the work of Friedrich Nietzsche, Jacob Burckhardt wrote: "I am more and more convinced that he had a special mission for our age. As the illusions of the 'Progress' which had dominated since 1830 come to disappear it is essential to have someone to tell us all that belongs to the kingdom of illusions and how to give up our vain hopes in time."[1] Commenting further on the "merciless optimism" of his age, Burckhardt predicted: "In the end there will be a pitched battle between optimism and—not pessimism—but 'malism' (forgive the silly word)."[2] Three years later, in his first encyclical letter, *Inscrutabili* (*On the Evils Affecting Modern Society*), Leo XIII appeared to be joining that battle prophesied by Burckhardt. Like Burckhardt, he found his age no occasion for optimism. "For, from the very beginning of Our pontificate," he wrote, "the sad sight has presented itself to Us of the evils by which the human race is oppressed on every side. . . ."[3]

The new Pope began his pontificate in a world he described as suffering from "this deathly mass of ills."[4] He saw mankind threatened by a ". . . deadly kind of plague which infects society in its inmost recesses, allowing it no respite and foreboding every fresh disturbances and final disaster."[5] In common with a host of critics who regarded modern society as menaced by the possibility of a "final disaster," Leo XIII shared that pessimism characteristic of much modern thought at the end of the nineteenth century. Leo separated himself from this camp, however, by the mission he established for himself and his Church. His success is resisting the "final disaster" was perhaps best acknowledged by the reception of his pontificate in Europe and America. Pius IX had begun his reign as something of a hero to Europe, but he ended it alienated from the affections of many of his contemporaries. Following Pius IX, Leo XIII had the good fortune not only to open his pontificate with the considerable sympathy of his generation, but to close his life and reign in 1903 with more than an unusual share of the love of his neighbors. For subsequent generations his historical personality has retained features that continue to evoke confidence in modern man's capacity to confront the problems peculiar to our age.

It is appropriate to have a collected appraisal of Leo XIII by scholars in America for the sesquicentennial of his birth on March 2, 1810. For no pontiff has ever received quite the attention from America equal to that Leo XIII enjoyed. Those who met in the spring of 1960 at Loyola University of Chicago to discuss Leo XIII's impact on the modern world were, in a sense, reaffirming their predecessors' judgments on the significance of his pontificate. Leo's career was followed closely by the popular and academic press of this country. This was true not only of the journals of the Catholic community, but also of the periodicals representing Protestant scholarship. The *North American Review, The Atlantic Monthly,* and *Harper's Weekly* were typical of the popular magazines that considered his activity of great interest.

The press, which was in agreement on the newsworthiness of Leo's reign, was not, as is to be expected, in total agreement on its presentation and evaluation of the Pope. There was a tone of genuine affection for Leo that grew as he advanced into great age. His person was in all of the press admired for the dignity and holiness of life he exhibited. Beyond this, there were decidedly flattering portraits. These exceedingly favorable portrayals were, in turn, complemented by descriptions drawn by critical eyes and hands not prepared to cover blemishes. Among the more critical and historically valuable examinations of Leo XIII's career were the inquiries conducted in the leading Protestant philosophical and theological journals.

The encyclical *Aeterni Patris (The Restoration of Christian*

Philosophy to Schools), issued in August of 1879, was, for example, interpreted as a step backward by Professor Archibald Alexander of Columbia College, in an article "Thomas Aquinas and the Encyclical Letter" published in *The Princeton Review* for January 1880. Professor Alexander believed that Leo XIII, in recalling the Church to the thought of Saint Thomas, was failing to face the realities of the modern age. There are, he wrote, "certain characteristics of scholastic thought of St. Thomas that makes it useless in modern times."[6] He argued that such a system—rooted in the psychology and physics of Aristotle—bore no true relationship to the philosophical thought that had developed from the Renaissance, and from Kant in a more modern period. A defective theistic system, a defective psychology, logic, and physics, could not, he thought, be a recommendation of St. Thomas's "wisdom."

The debate initiated by Professor Alexander was immediately joined by the Paulists' journal *The Catholic World*. And since 1880 the problems raised by the contestants of that day have had a continuing life both in Catholic and non-Catholic philosophical discussion. The ardor accompanying many a consideration of the modernity of Thomism has, however, often obscured a clear presentation of Leo XIII's original posture towards modern thought. Professor James Collins, in his contribution to this evaluation of Leo XIII, directs our attention to the primary issue of what was Leo's attitude toward modern philosophical inquiry and conviction.

In November of 1885 the encyclical *Immortale Dei* (*The Christian Constitution of States*) appeared. The *Andover Review,* published by the Andover Theological Seminary, was among the first to discuss this statement on the problems of Church and State. An editorial, "The Pope's Encyclical," was prominently placed in the January 1886 issue of the *Review.* It was the editor's impression that this letter reflected considerable change in the direction of papal thought from that expressed twenty-one years earlier in the Syllabus of Errors. He believed that the Pope was now accommodating, perhaps of necessity, the Church to the conditions of modern "civil society." "In its present gigantic development of good and evil" this society was not, he thought, "likely to be stayed by the voice from the Tiber."[7] Yet, he observed a note of "moral sanity" in the Pope's letter. And while he found Leo no Boniface VIII, or even a Clement XIV, he concluded: "But we do not know that since Clement XIV anything so worthy of him has proceeded from the Roman Chair."[8]

Leo XIII was of necessity concerned with the variety of political beliefs that attracted his age. Here a central question was that of Leo's understanding of the nature of liberty and the conditions governing its realization. This problem, the heart of the matter in all modern political endeavor, is considered in the essay "Pope Leo XIII and the Problem of Human Liberty" by the Most Reverend Egidio Vagnozzi, Apostolic Delegate to the United States. Leo's political counsel developed within a contemporary environment offering the Papacy and the Church some of their greatest trials. One such heart-breaking issue was the relationship of the Holy See to the Italian States. This, the famous "Roman Question," the painful legacy Pius IX was obliged to leave to his successor as a consequence of the loss of the Papacy's temporal power, is examined by Professor Samuel William Halperin, who has devoted many studies to this question and its historical unfolding.

The *Andover Review*'s interest in Leo's pronouncements was exhibited again in 1891 when the encyclical *Rerum Novarum* (*The Rights and Duties of Capital and Labor*) was issued in May of that year. In the August number lengthy editorial attention was given to "The Papal Encyclical on Labor." The editor wondered, this time, whether the Pope's statement, as it became less abstract and more concrete, was not like the thought of "any other man of modern times."[9] He further believed that the Pope in stressing the responsibility of the State to alleviate social distress was taking a stand similar to that "of the better socialist journals of Great Britain."[10] The editor was not, however, without some sympathy for Leo's position. Generously, he concluded: "One can but read the Encyclical on Labor with interest and satisfaction. Its influence will be felt toward freedom and elevation of the working class."[11]

In this judgment the *Review* was not in error, for no other state-

ment of Leo's had greater success in shaping the Church's approach
to modern society. The editor of the Andover periodical was equally
perceptive when he insisted that the encyclical be compared to the
social views of Leo's contemporaries. Monsignor Joseph N. Moody,
in his discussion of "Leo XIII and the Social Crisis," investigates in
depth this relationship, and the concrete realities that made urgent
Rerum Novarum. In suggesting that Leo's ideas were not unlike those
of current circulation in England, the *Andover Review* had also
accurately discerned another significant aspect of Leo's thought.
Leo XIII was especially interested in English efforts to meet the
social issues of his day. Eric McDermott, S.J., considers, in his
contribution, the scope of Leo's significant historical relations with
Great Britain.

The attention paid to Leo's word by the academic journals was
matched by that of the popular magazines of his time. In May of
1894, *The Atlantic Monthly* reviewed, in an article entitled "The
Encyclicals of Pope Leo XIII," his thought in the fifteen years of his
continuing pontificate. The Pope's "solicitude" in social matters was
appraised as that "which has seldom been surpassed."[12] *The Atlantic*
was particularly happy with the Pope's appeal to French Catholics
to support as good citizens the Third Republic as a legitimate form of
government. Commenting on *Au millieu des sollicitudes* of 1892, the
magazine noted: "The Church does not desire a political domina-
tion over the state, and all forms of government are good which tend
towards the common weal. That is the lesson of this epoch-making
Encyclical. . . ."[13] In his biographical treatment of Leo XIII,
Raymond Schmandt reconsiders Leo's relationship to France and
his equally important involvement in the evolution of religious-politi-
cal matters in Germany. These problems are all intrinsically related to the evaluation of Leo's impact on the world scene. When
The Atlantic was considering Leo's ultimate historical achievement,
the editor felt compelled to suggest that the Pope's influence on his
Church would not be reciprocated in the world at large. Raising a
problem of the first order for future historians, and for this volume,
The Atlantic concluded: "These are the facts which must be faced

8

in an impartial notice, and the inference they lead to seems to be that the influence of the papal writings on the collective activity of modern times is very slight."[14]

   Harper's, the great rival of *The Atlantic,* though not yet as sophisticated, followed the career of the Pope with marked affection. In July of 1903, as the Pope's life began to ebb away, *Harper's* ran a series of comments on his pontificate and the choice of a successor. Leo died on July 20 and the cover for *Harper's* of July 25 carried not the usual figure of the Statue of Liberty, but an "allegorical" representation of the cardinals in attendance at the Pope's deathbed. In addition to this cover, a series of special paintings, in full page and color, were commissioned and printed to review the life of the Pope. The editorial comment was one of deep appreciation for the late Pontiff, described as "a magnificent figure in the world's history." Special note was taken of the growth of the Church under the free institutions of America. "The feeling," it was observed, "gained strength that the Church was in no degree a menace to the country, but rather a bulwark, especially in its support of law and order."[15] The question of the Church and America, of such a concern to Leo's contemporaries, is also ours in the discussion of the Apostolic Delegate, and in the contribution of Father Thomas T. McAvoy, C.S.C., which traces out the tasks Leo faced with regard to the growth of the Church in America.

   The care taken by *Harper's* to mark Leo XIII's death was imitated and even surpassed by the *North American Review.* In 1903 the *North American Review* was one of the most brilliant literary journals in this country. The September issue of the *Review,* then in its eighty-ninth year, carried a lengthy co-operative article on "Leo XIII, His Work and Influence." This same number included a new play by the young Irish writer W. B. Yeats, "The Hour Glass: A Morality," and also part nine of the installments on the novel *The Ambassadors* by Henry James. The *Review* had, with great promptness, invited seven prominent religious leaders of varying faiths to discuss Leo's achievement. The resulting article was truly a predecessor of this appraisal. The contributors included Archbishop

John Ireland of Saint Paul; the Right Reverend Leighton Coleman, Episcopal Bishop of Delaware; the Reverend Robert F. Coyle, Moderator of the Presbyterian General Assembly; J. B. Thomas, professor of church history in the Newton Theological Institute; the well-known pastor Washington Gladden of the First Congregational Church in Columbus; the Reverend J. Wesley Johnston of the Old Street Methodist Episcopal Church in New York; and, finally, Dr. H. Pereira Mendes, rabbi of Sherith Israel Synagogue of New York.

Rabbi Mendes believed that "The glory of Leo XIII is that he recognized new times and new conditions. . . . He found the Church mediaeval; he left it awakening to modernism."[16] Washington Gladden, the Congregational minister, noted for his interest in labor, thought that "it is doubtful whether any occupant of the Papal throne since the Reformation had had a larger influence in the whole of Christendom than Leo XIII."[17] Professor Thomas regarded of special significance "the Papal laudations of American institutions," and that "none of our citizens are more profuse in reiteration of loyalty to all our political tenets than Roman Catholics."[18] Archbishop Ireland also centered his recollections on the Pope and America. He suggested that "the very special esteem he always had for America and its institutions arose from his deep comprehension of the modern age. . . ."[19]

Leo's contemporaries in America established a consensus on the issues and developments of the utmost importance in his reign. These issues remain the significant ones for our generation: the relationship of scholastic philosophy to modern thought, the Church's sense of the political and social needs of man, the Pope's thought as viewed in a democratic climate. With the advantage of hindsight, we may add two approaches to Leo's achievement that take on a heightened relevance for our own age. Father Gustave Weigel, S.J., considers in the final essay the direction which Leo XIII gave to Catholic theology at the start of the twentieth century. Professor Kenneth Scott Latourette opens our inquiry by reminding us that the Protestant and Catholic communities experienced many similar trials and victories in the world of the nineteenth century.

We may be free of some of the passions and limits of an earlier generation's response to Leo XIII, yet the perspective we enjoy today does not free us from our commitments, our separate allegiances, our divided loves. Thus, the impression of Leo XIII in James Hastings Nichols' *History of Christianity: 1650–1950* differs from that in Professor Latourette's *Christianity in A Revolutionary Age,* and both studies are to be distinguished from the writings of E. E. Y. Hales. These academic differences are not to be deplored. They are indeed a condition of our existence. The present, a time of perennial crisis, beats incessantly upon our consciousness, and it forms irresistibly our separate visions. It may be hoped, however, that in this historical approach to Leo XIII, we will merit his belief that history is a liberating discipline. It may also be desired that our understanding of his achievement might contribute to postponing the "final disaster" he labored to turn aside.

NOTES

1. Jacob Burckhardt, *The Letters of Jacob Burckhardt,* ed. and trans. by Alexander Dru (New York, Pantheon Books, 1955), p. 170 (Burckhardt to Friedrich von Preen, September 19, 1875).
2. *Loc. cit.*
3. See the text of this encyclical in Étienne Gilson, ed., *The Church Speaks to the Modern World: The Social Teachings of Leo XIII* (Garden City, Image Books, 1957), p. 278.
4. *Ibid.,* p. 279.
5. *Loc. cit.*
6. Archibald Alexander, "Thomas Aquinas and the Encyclical Letter," *The Princeton Review,* V (1880), p. 249.
7. Unsigned editorial, "The Pope's Encyclical," *Andover Review,* V (1886), p. 77.
8. *Ibid.,* p. 79.
9. Unsigned editorial, "The Papal Encyclical on Labor," *Andover Review,* XVI (1891), p. 177.
10. *Loc. cit.*
11. *Ibid.,* p. 178.

12. "The Encyclical of Pope Leo XIII," *The Atlantic Monthly,* LXXIII (1894), p. 692.
13. *Ibid.,* p. 699.
14. *Ibid.,* p. 701.
15. "Leo XIII," *Harper's Weekly,* XLII, pt. 2 (1903), p. 1218.
16. John Ireland *et al.,* "Leo XIII, His Work and Influence," *North American Review,* CLXXII (1903), p. 361.
17. *Ibid.,* p. 354.
18. *Ibid.,* p. 348.
19. *Ibid.,* p. 334.

The Life and Work of Leo XIII

RAYMOND H. SCHMANDT
Loyola University

VINCENT JOACHIM PECCI[1] was born March 2, 1810, at Carpineto, an eagle's-nest town situated in the mountains of central Italy about fifty miles south of Rome, within the Papal States and in the diocese of Anagni. Three brothers and two sisters had preceded Vincent into the world, and a fourth brother was born six years later.

Both Count Ludovico Pecci and his wife, Anna Prosperi-Buzi, from the nearby town of Cori, enjoyed their noble titles by custom rather than by strict right, for they held no patent of nobility. The Peccis originated as a bourgeois family in Siena. As a result of one of those obscure disturbances which every Italian Renaissance city experienced from time to time, some of the wealthy Pecci clan migrated into the Papal States. The Medici Pontiff, Clement VII, welcomed them to Carpineto, where they soon became leading citizens. Through the centuries Peccis served the Church with distinction in both ecclesiastical and civil capacities. In 1792 Count Ludovico entered the papal militia with the rank of lieutenant, just in time to play a small part in the political and military whirlwind that swept through the peninsula in the wake of the French Revolution and Napoleon Bonaparte.

In the life of young Vincent the first event of major importance was his departure from home in 1818, the year he entered the Jesuit boarding school at Viterbo. He continued under Jesuit tutelage for his advanced studies at the Roman College, also known as the Gregorian University, where he matriculated in 1825. Completing his philosophical studies five years later, he remained for graduate work in theology and received a doctorate in 1832. Next, after clarifying the matter of his irregular noble title, Joachim (as he now called himself) was accepted at the Roman Academy for Noble Ecclesiastics, a college for potential members of the papal diplomatic corps. Following three years of specialization in civil and canon law, as well as more theology, he received his degree from the Sapienza University on August 7, 1835, and was now ready, at the age of twenty-five, to embark on his career.

But what was his state in life to be? An insight into young Pecci's thoughts can be gleaned from the collection of 239 personal letters which he wrote between the ages of nine and twenty-seven and which were published with his approbation after he had become Pope.[2] In these letters there is scarcely a mention of a vocation to the priesthood. His mother, to be sure, had tried as early as 1821 to persuade both him and his older brother Joseph to take the first steps in this direction, but both had demurred. On his mother's deathbed in 1824, he apparently resolved to accede to her wish, for he soon afterwards received the tonsure. This decision, however, was unsupported by any real conviction. One theme runs consistently through his youthful letters to relatives and friends—the desire for fame for himself and renown for his family. In an age when literary self-revelation and emotional outpourings were definitely in style, young Pecci's letters are barren of any evidence of deep spiritual crisis or even concern.

Perhaps he was too busy. Despite his weak constitution, young Pecci worked with tremendous concentration at his studies, developing his unquestionable talents to the fullest. He always carried off the prizes and delivered the honorary addresses and declamations in the schools he attended. He also showed a talent for attracting the attention of influential people who could be of assistance to him. Cardinal Sala was his particular patron. Pope Leo XII became aware of him, and Cardinal Pacca personally recommended him to Pope Gregory XVI.

Pecci's entrance into the Roman Academy indicates the type of career he had chosen, and for this he had taken minor orders. Papal service, however, necessitated the further decision of whether to remain a layman or receive holy orders. In January 1837 Pope Gregory XVI granted him the rank of domestic prelate, and soon thereafter he was given positions on several of the congregations of the papal administrative machinery. Probably about mid-1837 Monsignor Pecci made up his mind to become a priest. While his motives seem not to have been spiritually profound or intense, his decision was obviously genuine and sincere. On November 17 and 24 he was ordained subdeacon and deacon, and on the last day of December he received the ordination to the priesthood. Thus qualified, he awaited his first significant assignment.

The diplomatic phase of Joachim Pecci's life lasted nine years. His initial post took him to Benevento, the southernmost province of the Papal States, where he served successfully as papal delegate, i.e., civil governor, from 1838 to 1841. In a similar capacity he labored for a year in Perugia, capital of the province of Umbria. Pleased with Monsignor Pecci's work, Pope Gregory XVI early in 1843 appointed him Papal Nuncio to the Kingdom of Belgium, an assignment that necessitated Pecci's promotion to the episcopate. On January 27 he received the consecration as titular Archbishop of Damietta, and three months later he arrived in Brussels.

At this moment, because of the situation then prevailing in the new Belgian kingdom, the Brussels nunciature represented a trying post for a fledgling thirty-three-year-old archbishop on his first appearance outside of Italy. Between the liberally inclined hierarchy and the conservative, Protestant King Leopold I, a distinct difference of opinion prevailed, a difference which the king expected the Nuncio to resolve on his behalf. Since Gregory XVI had already spoken critically of the Belgian hierarchy's policies, the bishops naturally distrusted the Nuncio. Archbishop Pecci's line of action, based on a too-literal reading of his instructions from the Vatican, was to hold himself aloof as much as possible, allowing the bishops freedom to guide their own affairs, but without associating himself with their principles. While King Leopold found Pecci personally affable and treated him very graciously, he found his official policy totally unsatisfactory. In November 1844 Leopold wrote to Cardinal Lambruschini, Papal Secretary of State, requesting the Nuncio's recall. This Lambruschini refused; however, he did urge on the Nuncio a more active role. "I have had to recognize," he wrote, "that you have done little more than restrict yourself to what I might call a negative line of conduct, whereas in various cases you should have shown greater perspicacity and greater energy."[3]

Six months later, June 23, 1845, the experienced but reactionary Austrian ambassador at Brussels, Count Dietrichstein, spoke of Pecci in a dispatch to his government in words indicating that the Nuncio had failed to overcome his deficiencies: "Well, we find in Belgium an excellent man, it is true, the best of men, full of good will and zeal, but young, sickly, languishing without means of action, without authority, without dexterity in dealing with the affairs that press upon him."[4]

In October of 1845 the Papal Secretary privately informed the Nuncio of his recall, although the public announcement was withheld until the following spring. At the same time, Pope Gregory offered Pecci the vacant bishopric of Perugia. Pecci dutifully accepted, realizing that this meant the close of his diplomatic career and the sacrifice of his hopes for a wider kind of fame than that open to a mere Italian bishop.

The thirty-one and a half years that Archbishop Pecci spent in Perugia (1846–1877) form an interlude between the beginning and the end of his life which both centered on Rome. While he did receive the cardinalate in 1853, promised to him eight years earlier, this appointment entailed no curial duties that might call him to Rome permanently. During these three decades his activity was local in scope and attracted little attention outside of Italy. Nevertheless, these important years transformed Archbishop Pecci into Pope Leo XIII. The indecisive, ineffectual young ex-Nuncio learned to exercise authority, to deal with men of every rank, to understand issues, and to cope with problems. He gained that invaluable experience of the world which manifested itself so realistically in the program of the future supreme pontiff. Nor should it be overlooked that the sacrifice of his personal aspirations was accepted by the Bishop without bitterness. This time in Perugia was Pecci's Damascus period. There he came to realize that it was God's work that had to be done, not the achievement of his own ambitious goals in life.

An analysis of Archbishop Pecci's episcopal activity reveals tendencies working in two directions.[5] On the one hand, the evidence points to a close agreement with the contemporary atmosphere in Rome under Pius IX. At times it almost appears that Pecci stood in advance of and even pointed the way for Pius to follow. Thus, a set of resolutions adopted by a provincial synod at Spoleto in November 1849, signed by Pecci among others, called for a doctrinal definition of the Immaculate Conception, specifically acknowledged papal infallibility, requested the Papacy to issue a point-by-point condemnation of current errors, and suggested an ecumenical council as the most apt means to these ends. Within a generation Pius IX had acted on all four of these resolutions. Some historians have seen in Pecci the real instigator of the papal Syllabus of Errors, partly on the basis of this synodal resolution.[6] In 1867 the Archbishop promulgated a small-scale syllabus of his own in the form of a pastoral letter to his diocese.

In 1860 the government of the Kingdom of Sardinia annexed Perugia along with other parts of the Papal State. Pecci protested in a strongly worded defense of the temporal sovereignty of the popes. Carefully avoiding conflict with the occupying government, the Archbishop nevertheless condemned one after another of the anti-clerical laws of the state, such as the suppression of religious orders, the secularization of education, compulsory civil marriage, and interference with the seminaries.

When Pius IX desired an expression of opinion on the calling of the Vatican Council, Pecci was among the thirty-four bishops secretly consulted in April 1865. In his response the Archbishop endorsed the suggestion most enthusiastically (*"toto animo"*), and even proposed an agenda based in part on the Syllabus and on *Quanta cura.*[7] At the Council he stood among the Infallibilists.

Paralleling these "conservative" attitudes we find expressions of

a more constructive outlook. The Archbishop showed great concern
for the education of his clergy, and ordered the seminary curriculum
modernized to admit the newer scientific thought. Personally an
admirer of Dante, he revoked the regulation forbidding seminarians
to read the *Divine Comedy*. Through an Academy of St. Thomas
Aquinas and the seminary reform he promoted the scholastic revival
within the diocese of Perugia. A document that attracted attention
even beyond the Italian borders was Pecci's pastoral letter for Lent
1877, on the subject of "The Church and Civilization." Defending
the Church against the frequent charge of opposing modern civilization, the Archbishop enthusiastically praised the material achievements of the last decades. Even the idea of progress, that idol of
nineteenth-century thinkers, received its share of warm commenda-
tion: "Society, then, being composed of men essentially capable
of improvement, cannot stand still; it advances and perfects itself.
One age inherits the inventions, discoveries and improvements
achieved by the preceding one, and thus the sum of physical, moral
and political blessings can increase most marvelously."[8] Not many
contemporary bishops expressed such sentiments.

In September 1877 Pope Pius IX appointed Cardinal Pecci to the
office of Papal Chamberlain, and the duties of this office compelled
him to take up his residence permanently in Rome. It has been
suggested that Pius sought by this honor to compensate Pecci for the
oblivion in which the Cardinal had been kept through the efforts of
the late Cardinal Antonelli, for many years the power behind the
papal throne.[9] Although there were traditions to the contrary, Pius
may have also intended in this way to direct the attention of the
College of Cardinals to the new Chamberlain as a possible candidate
for the papal tiara.

Pius IX died February 7, 1878. During the interregnum it fell to
the Chamberlain to administer papal affairs, prepare for the funeral
of the late Pontiff, and supervise the arrangements for the Conclave
of the Sacred College, all of which Pecci accomplished with firm
courage and efficiency. Assured by the Italian government of full
liberty, the Conclave opened in Rome within the prescribed time on

February 19. All but three of the sixty-four cardinals attended. As in all the conclaves of the nineteenth century, the Sacred College was in general divided into two camps with divergent views on the political and social program which the Church should pursue, and therefore on the choice of the man most suitable to execute that program. Among those who might be called the progressives Pecci stood out as the obvious candidate. Perhaps his advanced age recommended him to the conservatives also, since they were quite unsure of themselves. On the third ballot in the morning of February 20, 1878, Joachim Cardinal Pecci received the required majority with forty-four of the sixty-one votes, and took the name of Pope Leo XIII. The ceremony of the coronation was performed on Sunday, March 3, the day following his sixty-eighth birthday.

Carlton J. H. Hayes has described the position of the Church at Pope Leo XIII's elevation as follows:

... the Catholic Church seemed to be at losing feud with the whole modern world, intellectually, politically, and morally. Its influence on the life and thought of the fashioners of public opinion—leading men of letters, journalists, educators, and scholars—was fast disappearing, and its hold was gone on a large fraction of the bourgeoisie and on the bulk of the urban proletariat. It appeared impotent to dike anywhere the flood tide of "science," liberalism, Marxism, anti-clericalism, and secularization.[10]

Everywhere the ancient bases of society were being undermined by the forces unloosed by the Enlightenment, the French Revolution, and industrialism. We glibly name these movements liberalism, socialism, or nationalism, yet behind these simple terms lay a tremendously complex network of ideas and attitudes, having little in common beyond a more or less blind determination to transform this or that aspect of the established order. It was a revolutionary age such as the world had seldom seen, and the offensive forces enjoyed a spectacular *élan* and seeming inevitability which were lacking to the embattled defenders of traditional positions, including the Church.

In his own way, Pope Pius IX had performed an essential service

by indicating forcefully and with precision the inherent dangers of the
new political and philosophical currents. Wholly unable to stem
the tide, he had at least kept the bark of Peter afloat. However, a
negative policy of the kind pursued by Pius could achieve only
limited results. To condemn the solutions offered by the radicals to
the problems of the times sufficed with some observers, but to imply
that the problems did not even exist by failing to offer meaningful
counterproposals simply courted disaster. It was to be Leo XIII's
task to come to grips with the great issues of the century in a constructive way, to draw on the deep reservoirs of Catholic strength,
and to give hope and a program for the future.

Those liberals in many lands who had hailed the elevation of
Leo XIII saw their hopes dashed when the new Pontiff's first
encyclical, *Inscrutabili,* April 21, 1878, failed to proclaim any
departure from the policies of his predecessor. In unexciting platitudes Leo diagnosed the evils of the times as springing from the fact
that "the holy and venerable authority of the Church . . . has been
despised and set aside."[11] The one specific issue dealt with at some
length was the Roman Question; here too Leo pledged adherence to
his predecessor's principles.

Undoubtedly the Roman Question held the foremost place in
Leo's thoughts. It caused him more concern than any other of his
political problems, and in fact it determined the entire course of his
international relations. Whether engaged with the Catholic or the
Protestant states, Leo's diplomatic program was shaped by the
Roman imbroglio. Ironically, this was the area in which he sustained
his gravest defeat. Leo's fine diplomatic sensitivity did not serve
him so well when Rome was in question, for this became a matter
of emotion rather than reason.

Obstructing Leo's approach to the Roman Question was the
fundamental difficulty of not knowing exactly who was the enemy.
Leo was convinced that all attacks on Catholicism, including the
annexation of Rome by Victor Emmanuel II, sprang from a mam-
moth, far-flung conspiracy of secret sects under the leadership of
the Masonic society.[12] Here he saw the roots of the doctrines of

socialists, communists, liberals, and indeed all of the anti-Christian groups. It was obvious that Cavour, Crispi, and many other prominent Italian statesmen or intellectuals were Masons, and that their lodge affiliations encouraged their attacks on the Church. Nevertheless, it was not quite so simple. Leo totally missed the significance and underestimated the strength of nationalism. In all of his writings there is no passage that examines this elusive, potent factor in modern political life; yet it was precisely nationalism that had effected Italian unification. Nationalism infected Catholics as well as anti-Catholics; probably there were more good Catholics than atheists among the advocates of Italian unification. Nevertheless, as late as 1887 Leo XIII publicly denied that national unity was either necessary or desirable for Italy, since he could point out historical examples of prosperous and mighty nonnational states.[13]

Failing thus to come to grips with the basic issue, Leo allowed his attention to be diverted to secondary considerations on which he expended his energy in vain. His tactical blunder in continuing the *non expedit* of Pius IX, and in fact changing it into the *non licet* in 1895, thereby preventing Italian Catholics from expressing their opinions at the polls or in parliament, entailed the surrender of the government into the hands of the anti-Catholic minority. The least that can be said is that Leo's intransigent attitude kept alive papal claims. The same advantage was won through Leo's steady stream of appeals to foreign governments for intervention on his behalf. On the other hand, the Pope failed to check the secularistic, anti-Catholic wave, and in fact his attitude contributed, albeit accidentally, to the rise of Fascism.

Leo never ceased to insist on the restoration of the temporal sovereignty of the Papacy. At times he thought it possible to recover the entire Papal State, at others only a portion of it. His minimum demands exceeded the boundaries of the ancient city of Rome, even with a corridor to the sea.[14] Although he apparently never presented his minimum expectations to the Italian government, it was unrealistic of him to believe that all of Rome could be returned to the Papacy.

At the basis of Leo's attitude was his firm conviction that the temporal sovereignty was sanctioned by divine right. In *Inscrutabili* he described it as "that condition of things in which the design of God's wisdom had long ago placed the Roman Pontiffs." Nine years later he wrote: ". . . in the intention of Providence, the temporal sovereignty of the Popes is still to be regarded as a means to the regular exercise of the Apostolic power, inasmuch as it constitutes an effective guarantee of their freedom and independence."[15] Thus for Leo XIII it clearly remained a question of the means to an end. He disavowed political ambition for its own sake; his only thought was the obvious necessity of securing complete religious liberty. The tendency of Italian politicians to ignore the Law of Guarantees which the government had offered to Pius IX confirmed Leo's conclusions. Furthermore, Leo was well aware of the fact that among liberals of the day it was commonly assumed that the elimination of the temporal power presaged the eventual overthrow of the spiritual as well. With such an estimate of the situation, and faced with the petty anticlericalism and vindictive stubbornness of the Italian government, Leo XIII's attitude seems almost reasonable.

From the vantage point of historical perspective, however, it is readily apparent that the Papal State as it had been constituted under Pius IX was an anachronism which had to be swept away. In today's world of atomic weapons and international politics, of complex social and economic issues, the Papal State would have been an insufferable burden. Just as the dissolution of the numerous ecclesiastical principalities in Germany at the beginning of the nineteenth century paved the way for the strengthening of Catholic life north of the Alps, so did the emancipation of the Papacy from the onus of its civil responsibilities allow the concentration on basic moral problems and the encouragement of the liturgical reforms of the twentieth century.

Sharply contrasting with Leo XIII's failure in Italy is the eminent success of his German relations. In method too the differences are great: the Leo XIII who engaged in a skillful diplomatic duel with Otto von Bismarck seemed not to be the same man as the inflexible, suspicious Pontiff who dealt with the government of Italy. In part the explanation lies in the character of his opponents. Bismarck, with all his faults, rose far above the petty, anti-Christian Italian politicians.

When Leo XIII became Pope, the Kulturkampf in Germany and Prussia was already seven years old. This misnamed "struggle for civilization," in reality a contest between advocates and opponents of a monistic and authoritarian concept of state power, had reached a point where both sides sensed the need for a change of course. A set of oppressive laws, the expulsion of most religious orders, and the numerous vacancies in the German episcopate testified to the Church's difficulties. On the other hand, the mounting strength of the Center Party frustrated the Iron Chancellor's hopes for complete mastery of the domestic political scene in the Reich at the very time when he was about to break his alliance with the National Liberals, his loudest supporters in the attack on the Catholic Church.

Leo XIII took the initiative. Within twenty-four hours of his election he wrote a personal letter to Emperor William I informing him of his elevation and expressing hope for a solution to the controversy. Again on April 17, 1878, Leo sent his condolences to the Emperor, whom a would-be assassin had seriously wounded. William's reply to this second letter, countersigned by Bismarck, indicated a willingness to explore the possibility of a compromise. Thus began a diplomatic hide-and-seek that endured for a full decade.

Since diplomatic relations between Berlin and the Vatican had been ruptured, Leo entrusted the preliminary negotiations to his Nuncio in Munich, Monsignor Masella, whom Bismarck invited to Bad Kissingen in July 1878. In September the Chancellor conferred with Cardinal Jacobini, Nuncio to Vienna. The friendly atmosphere generated by these conversations was not disturbed by the death of Leo's Secretary of State, Cardinal Franci, since Leo himself directed the German negotiations. Few concrete results were attained, however, beyond the dismissal shortly afterwards of Falk, the anti-Catholic Prussian Minister of Worship. Undismayed by the slow progress, Leo employed every device to keep the negotiations open. Bismarck responded warily, yet he soon came to have a high regard for the Pope both personally and politically, and always treated him with precise correctness. The Chancellor's diplomatic adroitness and understanding of Leo's position permitted him an occasional fine gesture. Thus, on June 18, 1880, he addressed a letter to Leo with the salutation "Sire," the customary form for sovereign princes—a skillful touch which gratified and encouraged Leo in his struggle with Italy. In 1880 Cardinal Jacobini succeeded Cardinal Nina as Papal Secretary of State, a move designed to please Berlin, where Jacobini was highly regarded. Two years later, in April 1882, Leo had the pleasure of welcoming to the Vatican after a ten-year lapse a new German ambassador, Kurd von Schlözer, whom Bismarck brought from the Washington embassy. Schlözer made many warm friends among the Roman prelates, despite his own Protestantism, and proved invaluable in the negotiations.

Throughout his dealings with Germany, Leo XIII's attitude and conduct were those of a true statesman. Without by any means ignoring the basic issue of the freedom of the Church, the Pope preferred to deal in the pragmatic realm of concrete situations, trading specific concession for concession, recognizing the limitations imposed on Bismarck by the domestic situation in Germany, and always accepting the Iron Chancellor's words at face value.

Opposition to Leo's policy expressed itself in the Curia through a group of cardinals—Bilio, Ledochowski, Oreglia, Pitra—and in Germany among the bishops and the Centrists. The Center, with its solid base in the Reichstag, had constitutional as well as religious interests to protect, and insisted that the only acceptable attitude for the Papacy was to demand complete surrender from the government. For his part Bismarck was not above using the contacts with the Vatican as an instrument for whipping the Centrists into line. Pope Leo rejected the Center's solution and tried indirectly and unsuccessfully to influence Windthorst and other Party leaders to moderate their demands on the Chancellor. At the same time, Leo refused Bismarck's request for a papal decree disbanding the Center Party. On the crucial issue of the May Laws, Leo long failed to win from

Bismarck any modification, although the Chancellor did gradually ameliorate the severity of those laws in their application, and he even repealed some of the minor anti-Catholic measures. Leo in turn agreed, reluctantly, to sacrifice Archbishops Melchers of Cologne and Ledochowski of Gnesen-Posen, both outspoken foes of Prussian policies. When Leo conceded to the government the right of approval of ecclesiastical appointments, the vacant bishoprics were filled one by one. In some circles Leo's tactics met with violent disapproval; Windthorst commented on one such occasion that the Pope's action was "a shot in the back."[16]

In September 1885 Bismarck requested Leo XIII's mediation of a dispute between Germany and Spain concerning the Caroline Islands. Although the papal commission's decision favored Spain, Bismarck acquiesced without protest. The Holy Father was overjoyed at this acknowledgment of his authority, recalling as it did the happier days of papal history. He expressed his pleasure by bestowing a papal decoration on Bismarck, whom the Pope grandiloquently addressed as *"Excelso viro . . . Imperii Germanici Magno Cancellario."* The incident considerably improved papal prestige on the international level.

As a further concession, Leo XIII intervened directly in domestic German affairs to urge the Center Party to pass the septennate bill of 1887 increasing the size of the German army. Bismarck had requested this intervention, with the hint that the government would then support additional revisions in the May Laws. Such revisions, enacted in 1887 and following those of the previous year, were generally interpreted in Germany and in the Vatican as marking the end of the Kulturkampf. The German government retained its right to supervise Catholic education and to approve clerical appointments; the anti-Jesuit laws remained. However, for the remainder of the Second Reich the German Church flourished in peace. The Center accepted the situation, and soon proved itself the strongest support of the monarchy. Leo XIII had shown himself a match for the Iron Chancellor, who had painlessly found his way to Canossa.

Nevertheless, in one significant respect Pope Leo suffered a disappointment. His relations with Germany had always been conducted with an eye to the Italian situation. He desired peace for the sake of the German Church, but he also aspired to use German goodwill against Italy. While the Papacy undoubtedly benefitted from German friendship, neither Bismarck nor William II would consent to direct intervention in Italy on behalf of the temporal sovereignty. This was made unmistakably clear to the Pope on the occasion of William II's state visit in October 1888 (the first of three visits to the Vatican), and on subsequent occasions. As early as 1881 and 1882, when the Triple Alliance brought Germany, Austria-Hungary, and Italy together, the Vatican had shown concern. The renewal of this treaty in 1887 confirmed Leo XIII's fears. In vain he demanded that the Catholic Emperor Francis Joseph of Austria-Hungary formally declare that the treaty implied no recognition of Italy's right to the Papal State. During an interview with Count Paar, the Austrian ambassador, Leo spoke of his betrayal by the Germanic powers. Papal relations with Austria-Hungary were already strained because of Leo's vigorous missionary interests in the Balkans, which Austria feared would provoke Russia to war. Hence Leo received no satisfaction from the Emperor.[17]

As a result, papal diplomacy underwent a change which took concrete form in the appointment in 1887 of Mariano Cardinal Rampallo as the fourth and last of Leo XIII's Secretaries of State. One of the newer cardinals, Rampolla advocated turning away from the Germanic powers and effecting a shift toward France. Leo embraced this proposal and began a campaign to gain in Paris what was denied in Berlin and Vienna.

The beginning of Leo XIII's pontificate coincided with the stabilization of the Third French Republic, which at once inaugurated a period of extreme difficulty for the Church. French political life revolved around the bitter hostility of the republicans and the monarchists, and between them they ground the Church into the dust. Republican sentiment was encumbered by a long tradition of anticlericalism rooted in a fundamentally secularistic, liberal philosophy. For its part, the Church and its spokesmen generally condemned republicanism and aligned themselves with the forces of reaction and monarchism. Aristocratic and conservative royalists, mindful of the advantages they had reaped from the alliance of throne and altar, loudly identified their cause with Catholicism. On the social and economic levels, the Church suffered from the complete estrangement between itself and the growing numbers of the proletariat. Since Catholicism supported the wealthy vested interests which refused concessions to the downtrodden workers, the workers preferred to ally with the anticlerical republicans and socialists. Even the peasants wavered in their traditional Catholicism. The Catholic press screamed raucously in language suitable for the poorly educated clergy, but which further alienated the intellectuals from the Catholic camp.

The new republican government opened its attack on the Catholic-Conservative alliance with a series of measures removing clergy from the administration of hospitals and suppressing military chaplaincies. Turning to education and the control of the minds of future Frenchmen, the anticlericals aimed, by a series of measures from 1880 on, to achieve a public school system completely free of religion in curriculum and teachers. Pope Leo XIII, through his Nuncio, Monsignor Czacki, joined the bishops in protest; he attempted without success to discover some ground for compromise. In an encyclical *Nobilissima Gallorum gens,* February 1884, Leo lamented the course of events and encouraged French Catholics in their efforts to maintain religious influence in education through parochial schools. Count Albert de Mun, an ardent royalist but sincere Catholic with a genuine sympathy for the working class, announced in 1885 his intention of building a Catholic political party on the model of the German Center. Lively discussion followed, showing the Catholics hopelessly divided on the question of the proper political coloring for such a party. Abruptly De Mun dropped his scheme; his explanation was that "Leo XIII stopped me with a firm hand."[18]

At that moment the Holy Father was trying to work out a more fundamental approach to the French situation, namely, the reconciliation of French Catholics with their republican government in

order to break the calamitous association of the Church with the
cause of monarchy. The first harbinger of Leo's plan appeared in
Immortale Dei, published in 1885. There Leo wrote: "The right to
rule is not necessarily, however, bound up with any special mode of
government. It may take this or that form, provided only that it be of
a nature to insure the general welfare." The royalists, including most
of the French hierarchy, ignored the Pope's advice. The Boulanger
crisis of 1888-89, during which Leo XIII instructed the Parisian
Nuncio to preserve strict neutrality, implicated the Catholic cause
in a plot to overthrow the government by a *coup d'état,* thereby inviting reprisals from the republican government. On January 10,
1890, Leo reiterated in *Sapientiae Christianae* his advice of five years
earlier about the Church's indifference to forms of government.
Perceiving no palpable success, Leo decided on a more direct approach.

In October 1890 Leo summoned the foremost liberal prelate of
France, Cardinal Lavigerie, Archbishop of Algiers, to the Vatican.
Plans were laid for a spectacular move to counter the effects of the
Boulanger crisis. The initiative was Leo's but the Cardinal co-oper-
ated fully. Returning to Algiers, Lavigerie invited the officers of the
French fleet to a banquet on November 12. With a great flourish,
the Cardinal offered a toast pledging allegiance to the French Republic, after which the band, composed of priests of the White
Fathers congregation, struck up the Marseillaise, the anthem of the
Republic and of revolution in general. A storm of controversy swept
France as a result of Lavigerie's action. Leo XIII made it perfectly
clear that the Cardinal had acted as his spokesman. In a barrage of
papal directives, Leo clarified his position even further. Some sign of
success appeared when the five other French cardinals issued a public
statement on January 22, 1892, reluctantly embracing the Pope's
sentiments.

Less than a month later, on February 16, Leo XIII published the
encyclical *Au milieu des sollicitudes,* written in French and devoted
entirely to French affairs. In the encyclical Leo admonished the

French that it was their duty as Christians to obey their lawfully constituted government, the Republic. Forms of government, he wrote, are the result of historical contingency, and "whatever be the form of civil power in a nation, it cannot be considered so definite as to have the right to remain immutable. . . . But, in regard to purely human societies, it is an oft-repeated historical fact that time, that great transformer of all things here below, operates great changes in their political institutions." Should Frenchmen continue to believe that republicanism is inherently anti-Christian, Leo reminded them of the distinction between *constituted power* to be obeyed and *legislation* to be enacted or amended according to Christian principles. Lest there be any misunderstanding of his meaning, the Holy Father at this same time granted an interview to a French journalist representing a popular secular newspaper, during which he reiterated his prorepublican recommendations. In this way the contents of *Au milieu* reached circles which papal encyclicals seldom penetrated.

Au milieu marked the climax of Leo XIII's efforts to rescue Catholicism in France. His program came to be called the *Ralliement,* and it envisaged the full integration of Catholics into their national life, with the ultimate goal of re-Christianizing society. *Ralliement* was in part successful; at least the majority of the hierarchy now ceased active opposition to the Republic, and the younger clergy began to take a more liberal stand. There were even promising signs of a reawakening social conscience among French Catholics. However, the ingrained prejudices against the Republic remained among the royalist minority, to whom the Church was actually a mere tool. They denounced the *Ralliement* through their influential newspapers and vilified the *Ralliés*. Their participation in the anti-Semitic hysteria of the Dreyfus case, in which the Republic was on trial, further discredited Catholicism and encouraged stronger measures from the radical Left.

Pope Leo continued to urge conciliation. He counseled acceptance of the severe taxation of ecclesiastical property imposed by a law of 1895; although he protested, he advised submission to the Asso-

ciation Law of 1901 banning most of the religious orders. Due to
Leo's efforts, the Concordat of 1801 remained in effect, and the
French embassy at the Vatican continued to function, with advantages to the Papacy in regard to the Roman Question. But in
refusing to heed the Pope's sound advice French Catholics brought
destruction upon their own heads. Fortunately, Leo XIII did not
live to witness the final debacle in 1904 and 1905.

With other governments of the world Leo XIII's diplomatic relations presented less knotty and protracted problems. Although there
was some public discussion of the subject, England did not accredit
an ambassador to the Vatican. Official contacts were generally
limited to mutual congratulations on the jubilee of Queen Victoria
or the various jubilees of Leo XIII. This disappointed the Pope, since
he had advised the Irish to adopt a more moderate attitude toward
English rule, partly in the hope of a warmer attitude from London.
Spain and Portugal presented few problems, and the religious ten-
sion eased in Switzerland. Belgium recalled its ambassador in a
moment of anticlerical pique in 1880, and then sent him back five
years later. To placate France, a Chinese offer to establish regular
diplomatic relations was rejected. The United States had long since
broken off official contact, although Leo XIII and President Taft
co-operated to solve Philippine problems. Russia's ambassador had
been recalled as a consequence of the Polish uprising of 1863, for
which Russia blamed the Papacy. Leo XIII strove to restore relations as a means of removing persecution from Catholic and Uniate
subjects of the czar. Diplomatic relations were re-established in 1884,
but anti-Catholic measures did not cease entirely. The full story of
the Papacy's role in bringing France and Russia together in the
alliance of 1894 cannot be known until the papal archives are made
available.

Theobald Chartran, who painted perhaps the best portrait of Leo
XIII, described the Holy Father's impression on him in these
words:

His height, the supreme distinction of his entire person, his counte-
nance at once energetic and mild, his spiritual and delicately-drawn lips,
his hands so thoroughly aristocratic, his deep but melodious voice,
and above all, those eyes so full of youth, life and will; in fine, a very
unique combination makes the wonderful Pontiff the most completely
interesting model that an artist could desire.[19]

Behind Leo's kindly, smiling visage lay a strong will and a keen
mind that retained its acuteness to the very end of his long life. His
memory too was extraordinary. Leo felt the greatness of his office
transcending his own person and investing him with self-confidence
and optimism. Although occasionally he showed a certain im-
periousness and irritability, he generally mastered his emotions completely. Simplicity, dignity, and kindliness are the words most frequently used by those with whom he came into contact. Except in
intimate circles, however, Leo tended to be somewhat cold, rigidly
insistent on etiquette in true aristocratic fashion. Officially he valued
pomp and ceremony, but in his private life he lived most frugally.
There were times when his household felt that his personal frugality
approached too closely to parsimony; however, the charities to
which he contributed defy enumeration.

Leo granted comparatively few audiences either to groups or to
individuals. He disliked improvising, and it required too much time
to prepare and memorize allocutions. Also, audiences were a drain
on his strength. He had never enjoyed robust health, hardly the best
preparation for a pontificate extending from his sixty-seventh to his
ninety-third year. Nevertheless, Leo responded appreciatively to the
sentiments of devotion expressed by such groups as the pilgrimages
of French workingmen whom Count de Mun or Léon Harmel
brought to Rome, and he was genuinely pleased with the expressions
of affection that came from many quarters on the occasions of his
jubilees: the fiftieth anniversary of his episcopal consecration in
1893 and the twenty-fifth papal anniversary in 1902, as well as
during the Holy Year of 1900. As was customary, he utilized the
opportunities presented by such occasions to deliver speeches or allocutions expounding officially his thoughts on this or that subject.

In his capacity of teacher of Christendom, Leo XIII made his most significant and enduring contribution to the Church and to civilization. His teachings are embodied in his encyclicals and addresses on political, social, intellectual, and spiritual subjects. They form an imposing corpus of ideas and interpretations, comprising seven volumes in the standard editions.[20] The major encyclicals are all Leo's own work. Although he employed various advisors and secretaries (such as Monsignori Boccali, Volpini, Angeli, and Marzolini), and drew the inspiration for his thoughts from a great many sources, those thoughts and in many instances the language of the finished pronouncements were his own.

What especially lends value to Leo XIII's writing is its generally realistic character, for it was grounded in a sound comprehension of contemporary affairs. The Holy Father was an avid reader of newspapers; he made a special effort to keep in touch with the daily affairs and opinions of the world himself rather than relying on second-hand reports. This helped to overcome the dangerous self-imposed isolation of the "Prisoner of the Vatican," and it served to balance the inherently conservative attitude of the majority of the curial officials with whom Leo had to work. However, the experience of his thirty-two years as Bishop of Perugia must also be regarded as an essential factor in Leo's outlook. Had he remained in the diplomatic corps, or had he spent his best years in the papal bureaucracy, Leo would never have acquired the practical kind of experience that is reflected in his writings. Indeed, his episcopal acts accurately foreshadowed many facets of his papal career. Thus he could focus his mind, steeped in the eternal teachings of the Fathers of the Church and refined by a sense of the relativities of history, on the problems of his own time.

Because of the fact that he wrote in the midst of a particular set of circumstances and under the impact of very specific day-by-day aspects of the problems he investigated, there is always a certain ephemeral element in Leo XIII's writings, and they can only be viewed satisfactorily within the framework of his own times. When Leo was speaking in condemnation of errors or opinions of his own day, his pronouncements have only a historical interest whenever those opinions have lost their vitality. In the process of analyzing current thought, however, Leo had to give positive, modern interpretations to the age-old Christian doctrine; it is this part of his work that has passed into the permanent heritage of Christendom.

Ideologically, Leo XIII does not stand among the extremists. He was neither a reactionary nor by any means a doctrinaire liberal. Perhaps the more neutral term "progressive" best characterizes him. Leo pledged himself to continue the program of his reactionary predecessor Pius IX; this he did. He never repealed any of Pius's enactments or spoke critically of his opinions. Many of Leo's own accomplishments might well have emanated from his predecessor's circle. The new decree on the Index of Forbidden Books (*Officiorum ac Munerum*), the encyclical *Divinum Illud* on the Holy Spirit, *Arcanum Divinae* on Christian Marriage, and others, regardless of their merit, could just as easily have been composed by popes other than Leo XIII. Even the indiscriminate language of Leo's *Quod Apostolici Muneris* on socialism, communism and nihilism is redolent of the negative and extreme attitudes of former pontiffs:

We are alluding to that sect of men who, under the motley and all but barbarous terms and titles of Socialists, Communists, and Nihilists, are spreading abroad throughout the world and, bound intimately together in baneful alliance, no longer look for strong support in secret meetings held in darksome places, but standing forth openly and boldly in the light of day, strive to carry out the purpose long resolved upon, of uprooting the foundations of civilized society at large.

While it is true, therefore, that Leo XIII's pontificate witnessed no sharp break with the past, and that earlier principles were maintained —in fact, had to be maintained—there did nevertheless occur a very significant change in attitude. The whole climate of the Papacy differed from the previous pontificate. The tactics of denunciation yielded finally to an approach that sought positive, constructive measures within the framework of traditional doctrines. Leo's sounder grasp of the nature and complexity of modern problems produced a greater sympathy for bewildered mankind. His flexibility allowed a smoother adjustment to new situations. We have already seen an example of the Pope's method in his sane approach to the French problems. One of the cardinals, speaking for Leo, stated succinctly the ideas that determined the Holy Father's technique:

It is the special property of human institutions and laws that there is nothing in them so holy and salutary but that custom may alter it, or time overthrow it, or social habits bring it to naught. So in the Church of God, in which changeableness of discipline is joined with absolute immutability of doctrine, it happens not rarely that things which once were apposite and suitable become in the course of time out of date, or useless, or even hurtful.[21]

Leo, who found so much to admire in contemporary civilization, set himself the task of demonstrating to the Catholic world what was or was not compatible with traditional Christianity.

For the sake of analysis, Leo XIII's works may arbitrarily be divided into categories of intellectual, political, social, and spiritual. In his statements, however, there is much cross reference and overlapping of subject. The four most important encyclicals are probably *Aeterni Patris, Libertas Praestantissimum, Immortale Dei,* and *Rerum Novarum.* The others elucidate or expand the thought of these four.

Leo established his ideological orientation in *Humanum Genus* (1884). Although this encyclical had Freemasonry for its subject, it explained that the Church's condemnation of this group rested on the naturalism which was its philosophical base. Naturalism insists that human nature and human reason alone are sufficient guides to human conduct, without leaving any room for the supernatural. For Leo XIII, the existence of God, the truths of revelation, and the reality of the supernatural were the touchstones for all human actions. Because of the relationship between naturalism and rationalism, the foremost characteristic of late nineteenth-century thought, it is evident that Leo could find much to criticize in the diverse intellectual currents of his time.

Libertas Praestantissimum (1888) investigated current notions about liberty, another rallying cry of the century's thinkers. Leo's starting point was the philosophy of liberalism, which he attacked on the grounds that it allowed equality of truth and error, denied all objective standards of truth, and placed the individual beyond the reach of all authority. Careless thinking, he insisted, had confused liberty with license, the abuse of freedom. The Holy Father analyzed specific liberties of worship, speech, press, and conscience, showing the necessary limits that applied in each case. Emphatically he asserted that the Church had ever been a staunch champion of liberty, which he described as "the highest of natural endowments."

The positive side of the encyclical was Leo's definition of liberty as "the faculty of choosing means fitted for the end proposed," and his demonstration of the dependence of liberty on reason and law. "Therefore," he wrote, "the true liberty of human society does not consist in every man doing what he pleases, for this would simply end in turmoil and confusion . . . ; but rather in this, that through the injunctions of the civil law all may more easily conform to the prescriptions of the eternal law." The Holy Father concluded with some considerations on tolerance and the willingness whereby the Church "usually acquiesces in certain modern liberties" in the name of prudence. This attitude Leo contrasted with the intolerance of the doctrinaire liberals.

Whether or not he consciously intended it, Leo XIII encouraged more than a revival of scholastic philosophy when he published *Aeterni Patris* in 1879, for the impetus he set in motion was felt in the whole range of Catholic intellectual activity. As he saw it, the chief cause of the problems of the nineteenth century was its confused philosophical foundation, with the result that "False conclusions concerning divine and human things, which originated in the schools of philosophy, have crept into all the orders of the State, and have been accepted by the common consent of the masses." Thought precedes action; of this Leo entertained no doubt. Hence the only way to effect a basic reorientation of modern life was to put it on a sound philosophical foundation. Even in the physical sciences which were progressing so marvelously and stridently challenging theology, "the investigation of facts and the contemplation of nature is not alone sufficient for their profitable exercise and advance." Surveying European thought through the centuries, Leo XIII demonstrated in *Aeterni Patris* that the Church had always fostered philosophy as a prerequisite for sound theology as well as for its apologetic value.

Many years earlier Leo had developed an interest in the philosophy of St. Thomas Aquinas; as Bishop of Perugia, he had insisted that Thomism be expounded in his seminary. Leo did not stand alone in this regard, for others such as the philosophers Kleutgen and Taparelli had also begun an effort to rehabilitate Thomism. The special attraction which this system held for Leo was its reconciliation of reason and faith, the major intellectual problem of his time. As Leo expressed it in *Aeterni Patris:*

Again, clearly distinguishing, as is fitting, reason from faith, while happily associating the one with the other, he [St. Thomas] both preserved the rights and had regard for the dignity of each; so much so, indeed, that reason, borne on the wings of Thomas to its human height, can scarcely rise higher, while faith could scarcely expect more or stronger aids from reason than those which she has already obtained through Thomas.

Therefore, Leo concluded, the Catholic world should return to St. Thomas and adopt his system as its own "official" philosophy. Thus equipped, Catholic teachers in general and the clergy in particular should better be able to cope with the challenges of modern thought.

In some circles, *Aeterni Patris* was greeted as a typical pronouncement from a Church immured in its medieval past, and to the nineteenth century "medieval" implied obscurantism. It is true that Leo XIII often did glorify the Middle Ages in uncritical fashion; it was no accident that he built a splendid mausoleum in St. John Lateran for the remains of Pope Innocent III. However, the encyclical itself shows definitely that Leo did not imagine that in the intellectual sphere it was advisable to return blindly to the past, however glorious. He had too much respect for the genuine achievement of his own century to reject it outright. He advised that "every word of wisdom, every useful thing by whomsoever discovered or planned, ought to be received with a willing and grateful mind," and if there is anything in scholasticism that "ill agrees with the discoveries of a later age," this should be discarded.

On November 18, 1893, Leo XIII published *Providentissimus Deus* (*The Study of Holy Scripture*). The historicity and divine inspiration of the Scriptures were under attack from the so-called "higher criticism," an offshoot of rationalism. Lamenting these attacks, the Pope urged Catholic scholars to come to the defense of the Scriptures. He called upon them to take up the study of the Oriental languages and the techniques of criticism in order to turn the weapons of the critics on themselves. Leo expressed unlimited confidence in their ability to vindicate the traditional doctrine of the Church. He again demonstrated his willingness to accept all the latest discoveries and techniques when he advised Catholic Scriptural scholars that

none of the recent discoveries which the human mind has made is foreign to the purpose of their work. On the contrary, let them make haste in any case where our times have discovered something useful in the matter of biblical exegesis to avail themselves of it forthwith and by their writings to put it at the service of all.

This admonition is contained in the instructions by which Leo in 1902 set up the Pontifical Biblical Commission in Rome to implement *Providentissimus.*

Further examples of Leo's zeal for educational and intellectual progress could easily be cited. *Immortale Dei* contains some fine passages expressing his confidence in intellectual endeavor; he wrote that "every newly discovered truth may serve to further the knowledge or the praise of God. . . ." In 1881, against the opposition of the Curia, he opened the secret archives of the Vatican, down to the year 1831, with the comment that "we have nothing to fear from the publication of the documents." This won high praise from historians who were just then beginning the scientific study of history. Some half-dozen countries soon established institutes in Rome for the exploration of the archives. For the Vatican Library Leo employed such eminent scholars as Denifle, Ehrle, and Hergenroether. Leo saw to it that the Vatican Observatory became one of the best in the world, with all the latest apparatus and a distinguished staff. Among the schools which Leo founded or strengthened may be mentioned the national colleges in Rome for the clergy of Poland and Russia, for the Melchites, Copts, Syro-Chaldeans, Armenians, Bulgars, and Greeks. In 1890 he saw to the foundation in Kandy, Ceylon, of a seminary to train secular priests for that island and for India. Pontifical universities under his patronage arose in Washington, Ottawa, Lyons, Toulouse, and Beirut.

In *Rerum Novarum* (1891) Leo XIII turned to the area of social and economic problems. Although this encyclical was the first official and constructive papal pronouncement about this difficult subject, Leo had ready to hand an extensive Catholic literature and accumulated experience to build on. Manning in England, Gibbons in the United States, Ozanam and De Mun in France, and the Germans Von Ketteler and Kolping had already shown an abiding concern for the working class. Organizations too had been founded to integrate the various investigations into the implications of industrialism. Even before his elevation to the Papacy, but more closely afterwards, Leo XIII followed these efforts. Perhaps because of the lateness of the Industrial Revolution in reaching Italy, the popes had been reluctant to go beyond the point of condemning the program of the socialists. But conditions showed little sign of improving, and many of the poor were already moving into the more extreme Marxism. Hence the significance of *Rerum Novarum* lay in part in its timeliness, but chiefly in its candid recognition of the existence of the social problem. For decades, the working class had heard papal condemnations of others' ideas for curing social evils, but they had despaired of any real understanding, any concrete guidance from the Vatican. Leo XIII changed all this, and for his efforts he became known as "The Pope of the Workingman."

At the start of *Rerum Novarum* Leo acknowledged the existence of the social problem and the need for an immediate solution for "the misery and wretchedness pressing so heavily and unjustly at this moment on the vast majority of the working classes." He realized that this situation arose from the new industrial organization and was thus totally different from anything the Church or society had experienced before. Nearly one-third of the encyclical was devoted to proving that socialism did not possess the answer, since it would hurt the workers as much as it would help them. Most emphatically Leo insisted that "The first and most fundamental principle, therefore, if one would undertake to alleviate the condition of the masses, must be the inviolability of private property." At the same time, Leo declared that economic liberalism had also to be rejected; thus he courageously eliminated the dangerous possibility of too close an alliance between the Church and the bourgeoisie.

Because of the nature of man and the question of justice, Leo affirmed that the voice of the Church should be heard on economic matters. No practical solution is possible, he said, without taking the Church into consideration. In regard to concrete issues such as the wage question, Leo deduced from the injunctions of Scripture and the traditional thought of the Church the norm that a sufficient wage represented enough to enable the worker to maintain himself and his family "in reasonable comfort," and to accumulate some savings. More precise than that he could not be. Leo clearly preferred that this and other issues be settled between employer and workers themselves on the basis of the moral principles binding on each. As more workable remedies Leo advised two things: 1) the formation of labor unions, which Leo hoped would "become more numerous and more efficient," and 2) intervention by the state. While Leo carefully outlined limits beyond which the state should not go, he wrote that "The richer class have many ways of shielding themselves . . . ; whereas those who are badly off have no resources of their own to fall back upon, and must chiefly depend upon the assistance of the State." By assistance he meant more than organized charity.

Rerum Novarum was a trumpet call for justice in the economic sphere. Leo XIII's contemporaries saw in it mainly an attack on socialism. The next generation realized that it also condemned capitalism, and so there were those who described Leo XIII as the socialistic Pope. Later still, liberalism, having evolved full circle from its original position, hailed Leo as a pioneer in the welfare-state ideology. The least that can be said is that with *Rerum Novarum* Leo XIII set to work to win back the working class for Catholicism.

A goodly portion of Leo XIII's collected writings is devoted to the political order. *Immortale Dei* (*The Christian Constitution of States,* 1885) holds first place here, but close behind come *Diuturnum* (1881), *Sapientiae Christianae* (1890), *Au milieu des sollicitudes* (1892), and *Graves de Communi* (1901). Many other pronouncements touch on aspects of the political life. John Courtney Murray, S.J., the most penetrating interpreter of Leo XIII's political views, has counted ninety-seven statements in Leo's writings dealing with Church-State relations.[22] Other aspects which Leo discussed in greater or less detail are the origin of political authority, forms of governments, and the limits of state action. In each of these areas Leo's considerations are "dated" by virtue of the special historical situation that called them into being, while at the same time they propound permanent and basic principles. Americans should note that Leo almost always wrote without specific reference to the United States.

Leo XIII viewed the political scene through his belief in the existence of an objective order of truth and morality against which human affairs must be judged. He insisted that political power has its source in God, citing the traditional quotation from St. Paul's *Epistle to the Romans* in support of his position. Whoever exercises power, therefore, may not do so without restraint, but rather under the restrictions imposed by the Creator. In other words, Leo stood firmly in opposition to the secularization of politics which had been in formation since Machiavelli. In *Diuturnum* he spoke out strongly against such theories on the origin of the state as had been developed by Rousseau. In disapproving of Rousseau's concept of popular sovereignty, Leo foresaw the risk that the democratic state might be perverted into modern totalitarian democracy.

Republicanism as a form of government met with the Holy Father's approval, as did any other form as long as it had no intrinsic qualities that obstructed justice. *Immortale Dei* declared unequivocally: "The right to rule is not necessarily, however, bound up with any special mode of government. It may take this or that form, provided only that it be of a nature to insure the general welfare." Leo's personal preference, conditioned by his aristocratic background and experience, was for monarchy; however, as his attitude toward the French Republic revealed, he admitted that other circumstances demanded other forms. Leo thought of government in paternalistic terms. For this reason he permitted broad powers in the regulation of the lives of the citizens. Here too his own experience was determinative, and his thoughts on liberty must be studied against this background.

In Church-State relations Leo's goal was always harmony or concord. In the traditional manner he described Church and State as two distinct, philosophically perfect societies, both deriving their existence from God, and each supreme in its own area. Because of their common origin and the fact that they have jurisdiction over the same subjects, they have the duty to co-operate to assist each other to achieve their own ends. Through co-operation or harmony, Leo insisted, they can solve problems arising in the concrete situations where their jurisdictional divisions lack precise delimitation. For these reasons Leo XIII condemned separation of Church and State. Here again the decisive factor was his European experience, since in this milieu separation involved subjection of the Church and restriction of its activity by the State, together with the State's complete abdication of its responsibilities to the Creator, namely, the promotion of morality and religion. In the abstract, and on the basis of the contingent historical data that shaped Leo XIII's thought, he declared in *Immortale Dei* that it was "unlawful to place the various forms of divine worship on the same footing as the true religion," that is, Catholicism. However, since not everyone recognizes Ca-

tholicism as the true religon, Leo "does not, on that account, condemn those rulers who, for the sake of securing some great good or
of hindering some great evil, allow patiently custom or usage to be a
kind of sanction for each kind of religion having its place in the
State."

A fourth, heterogeneous category of Leo XIII's labors includes
his spiritual, theological, and missionary activities. Leo's accomplishments in these areas are frequently overshadowed by his other, more
spectacular acts, but they should not be overlooked. He devoted
eleven encyclicals to the Blessed Virgin and the Rosary. The closing
years of Leo's life witnessed his consecration of all mankind to the
Sacred Heart of Jesus in 1899, and the profoundly spiritual encyclicals on Christ the Redeemer and the Holy Eucharist in 1900 and
1902, respectively. He instituted the feast of the Holy Family, and
encouraged devotion to St. Joseph. Among his canonizations were
Saints John Baptist de la Salle, Peter Claver, John Berchmans, and
Alphonsus Rodriguez; among his beatifications were Blessed Thomas
More and Blessed John Fisher. His interest in the cause of the reunion of Christendom did not produce concrete results; in fact, this
cause suffered a setback when he found it necessary in 1896 to declare the invalidity of Anglican orders, thereby stemming the talk of
accord with Canterbury. Some small successes were enjoyed among
the schismatic Oriental groups.

European imperialistic expansion proffered new opportunities for
missionary endeavor which Leo XIII eagerly seized upon. His
pontificate witnessed a far-flung expansion of Catholicism. Altogether, Leo established 248 episcopal and archiepiscopal sees, 48
vicariates or prefectures apostolic, and two patriarchates. The Dark
Continent attracted particular attention. One of his first papal acts
in 1878 involved authorizing the mission of the White Fathers
in central Africa. The following year the prefecture of Senegal and
the apostolic vicariate of the Gold Coast were established, followed
by the prefectures of Dahomey, Fernando Po, Upper Niger, Lower
Niger, the Ubanghi, French Guinea, and the apostolic vicariate
of the French Congo. Regular hierarchies were provided for the

Church in North Africa in 1884, India in 1886, and Japan in 1891. Leo paid close attention to the Eastern Rites of the Church such as those in India and among the Slavic people of Eastern Europe. After a lapse of centuries, the hierarchy was restored in Scotland. In 1899 a national council of the South American bishops convened at Leo's invitation in Rome, since they could not agree on a site closer to home.

Officially, the United States remained mission territory throughout the nineteenth century. Leo XIII carefully watched the rapid development of the Church there and made the necessary administrative adjustments as they became necessary. He created three new metropolitan sees at Chicago, Saint Paul, and Dubuque, and increased the number of dioceses by twenty-eight. Against the wishes of the American hierarchy, Leo in 1893 appointed Archbishop Satolli as the first Apostolic Delegate to the United States, a move designed to establish direct and regular communication between the Vatican and the American Church, which was then going through a particularly stormy period. The Holy Father won the gratitude of American Catholic workingmen by refusing, at the vigorous urging of Cardinal Gibbons, to forbid Catholic membership in the Knights of Labor, the first major American labor organization. His two chief documents to the American hierarchy are the encyclicals *Longinqua Oceani,* January 6, 1895, and *Testem Benevolentiae,* January 22, 1899. In the former, commemorating the Columbian Exposition, Leo XIII congratulated the hierarchy on the progress of their country and Church, and commented on aspects of the American scene. *Testem Benevolentiae* exonerated American Catholicism of the "phantom heresy" of Americanism.

Leo's curiosity about the United States is glimpsed in one of Archbishop Ireland's anecdotes: "One of my hardest experiences with Leo was when I was asked to tell him in brief summary the exact radical difference between our two American political parties, the Republican and the Democratic."[23] In his various encyclicals the Holy Father frequently alluded to the United States, albeit superficially. Here he saw a concrete example of the Catholic Church adapting itself successfully to modern civilization—the foremost goal of his own life's work. From this he took courage. As he wrote in his letter to Cardinal Gibbons and the hierarchy on April 15, 1902: "Therefore, while the changes and tendencies of nearly all the nations which were Catholic for many centuries give cause for sorrow, the state of your churches, in their flourishing youthfulness, cheers Our heart and fills it with delight." In Archbishop Ireland's words: "Speaking of America, he would say with manifest admiration, *'L'avvenire'*—'The Future.' "[24]

As his life drew to a close, Leo was aware of how much remained to be done and of how tenuous were some of his achievements. He knew the strength of the opposition elements in the Curia that had looked askance at his progressive pace. The task that he had sought to accomplish had to be continued, for the Church in each generation faces the problem of reconciling its principles with the peculiar features of worldly civilization. When Leo received a delegation of French workmen who came to thank him for *Rerum Novarum,* he told them: "Realise in deeds those things of which the principles have been placed beyond dispute. If in regard to the application of such principles, there are still obscure aspects and doubtful points, as is inevitable in problems of such complexity, we must leave the solution to time and experience."[25] Subsequent events substantiated the opinion of many of Leo's contemporaries that his pontificate, on the whole, had been a success. He died on July 20, 1903. The historian can only lament that an earlier generation has pre-empted the appellation "The Great" for its own Leo.

NOTES

1. This is the order of names given on the baptismal certificate as translated in Charles J. O'Malley, *The Great White Shepherd of Christendom* (Chicago, 1903), p. 30. There is considerable confusion among the biographers, since Pecci dropped the Vincent from the time of his secondary schooling.

2. Boyer D'Agen, *Die Briefe des jungen Joachim Pecci,* trans. from the French (Regensburg, 1897), as used by W. Lorenz, "Die Jugend Leos XIII.," *Stimmen der Zeit,* 165 (1959/60), pp. 415–423.

3. Eduardo Soderini, *The Pontificate of Leo XIII,* trans. by Barbara B. Carter, I (London, Burns, Oates and Washbourne, 1934), p. 48.

4. *Ibid.,* p. 54.

5. P. A. Baumgartner, "Bischöfliche Actenstücke des Cardinals-Erzbischofs Joachim Pecci von Perugia, jetzt Papst Leo XIII.," *Stimmen aus Maria-Laach,* XVII (1879), pp. 333–352, 479–496.

6. J. B. Bury, *History of the Papacy in the 19th Century (1864–1878),* (London, Macmillan, 1930), p. 2; Lorenz, *op. cit.,* pp. 422–3.

7. L. Petit and J. B. Martin, *Collectio Conciliorum recentiorum* (Arnhem, 1923), vol. 13 (vol. 49 in Mansi series), c. 150.

8. Pope Leo XIII, *The Church and Civilization* (New York, 1878), pp. 10–11.

9. Soderini, *op. cit.,* pp. 20–21.

10. Carlton J. H. Hayes, *A Generation of Materialism 1871–1900* (New York, Harper, 1941), pp. 141–142.

11. All quotations from the encyclicals of Leo XIII, unless otherwise indicated, are from the edition by John J. Wynne, S.J. *The Great Encyclical Letters of Pope Leo XIII* (New York, 1903).

12. Cf. Encyclical *Humanum Genus* and others.

13. A. C. Jemolo, *Church and State in Italy 1850–1950,* trans. by David Moore (Oxford, Blackwell, 1960), p. 78.

14. Eduardo Soderini, *Leo XIII, Italy and France,* trans. by Barbara B. Carter (London, Burns, Oates and Washbourne, 1935), pp. 3, 64–65.

15. Jemolo, *op. cit.,* p. 78.

16. Georg Franz, *Kulturkampf* (Munich, Callwey, n.d.), p. 260. Cf. also F. Hanus, *Die Preussische Vatikangesandtschaft 1747–1920* (Munich, Pohl, 1954), pp. 319 ff. for Schlözer's role.

17. Cf. F. Engel-Janosi, *Oesterreich und der Vatikan 1846–1918,* I (Graz, Verlag Styria, 1958); also Alois Hudal, *Die Oesterreichische Vatikanbotschaft 1806–1918* (Munich, Pohl, 1952), pp. 219 ff.

18. Cited in Joseph N. Moody, *Church and Society* (New York, Arts, Inc., 1953), p. 236.

19. Letter to Boyer d'Agen, April 11, 1892, cited in Reuben Parsons, *Studies in Church History,* VI (New York, 1900), p. 201.

20. *Leonis Papae XIII Allocutiones, Epistolae, Constitutiones,* 7 vols. (Paris, Desclée, 1887); *Lettres Apostoliques de Léon XIII, En-*

cycliques, Brefs, etc., Texte latin avec traduction française, 7 vols. (Bruges, Maison de la Bonne Presse, n.d.).

21. Cited in John Courtney Murray, S.J., "Leo XIII on Church and State: The General Structure of the Controversy," *Theological Studies*, 14 (1953), p. 16.

22. *Ibid.*, p. 1; see the full series of four articles in *Theological Studies*, 14 and 15 (1953, 1954).

23. John Ireland *et al.*, "Leo XIII, His Work and Influence," *North American Review*, DLXII (September, 1903), p. 327.

24. *Ibid.*, p. 34.

25. Soderini, *The Pontificate of Leo XIII*, p. 202.

2 The Church and the World in the Nineteenth Century

KENNETH SCOTT LATOURETTE
Yale University

THE NINETEENTH CENTURY presented a striking contrast. On the one hand, forces were at work which seemed to threaten the very existence of Christianity. On the other hand, the Church, at the outset seemingly weak and decadent, ill-prepared to meet the threat, displayed an amazing vitality which made it more potent in mankind as a whole than it had been in any previous century.

The threat was—and still is—multiform. One of its most striking features was that it arose in historic Christendom. Indeed, much of it had at least part of its source in perversions of what had come from Christianity. It seemed that Christianity was giving rise to forces which were making it an anachronism—as though it was digging its own grave. One of the threats was a secularized democracy. Democracy had among its sources the Christian faith, with its emphasis upon the value and dignity of each individual, possessed as the individual is with a soul which, although now sadly marred, was created in the image of God and has before it an eternal destiny, with the possibility of infinite weal or of infinite woe. Yet, at the outset of the nineteenth century and through all the ensuing decades, democracy has repeatedly had secularized forms which have either ignored the Christian faith or have labeled the Church as a menace to the welfare of mankind and an obstacle to progress. That was seen in the French Revolution and in some of the self-styled "liberal" movements of the nineteenth century which, by espousing what was called "liberty," professed to free mankind from the shackles imposed by the Church—and, indeed, by all religion. Communism, which creates governments that it calls democratic, was first formulated in the nineteenth century by men who had once thought of themselves as Christians and is characterized by a secularized perversion of Christian apocalypticism and eschatology. The science of the nineteenth century, as of the twentieth century, had rootages in a Christian view which regards the cosmos as an orderly universe, not chaos, created by God and which men can confidently seek to understand and to utilize for their well-being. Yet, like democracy, it has been ambiguous and has been furthered both by reverent Christians and by men who have attacked Christianity as untenable by intelligent minds. The construction of mechanical devices which, utilizing science, have enabled men to master much of their environment and to harness steam, electricity, and now the atom issued in the vast industrialization of human society, with its factories, its means of transporation and communication, and its huge cities in which men tended and still tend to drift away from the Church and its faith. The peoples of Western Christendom, equipped with these devices, expanded into all the globe, settled its vacant lands, brought great and small nations under their rule, and ransacked the planet for markets and raw materials. Through them the revolution in all aspects of human life begun in Western Christendom spread through all the earth and continues to mount.

At the dawn of the nineteenth century the Catholic Church appeared to many to be moribund and inextricably bound to a social and political structure which was passing. It was tied hand and foot to monarchical governments which were about to be either drastically weakened or swept aside by the revolutionary currents of the day. The administrative authority of the Papacy was all but nullified by Gallicanism, Josephism, the power of the Crown in Spain and Portugal, and Febronianism. The higher clergy were largely wealthy and from a nobility which was being destroyed by the political phases of the revolution. Many of the parish clergy were poverty-stricken and at odds with their ecclesiastical superiors. On the geographic frontiers to which the faith had been carried by the missionary urge of the sixteenth and seventeenth centuries, the Catholic Church appeared to be retreating. During those centuries intrepid missionaries had planted the cross over a wider area than ever before and, indeed, among more peoples than any other religion previously had been represented. Yet a variety of factors had militated against the expansion of the faith—among them the declining vigor of Spain and Portugal, the Enlightenment with its cooling of missionary ardor, the dissolution of the Society of Jesus (only temporary, but crippling while it lasted), the French Revolution, and the Napoleonic Wars. Then, early in the nineteenth century, came the independence of Spanish America and the prolonged struggle between the successor states and the Spanish Crown to control the Church. Combined with secularizing influences from Europe, they dealt blows from which the Catholic Church in that vast area has not yet fully recovered.

But, and here was one of the most striking features of the nineteenth century, the Catholic Church not only survived but displayed a vigor that made it more of a power in the human scene than in any era in the past. That story should be familiar to all Catholics, but may I venture to rehearse it? First of all, the Papacy became a more effective center of the Catholic Church's life than even at the apex of the Middle Ages. Not only was the Pope's infallibility in questions of faith and morals emphatically affirmed and accepted by all the bishops, but the Pope's administrative authority in the Church was more effectively exercised than in any earlier century. For the latter a number of causes can be ascribed. One was the blows given the Catholic Church in several countries, which made the bishops more ready than before to seek the reinforcement of the collective strength of the Church, centering as it did in the Pope. Another was the improved means of communication due to the science and mechanical devices which were often adverse to the faith, but which made it physically more possible for the Pope to keep in touch with his widely flung spiritual domain than in any earlier age. Still another was the formal recognition by the Vatican Council. Politically, the Papacy still seemed to be weak. It is sobering to reflect that the Vatican Council, which defined Papal infallibility and recognized the adminstrative authority of the Pope, was adjourned rather than officially terminated because of the occupation of Rome by the Kingdom of Italy. Yet, a generation earlier the rule had been established that the papal nuncio had precedence in the diplomatic corps in any capital to which one was accredited, and in the decades which followed the Vatican Council the Pope won the Kulturkampf against Bismarck, the most powerful statesman of the Europe of his day.

Next we must note the revival of existing orders and congregations and the founding of new congregations. As we all know, one index of the devotion of Catholics is dedication to the religious life as expressed in orders and congregations. In the nineteenth century not only were old orders and congregations renewed and strengthened after the blows dealt them by the Enlightenment and the French Revolution and in spite of the confiscation of much of their property by anticlerical governments, but in addition more new congregations came into being than in any preceding century.

Along with the resurgence of the religious went the foreshadowings of the devotion of the laity seen in the twentieth century in Catholic Action and through other channels which has led some to call this century the century of the laity.

The rising tide of devotional life had a number of manifestations —among them the first of the Eucharistic Congresses that have been a striking feature of the Catholic Church in the present century in expressing and stimulating the loyalty of both laity and clergy; the heightened devotion to Mary seen not only in the enthusiastic reception of the proclamation of her Immaculate Conception, but also in the throngs that flocked to Lourdes and to other centers dedicated to her; the beginnings of the Liturgical Movement; and the popularity of such contemporary saints as the Curé of Ars.

We must not forget the revival in Catholic theological scholarship of which we are rightly to hear more in succeeding papers.

Nor can we ignore the fashion in which the Catholic Church addressed itself to the problems brought by the growth of industrialization and the kind of society which emerged from it. To this, too, a later paper is to be addressed. We do well to recall that Leo XIII gave impetus and leadership to Catholic movements which were already in progress in more than one country.

Fully as striking as any of the features of the nineteenth-century revival in the Catholic Church was the geographic extension of its borders. That was partly by emigration to the Americas, Australia, and New Zealand. The holding to the faith of the millions of this vast hegira was not automatic. It was accomplished only through devoted clergy and laity, some from the first generation of emigrants or specially recruited in Europe, or by the faithful of the second and later generations born in the lands of their adoption. The extension was also by missions among non-Christians, mainly in Asia, Africa, and the islands of the Pacific, but among the Indians of the Americas as well. Here was an outpouring of missionary zeal previously un-equaled in numbers and issuing in planting the Catholic Church among more peoples even than in the heyday of the sixteenth and seventeenth centuries.

Another feature of the amazing vitality of the Church in the nineteenth century was the remarkable awakenings in Protestantism and the renewal of life in some of the Eastern Churches. I am quite aware of the questions with which Catholics will greet the inclusion of these movements of Christian origin under the designation of the Church. However, as a Protestant, I have ventured to give to the word Church the inclusive scope accorded it by some Protestants— that implied in the phrase "the family of God" and in one of the prayers in the Anglican Liturgy, "the body of Christ, which is the blessed company of all faithful people." Many Protestants, I among them, regard the "family of God" and that "blessed company" as the Church. We believe that it is to be found in all the ecclesiastical bodies which bear the name of church and even outside them, and that only God knows, and I say that reverently, who are of it.

At the beginning of the nineteenth century, Protestantism, even more than the Catholic Church, seemed ill-prepared to meet the challenge of the new day. In contrast with the Catholic Church, with its wide geographic extension in Europe, the Americas, Asia, and the shores of Africa, it was almost entirely confined to north-western Europe and the British Isles, with a slight representation in the Atlantic seaboard of North America and a few enclaves on the African coast and in India, Ceylon, and the East Indies. It seemed to be aptly described by a later phrase, attributed to the Anglican Dean Inge, as "the reaction of the Teutonic mind to Christianity." Moreover, it appeared to be hopelessly divided and, except for a few minorities, to be tied to the State, whether in Germany, Scandinavia, England, or Ireland. In the Church of England pluralism and absenteeism were prevalent. On the Continent and in the British Isles, deism and the Enlightenment had largely reduced preaching to moral platitudes and had undercut belief in the Incarnation and the Trinity.

Yet in the nineteenth century that seemingly sterile and dying Protestantism experienced remarkable awakenings, had an even more spectacular geographic expansion than the Catholic Church, made an outstanding impact on human life both within and outside Christendom, and experimented in novel ways toward attaining the unity of Christians—all of them movements which have continued and even mounted in the twentieth century.

The awakenings took the form chiefly of what on the Continent of Europe is known as Pietism and in the Anglo-Saxon world as Evangelicalism. They were not confined to any one denomination but permeated many. From them came most of the men and women who led in holding to the faith the millions of Protestant ancestry in the migrations that marked the past century and the majority of those who planted Protestantism in non-Christian lands. For example, the vast majority of Protestants in the United States owe their faith to Pietism and Evangelicalism. Pietism and Evangelicalism have displayed many variations, but they have in common the distinctive Protestant principles of salvation by faith alone and share with Catholics belief in the Incarnation, the Deity, the atoning death and the resurrection of our Lord Jesus Christ, in the work of the Holy Spirit, and in the inspiration of Holy Scripture. Because of the admittedly dangerous conviction of the right and the duty of individual judgment which is also characteristic of Protestantism but not always consistently followed, many interpretations of these doctrines have been made—numbers of them deemed by the Catholic Church to be invalid and harmful. Yet in the main Protestants have held to these doctrines. Other forms of the awakenings, but affecting smaller numbers than Pietism and Evangelicalism, were the emphasis by some Anglicans on the elements in their tradition derived from the Catholic Church of the early centuries and the stress placed by many Lutherans on doctrines formulated by their predecessors of the sixteenth and seventeenth centuries.

Through its geographic expansion, by the close of the nineteenth century Protestantism was no longer a regional faith but had become world-wide. It became and remains the religion of the majority who have called themselves Christians in the United States, Canada, Australia, New Zealand, and South Africa. It was and is represented by minorities, some of them rapidly growing minorities, in every Latin American country, in every country in Africa south of the Sahara, in North Africa, western Asia, Madagascar, Japan, China, Korea, the islands which fringe the southeast coast of Asia, and almost all the islands of the Pacific. As was true of the Catholic Church, most of this geographic growth of Protestantism was by emigration from Europe and the British Isles of traditionally Christian peoples and by missions among peoples of non-Christian religions. As was also true of the Catholic Church, the growth through both channels was evidence of profound religious conviction and indubitable religious vitality. For instance, the rootage through emigration was not the result of inertia, the automatic retention of the ancestral faith. In the United States, as an example, a chronic trend among Protestants as they came from Europe or as they moved westward from the older states was to allow such church ties as they possessed to lapse. Yet percentagewise the proportion of Protestant church members in the white population mounted and still mounts fairly steadily from decade to decade, the majority of Negroes, pagan when their ancestors were brought to the country, have become professed Protestants, and among the Indians, Protestants and Catholics are about equal in numbers. The spread of Protestantism in the United States among both immigrants and pagans has come about chiefly through those deeply committed to the faith. The same is true in countries and regions other than the United States.

As to the effect of Protestantism upon human life both within and outside the Churches, we need only remind ourselves of such examples as the abolition of the African slave trade and of Negro slavery in the British Empire and the United States, the initiation and growth of the Red Cross, and repercussions through such figures as Gandhi and Sun Yat-sen, the former never calling himself a Christian but profoundly impressed by Christ and the latter baptized, both through contact with Protestants.

Efforts of Protestants to achieve the unity of those who profess and call themselves Christians have been and still are attempts to contribute to the answer of our Lord's prayer for the unity of all who believe in Him that the world may believe. Characteristically Protestant in their variety of expressions, they mounted in the nineteenth century, and in the twentieth century have gained momentum. Historically, they arose primarily from the desire to see all men acknowledge the kingship of Christ.

Significantly, William Carey (1761–1834), who is usually regarded as the major pioneer of the Protestant missionary movement of the past century and a half, proposed that Protestants of whatever denomination who were concerned for the world-wide spread of the faith come together every ten years for co-operative planning. He had the courage to suggest this during the Wars of Napoleon, those stormy near-global predecessors of the World Wars of the present century. His appeal was dismissed by one of his closest friends as "Carey's pleasant dream." It was almost forgotten, but during the nineteenth century a number of efforts were made toward co-operation on a regional or global scale in fulfillment of Christ's command to bring all men to discipleship.

What proved to be a training school for future leaders in the efforts for unity sprang immediately from students of Evangelical and Pietist background and convictions. What was called the Student Volunteer Movement for Foreign Missions arose from a gathering in 1886 convened under the notable lay evangelist, Dwight L.

Moody. That movement had as its watchword the daring phrase "the evangelization of the world in this generation." By it was meant not the conversion of the world but the presentation of the gospel by each generation of Christians to all living in their day. It enlisted thousands, not only in the United States and Canada, but also in the British Isles, the Continent of Europe, and some other countries and regions. They were from many denominations but were predominantly from Evangelical or Pietist circles. The long-time chairman of the Student Volunteer Movement in the United States and Canada was John R. Mott, a Methodist layman. In 1895 Mott led in the formation of the World's Student Christian Federation, which had and has as its motto *Ut omnes unum sint* and which sought and still seeks to unite the Christian students of the world irrespective of their denomination in efforts to win their fellows to Christ. Mott was its first general secretary and then for many years its chairman. Through him units of the World's Student Christian Federation were organized in many countries and world conferences were held. At present, under the Federation, an ambitious program for worldwide evangelism among students is in progress under the general title "The Life and Mission of the Church."

In 1910 what was called "The World Missionary Conference" was held in Edinburgh. Mott was the chairman and headed the Continuation Committee, out of which came the International Missionary Council and a number of what were and are called National Christian Councils. J. H. Oldham, like Mott a layman, a product of the Student Christian Movement of Great Britain and Ireland (which was a direct outgrowth of the Student Volunteer Movement), was the secretary of the Edinburgh gathering and one of the first two secretaries of the International Missionary Council.

Important, too, has been the achievement of the Young Men's Christian Association. Like the Student Volunteer Movement and the World's Student Christian Federation, the YMCA arose in the nineteenth century from Evangelical and Pietist Protestantism. Nonecclesiastical, predominantly lay in its leadership, and disavowing any desire to be a church or to change the ecclesiastical loyalties of its members, and indeed, seeking to strengthen those loyalties, it has enrolled Protestants from many denominations, and in some countries the majority of its members are Catholics and in others are communicants of one or another of the Eastern Churches. It has sought to be a world-wide brotherhood expressing its faith in the kind of actions in which all Christians can join without altering their theological convictions. Mott was caught up in it in his student days and for many years was prominent in it.

The World Council of Churches, a twentieth-century creation, is deeply indebted to the Edinburgh Conference. It combines the World Conference on Faith and Order, to which Edinburgh gave a major impulse, and the Universal Christian Conference for Life and Work, which had as its main creator Nathan Söderblom, Primate of the (Lutheran) Church of Sweden, and who in his youth first caught the vision of a fellowship more inclusive than his own church at a student gathering in Northfield, Massachusetts, led by Moody. After Söderblom's death Oldham became the most inspiring figure of the Life and Work Movement. The tentative constitution of the World Council of Churches was drafted by a committee of about a hundred, representing most of the major Protestant denominational families and which met at Utrecht in 1938 under the chairmanship of William Temple, who had been enlisted in his student days in the Student Christian Movement, had been present at Edinburgh, was created Archbishop of York in 1938, and died as Archbishop of Canterbury, the ranking prelate in the Anglican Communion. Because of World War II, the World Council of Churches was described for ten years as "in process of formation," and was formally organized in Amsterdam in 1948. Mott was its first honorary president, and it has had as its first general secretary a former officer of the World's Student Christian Federation. To insure that the World Council of Churches shall have the missionary purpose at its heart, the International Missionary Council will probably be integrated with it.

The World Council of Churches is described in its constitution as a "fellowship of churches which accept our Lord Jesus Christ as God and Saviour." Although some of its supporters hope that it will

eventually effect the formal union of all the churches, it is not a
"superchurch," and its leaders do not wish it to be more than what it
claims to be—a "fellowship" of churches. At present it embraces
churches which enroll the overwhelming majority of the Protestants
of the Continent of Europe, the British Isles, Canada, Australia, and
New Zealand, the majority of the Protestants of the United States,
Asia, and Africa, and a minority of the Protestants in Latin America.
It includes in its membership the Old Catholic Churches and some
of the Eastern Churches, among them the Orthodox Church of
Greece.

The World Council of Churches is only the leading expression of
what its members call, with what must seem to Catholics unwar-
ranted presumption, the Ecumenical Movement. That movement has
many other manifestations, all with ties with the World Council of
Churches varying in their form and strength, some of them very
slight. Among them, in addition to the International Missionary
Council, are the World's Student Christian Federation, the World
Council of Christian Education, the World's Alliance of Young
Men's Christian Associations, the World's Young Women's Christian
Association, and various national councils of churches. Most of the
churches formed in the present century by unions of existing churches
are members. Among them are the United Church of Christ, the
United Church of Canada, the Church of Christ in China, the Church
of South India, and the Church of Christ in Japan.

We can take the time only for the briefest mention of the
nineteenth-century renewal of life in the Eastern Churches. At the
dawn of that century their conditon was even less promising than
that of the Catholic Church or Protestantism. The Russian Orthodox
Church was completely subservient to the State. In the seventeenth
century Peter the Great had allowed its patriarchate to lapse and had
substituted for it the Holy Synod, completely under the thumb of the
tsar. In the Balkans, Greece, western Asia, and Egypt, the Eastern
Churches were subject to Moslem rulers. In the nineteenth century
a fresh surge of the interior life was seen in the Russian Orthodox
Church, nourished by books of devotion. In the Balkans and Greece

the Turkish yoke was cast off, and the national churches, autonomous, began to recover the vigor which they had lost. Due to Communism, in the twentieth century that hopeful beginning has been partially negated, but life has not been quenched, and in the Greek Orthodox Church it continues to revive.

In concluding summary we can say that although many features of the nineteenth century were hostile to the Church and its faith and large elements in the historic Christendom were partially or entirely dechristianized, starting from a most unpromising condition the Church, whether Catholic, Protestant, or Eastern, experienced remarkable awakenings and by the end of the century was displaying a remarkable growth in inner vitality and in geographic extent. That growth has continued in the present century.

3 Leo XIII and the Social Crisis

RT. REV. JOSEPH N. MOODY
Ladycliff College

IT IS GENERALLY ACCEPTED that with Leo XIII the Papacy addressed itself constructively to the issues that confronted the Church in the modern world. This seems particularly true in regard to the problems that had arisen out of the technological changes which were transforming the social patterns of nineteenth-century Europe and which were soon to affect the whole world.

The central declaration of Leo XIII on the social question, *Rerum Novarum,* can be classified as a substantial contribution to the social thought of the late nineteenth century. But it cannot be understood except in the social crisis of its time. Pope Leo XIII was not an academic thinker. He was concerned with a precise historical situation. He had been called to guide the Church in a stormy period, and he kept his attention fixed on the issues which immediately touched her teaching mission. He could insist that the principles he cited were unchangeable because they were drawn from the revelation of Christ. But their exposition was contemporary, for Leo was applying them to an ensemble of conditons that he would designate as "the social crisis."

Leo located this crisis not in the problem of human want, which had been endemic in all human societies, but in the social consequence of machine technology. Specifically, he defined it as the plight of the industrial worker, and it is to this central issue that *Rerum Novarum* was primarily directed.[1] This basic emphasis links the thought of the Pope to that of Karl Marx, though the two differ radically in principle and perspective. Like Marx, Leo was aware that the revolution in production, transportation, and communications had occurred in a Europe that was undergoing a rapid expansion of population. He knew that this expansion provided the human material for the urban conglomerates that were the most visible evidence of change in industrial society. He was conscious that the mass movement to the factory towns had shattered customary social patterns and left the recruits isolated in an environment that offered them bad housing, marginal subsistence, and periodic unemployment.

If one would confine oneself within the narrow range of social analysis, there is a certain concurrence in the descriptions of Marx and Leo XIII. But the Pope added other factors that were not directly rooted in economic change. *Rerum Novarum* emphasizes the expanding expectations of those who felt that the new technology would remove all inequalities and bring immediate benefits to all. The new industrial workers were brought into contact wtih the whole fabric of optimistic political and sociological ideas which had been elaborated in the Enlightenment and which were a principal target of Leo's strictures. The Pope deplored the weakening or religion that accompanied the industrial transformation,[2] and pointed out its contribution to social discontent. The consequence was the growth of class conflict, stimulated by new ideas and by the close proximity of the industrial worker to evidences of increasing wealth.

It was not merely that the worker envied the conspicuous consumption of the rich, though this was a factor. More subtle was the workers' reaction to a change of values which preceded and accompanied the Industrial Revolution.[3] The more wealth became the standard of achievement in Western society, the greater the urge to share it. Establish virtue as the highest goal of the human person, and only a few will enter the lists; make proficiency in arms the index of status, and the candidates will still be in a minority; intellectual excellence was always a goal with limited appeal; and even the Greek ideal of skill in the affairs of the *polis* would leave some uninterested. Past societies were hierarchical for a variety of reasons; but the elite could remain reasonably secure, for not every one wished to scale the heights. But once possession of wealth was confirmed as the major mark of success and the key to the "good life," as in nineteenth-century Europe, all will want to share. For all men think themselves equally qualified to enjoy material goods. Given a society with a reasonable level of education and communication made possible by technology, and one of two results have followed: social pressure would force a welfare-state situation or it would explode in revolutionary discontent. This is implicit in *Rerum Novarum*,[4] it is shrill in Leon Bloy's prophecies of doom on the European bourgeoisie for crucifying the worker as they robbed him of his religious ideals.[5]

Leo is aware of another psychological factor that complicated the social question and which French commentators call *la capacité oeuvrière*. When the Pope notes that "the workers have more confidence in themselves,"[6] he was stating a fact that had vitiated much of the social idealism of European Catholics involved in the workers' condition. By the closing decade of the nineteenth century the European worker had access to a minimum of education and to expanding democratic ideas. He was in no mood to be patronized. He might remain pessimistic in regard to many features of his environment, but he shared the general optimism about building a "better world." He was certain that he could create this world by his own efforts.[7] The protests that shook working-class circles regarding "collaboration with the bourgeoisie" in the decade following the encyclical are only one indication of this rooted conviction.

Rerum Novarum not only mirrors these general features of working-class reaction to industrial society, it reflects the precise development of the time of its composition. Its opening sentences are a classic statement of class conflict. It would go on to deplore this condition and to suggest remedies; but it accepted it as a fact. Here again it differed from the Marxist view not in social analysis but in objective. The Pope was committed to mitigate the class war which he noted as a fact. The Marxist saw it as an opportunity, a means for final liberation, a condition leading necessarily to its resolution by revolution. Historically, the papal description of the social crisis is accurate. No longer was discontent evidenced in the sporadic outbreaks of violence that had marked the early industrial era. Now there was sustained bitterness in the European working class, reinforced by an aggressive ideology and by powerful Socialist parties. These were pitted against growing concentrations of industry, which were better organized by men determined to protect their interests. No longer was dissatisfaction confined to an elite of the workers who had been influenced by social thinkers. It had entered into the main stream of those employed in Europe's soaring industries.

A glance at the social map of Europe will confirm these observations. Britain was an exception to the trend in the European working class to mobilize in political and social organizations with a militant program of economic change. By 1891 the bulk of the growing trade unions in Britain had rejected revolutionary leadership and were still linked in an uneasy political alliance with the Liberals. On the continent there was a considerable conflict of ideas in the working-class movements, but the appeal of radicalism was unmistakable. In Germany the Christian trade unions had been solidly established in a minority position, and there was a still smaller Liberal group among some white-collar workers. France and Belgium had witnessed the first stirrings of Christian unionism.[8] But the overall picture was highly unfavorable to Christianity and to social stability. Marxism had made massive strides in the 1880's. Highly centralized Social Democratic parties had made their appearance in western and central Europe. For the most part their leadership remained committed to the destruction of the existing system and to the fashioning of a new order in the workers' interest. Not all Marxists were agreed on the program. Some in France were willing to limit their demands to the "possible." There was a tendency elsewhere to work for immediate gains and to relegate the utopia to some distant future. Yet, at the time of the encyclical, German revisionism had not been born. Nor had there yet occurred that large-scale domestication of Marxists into western European political life that was to mark the immediate pre-World War I period. Certainly there was no visible relaxation of hostility to religion in any brand of Marxists.

While the followers of Marx formed increasingly the dominant proletarian movement on the Continent, other types of protest continued to enlist the interest of the workers. Syndicalism was still expanding in France. Its adherents eschewed all parliamentary involvements. They hoped to develop the workers' militancy by strikes that would win concessions from employers and the state, but which were primarily designed to prepare for the day when the entire working class would lay down its tools, paralyze the nation by a general strike, destroy existing structures, and create the free society of the future. Even more intractable were the anarchists, who were more powerful in the industrially backward countries of southern and eastern Europe. These preached "propaganda by deed" and aimed to destroy every vestige of the bourgeois world.

Clearly the protesters were no longer a few utopian journalists and writers. They had swelled into an army that was divided in policy but united in its detestation of "capitalism" and in its scorn for its "ally," religion.

That these programs were not academic is apparent in the disorders that had marked European society since the beginning of Leo's pontificate. In 1889, after several preliminary attempts, two congresses met in Paris during the International Exposition to project the Second International. Both these competing bodies endorsed the proposal of the delegates of the American Federation of Labor that the workers use the first of May for strikes and protests for the eight-hour day. While some national bodies injected qualifications and each group interpreted the proposal in light of its assumptions, the adoption of the resolution and its consequences concentrated public attention on the "social question." On May Day 1890 there were extensive stoppages of work in most European cities and many demonstrations. Some of these were orderly, but in France, Spain, and Italy there were serious clashes with the police and some casualties. In 1891 the demonstrations and disorders were more widespread and more violent. On the eve of the encyclical many felt that the old order of economic liberalism was beginning to show alarming fissures.

All this is reflected in *Rerum Novarum*. The Pope evidences his awareness of the crisis in terse language:

> For the result of civil change and revolution has been to divide cities into two classes separated by a wide chasm. On the one side there is the party which holds power because it holds wealth; which has in its grasp the whole of labor and trade; . . . On the other side there is the needy and powerless multitude, sick and sore in spirit and ever ready for disturbance.[9]

It was an accurate description of the deepening social crisis. What was equally alarming was its geographical spread as new areas experienced the introduction of the machine. It was the proper moment for the official intervention of the Church with its universal interests.

It is this immediate background which explains why Leo's description of the divisions of society into two antagonistic classes appears close to that of the Marxist. This is the way it looked in 1891 to an acute observer. The Pope saw a conflict which verged on the revolutionary in many countries. He was correct, though had he written later his statements would have required qualification. It must be remembered that these descriptions of contemporary society are intended only as a framework for the moral teaching of the encyclical. Pope Leo XIII was not a sociologist. His purpose was moral. He was interested in the pathology of industrial society. Accordingly, *Rerum Novarum* does not provide a careful balance sheet which lists the advantages and disadvantages of industrialization.

Leo's moral preoccupation gives a different shading to the term "class" than that found in Marxist writing where it signifies a group which bears a certain relationship to the means of production. The Pope does employ the term as an equivalent for the workers as distinguished from the employers, and he does say that the former are exploited by the latter. But he also speaks of the "few rich" and the "many poor," the "rich" and the "proletarians," the "great" and the "small," the "two orders." In each of these cases the Pope is alluding to a group of privileged and another group whose lot is hard. The emphasis in his usage is ethical, not sociological.

Nor would the Pope agree with Marx that the mere existence of social classes is the cause of the crisis. What is wrong is not the structure but its misuse: the injustice done by one human group to another. Nor does Leo accept the surplus value theory of Marx, which makes the wage system necessarily exploitative and which insures the ultimate revolution. The Leonine emphasis is on the concrete, the Marxist on the abstract. In the latter theory it is the institution that is at fault—class, wage, property—and it is the institution that has the inner contradictions that makes certain its destruction. Leo's accent is on the actual, on the abuses that would make any human institution unworkable. Marx's determinism foresees necessary and automatic consequences arising from social relationships. Leo maintains the reality of human liberty, and sees the possiblity of correcting the evils and employing human initiative to establish a regime of justice. One could go further and say that Leo speaks of this happy result as a possibility, for there is an optimistic emphasis in *Rerum Novarum*. It is a realistic optimism since it is conditioned by the free action of men. It is in sharp contrast with Marx's radical pessimism in regard to "what is" and radical optimism on "what will be." Subsequent history has been an interesting commentary on the relative validity of the two approaches to the social crisis.[10]

While it is important to distinguish between the Marxist and papal positions on the nature of the crisis, it is equally necessary to note that *Rerum Novarum* is not a defense of the *status quo*. It does not preach simple resignation to the workers. It rejects the complacency of the economic liberals who would defend all by an appeal to the necessary operation of natural law. But it emphatically belongs to the evolutionary or reformist class of criticism of industrial society. Leo is unequivocally on the side of those who would repair, not destroy, the social structure. He has no sympathy with the myth that proclaims revolution as the savior of suffering humanity. Nor would he condone class conflict as a necessary step in the dialectic progress of mankind. Class conflict is seen for what it was: a regrettable consequence of social wrong which has obscured the reality of labor and capital's mutual dependence.

The social crisis to which Leo addressed himself in 1891 had been maturing in western Europe since the introduction of the machine. When the Pope came to frame the official position of the Church in *Rerum Novarum,* he had at his disposal more than a half century of pioneering social effort under Catholic auspices. It is important to grasp the character of this new concern. It was not a simple interest in the poor. That had been a characteristic of the Church at every time and in every area. What was needed under industrialism was not only a concern for poverty but a program to deal with its causes. The concept of justice, as well as charity, would have to be incorporated into any social theory that would meet effectively the industrial world. As Duroselle has pointed out,[11] two factors were needed before a social Catholicism could be born: (1) an understanding that the exceptional gravity of the social problems made it necessary to speak of poverty rather than the poor, and to prepare collective action for reform rather than to trust to individual charity; (2) a sufficiently optimistic attitude toward the future that would encourage the elaboration of theoretical solutions and practical proposals.

These preconditions were met by some Catholics as early as the 1830's, and a body of Catholic social thought was elaborated in the following decades. Some of the pioneers, as Von Ketteler in Germany and Ozanam in France, had as deep an understanding of social realities as their more numerous socialist contemporaries. Had Catholics generally accepted Ozanam's dictum "Avoid politics and concentrate on the social question," the widespread religious defection of the industrial workers might have been checked. But politics could hardly be avoided when the traditional position of the Church was under assault in every European country, when the struggle over education was at its height, and when the problem of the temporal power was in the forefront of Catholic consciousness. At root was an intellectual climate unfavorable to religion which drained from the Church many of the mentally vigorous and simultaneously poisoned the newly aroused urban workers.[12]

Thus, while Catholic social spokesmen were courageous and farsighted, they faced severe obstacles both within their own body and from their environment. The consequence was a twofold defeat: they attracted only a small minority of the workers and they did not win the majority of practicing Catholics to their views. They remained a minority in the Church, often regarded with suspicion as tainted with socialism. While their numbers grew and their doctrines became more precise, they were desperately in need of official support. Here lies the importance of Leo's intervention, which may be compared to the "capture" of the Papacy by the reforming elements in the eleventh century.

Contemporaries did not see the election of Pope Leo as the decisive event which we now consider it to be. The Marquis de Vogüé, an eyewitness of his coronation in 1878, wrote: "His coronation appeared to us as a parade of vanished realities, as the evocation of a ghost. We carried from the ceremony the impression of an institution that was dead."[13] Yet in the social question and in the other fields this Pope was to redefine the relations of the Church with the existing world and attempt to build a bridge over the chasm that had opened between them.

Leo's preparation had been adequate but not spectacular. In the early years of his priesthood he seemed certain of a promising diplomatic career when he became Nuncio to Brussels in 1843. The post gave him the opportunity to view the Continent's most rapidly industrializing nation in the melancholy early stage of the process. But his career was cut short and he was named Bishop of Perugia, where he remained for thirty-one years. His major development came here as a diocesan administrator. In his Lenten letter for 1877 he denounced the abuses in the current economic world and proposed two remedies: intervention of the civil authority and fidelity to the laws of God and the Church.[14]

The social crisis was only one of the problems which confronted Leo's pontificate. Often it seemed overshadowed by such issues as the liquidation of the Kulturkampf, the laic laws of the Third Republic, or the continued hostility between the Vatican and the Italian government.[15] But the Pope never lost sight of the social question.[16] Before the end of 1878, Emile Keller, a prominent figure in the French Conseil des Études, told his colleagues on his return from Rome that the Holy See was interested in social questions and had invited the group to communicate its findings to the Vatican. In 1882 Leo encouraged the creation of the "Roman Committee for Social Studies" under the presidency of Monsignor Jacobini. Monsignor Mermillod, the exiled Bishop of Geneva, was a formative influence in this group. He later set up a kind of Catholic International at the University of Fribourg in 1884. The Pope maintained an interest in the studies of this union of Catholic social thinkers, gave audiences freely to its members, and in 1890 received a report on its findings which became available for the drafts of *Rerum Novarum*. The international gatherings of socially minded Catholics at the Congresses of Liége in 1887 and 1890, under the presidency of Bishop Doutreloux, also won sympathetic attention from Leo.

In addition to this movement of ideas, which stretched back to Von Ketteler,[17] Leo observed the action of distinguished bishops who became involved in the cause of labor. He was impressed by Cardinal Manning's intervention in the London dock strike in 1889. His interest in the Knights of Labor case, presented by Cardinal Gibbons,[18] widened his perspectives of the trade union movement by acquainting him with American conditions. Of considerable importance was his reception of the French workers' pilgrimages, organized by Léon Harmel and Cardinal Langénieux. Starting in 1887 with 1,400 workers, the number reached 10,000 in 1889 and made a world-wide impression. Leo not only received the workers with affection, but he praised the organizers and the priests and employers who accompanied them, hinting that he would soon speak on this subject, the gravity of which he recognized. De Mun later described their impact as follows:

Then came our pilgrimages, and you recall the triumphant reception of the workers at the Vatican where they were greeted with princely honors and where the Pope received the men of the people in their working clothes. The crowd of workers took their place on the steps of the royal staircase, surprised at this new majesty which was taking the place of the sovereigns of old. It was an unforgettable spectacle. All those who saw it remember its splendor, but not every one can measure its depth. It was not only a great manifestation; it was the solemn meeting of the Head of the Church with the envoys of the people. It was the formation of the encyclical and the beginning of a new age.[19]

It may not be an exaggeration to say that these popular processions opened the road for the encyclical. Certainly, as a consequence of them, Harmel enjoyed immense prestige at the Vatican. The Pope saw him as the only one who could get concrete results of importance. Loyal to his faith, he had the affection of his workers and labored for their material and moral development.

Rerum Novarum may be regarded as a synthesis of much of this persevering work of Catholic social thinkers and reformers. New light has recently been thrown on the details of the process whereby these various streams were merged in the classic document. During World War II, Monsignor Tardini, then pro-Secretary of State, became interested in the background of the encyclical. A search revealed a large volume in the handwriting of Monsignor Volpini, private secretary of Leo XIII, which contained all the versions of *Rerum Novarum* from the first draft to the definitive text. Each version had its corrections and erasures. After study it was entrusted to Monsignor Antonazzi, who carefully prepared it for publication.[20]

We now know that Volpini received the first Italian draft on July 5, 1890 from the Jesuit P. Liberatore. In September he received a second in Italian from Cardinal Zigliara and at once began to translate it into Latin. "By order of a superior" he interrupted the work on October 28, and gave the second version to Cardinal Mazella and then to P. Liberatore, both of whom modified it. This third version was translated into Latin by January 31, 1891. But meanwhile it had been studied and recast by Monsignor Boccali. This was in turn translated on April 21 and was meant to appear on May 10. But it was subjected to important but limited changes and finally appeared, dated May 15.

The published volume contains the two original versions; then in parallel columns the corrected Zigliara-Mazella text, the Latin version of Volpini, the version of Boccali, and the definitive text. Footnotes provide all the corrections and variants, as well as the full critical apparatus employed in editing.

This volume allows us for the first time to study the progression of ideas in the formation of *Rerum Novarum*. Among other items, we can now understand the Pope's handling of the issue of corporatism, which was a serious subject of debate among the social Catholics of the period.[21] Liberatore was resolutely corporatist. In his draft we find approval for unions of employers and workers who would be joined in a single body for the defense of moral and material interests under the guidance of the Church. Initiative would come largely from the employers. These would enjoy a privileged status in public law and would be closely associated with the state. Along with these "mixed" unions would be larger groupings in religious associations in which all the members of the workers' families would participate and which would provide a wide variety of social, educational, and moral services. Funds for the associations would be provided by dues from the workers and contributions of the wealthy, since their possessions obligate them to charity. These are the ideas of La Tour du Pin, *L'Association catholique,* Léon Harmel's *Catéchisme du patron* (1889), and *Manuel d'une corporation Chrétienne* (1879). The Pope had apparently given support to this interpretation in his allocutions to the French worker pilgrims, although he always added such qualifications as "at least in regard to their substance . . . and under such forms as the new conditions of the time permit."

Zigliara renounced this "social Christian order" and emphasized the need of strictly professional working-class organizations. More specifically than in the final text, he insisted on their autonomy, and on their private and voluntary character. To preserve their liberty he gave them no function in the public order. He did not spare praise for the initiative of the employers and their efforts to aid the workers, but he placed accent on variety of methods to reach the objective. He was particularly interested in protecting the activities of these associations from the intervention of the State. Their rules and practices are to be a matter for the membership. Associations of employers and workers are commended and should provide for the needy in periods of unemployment, sickness, and distress. As for their other objectives, Zigliara placed emphasis on the religious goals.

The final text follows Zigliara rather closely. But there is one significant change with the addition of: "It is gratifying to know that there are actually in existence not a few associations of this nature, *consisting either of workmen alone,* or of workmen and employers together. . . ."[22] It has been thought that Leo himself must have given this new orientation to the encyclical at the last moment. Monsignor Antonazzi has established that, despite the many hands which went into the various redactions of the text, the Pope retained a firm grasp on the development of the encyclical and it was his thought, and his alone, which was expressed in the document. Though Leo wrote little, he carefully supervised its preparation and made verbal suggestions and corrections at every stage of its progress.[23]

It would seem nearly impossible to trace the influence to which Leo responded in his decision to put the strictly workers' union on the same basis as the "mixed union" in the text of his encyclical. Antonazzi shows that Toniolo had no role in the drafting of the document, but that he was highly regarded by the Pope and that he frequently saw the Pontiff in private audience during the period. It is known that Toniolo, while approving "mixed" unions, was one of the first European Catholics to see the necessity of strictly working-class organizations, and that he moved progressively toward this position as the social crisis unfolded. It is possible that his reservations on the possibility of combining employers and workers in the same organization might have persuaded the Pope.

It has also been advanced that Cardinal Gibbons may have been the decisive influence. The parallelism between the encyclical and the memorial of the Cardinal in defense of the Knights of Labor had been pointed out.[24] There is also evidence that he shared the confidence, and even the friendship, of the Pope. It may be that in his conversations with the American Cardinal the Pope realized that he must compose his text in a sense that would be acceptable to the entire world, and he knew that many of the terms, so dear to European social Catholics, would be meaningless, or worse, in America. He had a strong sense of history and may have grasped the direction of social development. As a realist, once he had grasped the distinctive character of the American scene, he could be presumed to make a place for it in the encyclical.[25]

Although Antonazzi's volume proves that corporatist doctrine was strong in the original draft of Liberatore, very little of it remained in the final text.[26] The encyclical insists on the voluntary nature of the workers' associations and the limited role of the state in directing them. In addition to this emphasis on the private nature of the associations—so alien to corporative theory—there is Leo's stress on the freedom of the workers. It would be impossible to read into the encyclical that the employer should organize *his* Christian corporation in his factory or a group of employers in *theirs*. The Pope encourages the employer to give aid but implies that it should be disinterested. It is not essential, because the workers' association is organized according to its own nature and can exist apart from the employer. Nor is the appeal for support directed to the employers as such, but to all the rich, whether or not they are directly connected with a group of workers. The differences between this approach and corporatism is obvious.

This partial disengagement of the Pope from some of the ideas of socially minded Catholics was of great importance for the future. There is no doubt that, despite their dedication and generous work, some of the Catholic champions of the working class, notably in France and Austria, raised serious barriers to their success. Their political ideas often classed them with the "emigrés of the interior" and could not possibly appeal to industrial workers. In spirit they were remote from the world they hoped to influence. They firmly rejected economic liberalism, and this was an advantage. But their economic ideas remained vague, and they lacked the talent for serious economic thought. Even more of a handicap was their paternalism. They had no thought of sharing leadership in their organizations with workers, and they failed to grasp the workers' growing self-confidence. Their major contribution was to remain indirect: their works were training areas where Catholics first came to grips with the social question and where important ideas could germinate.[27]

While the publication of the various drafts of the encyclical assists us in clarifying some disputed points in the text, it must be remembered that Leo did not wish to bind himself to any particular school of Catholic social thought. Soderini, the intimate friend of the Pope's personal secretary, gives this illustration of the Pontiff's caution: Count de Mun sent to the Pope a copy of one of his writings on the social question. The Pope responded in amiable and general terms. De Mun had expected a more specific approbation. Soderini made this known to Leo, who replied: "If I gave my approval to particular points on matters essentially economic, I would be restricting the liberty of men in an area where God left them entirely to themselves." Soderini goes on to quote further:

God has left the solution of many questions to the judgment of men. They have therefore the right to debate them among themselves in order to find the truth. And why ought the Church to prevent such discussions, even before they had begun, by imposing silence on all? Her intervention would be understandable if there was the question of the diffusion of some error, but it would not be at all when men discuss honorably opinions which can be supported in one or another sense. This would be an unjustifiable restriction on human liberty.[28]

Leo follows this policy throughout his encyclical. He is explicit in his rejection of economic liberalism and socialism, as both manifested themselves at the end of the nineteenth century. In their place he sought to project on the social plane a theology of man which would consider him in his relationship with God and his fellow men. He thus reintroduced ethics into the market place where it had been banished by the classical economists and the Marxists. Fundamental was his insistence on the personal dignity of every human being which "no man could outrage with impunity."[29] That is why labor cannot be a commodity, but must be regarded as a creative effort which fulfills the plan of God and is touched by the sacredness of the human. Since the poor can safeguard their right to live only through what they earn through their labor they must be compensated so that they can provide for themselves adequate housing, clothing, and bodily fitness. This is owed them in justice because of their great contribution to the community; for "it may truly be said that it is only by the labor of working men that states grow rich."

It is Leo's moral perspective which gives greater depth to his teaching than is found in competing systems, though it may not compare with them in technical detail. It could be argued that this ethical base is precisely what a large proportion of the industrial workers had sought during the nineteenth century. It was to have a powerful impact. One is tempted to speculate on its effect if it had been enunciated with this clarity and authority earlier in the century.

The absence of precise economic formulation has disturbed some commentators who would like to find in papal teaching more than the popes would claim. *Rerum Novarum* did set forth the right of the Church to restate for industrial society the moral view of man and his needs, leaving it to technical experts to apply it to changing situations.[30] In this Leo anticipated the call of more recent popes for the lay apostolate; for, while he was insistent on the authority of the hierarchy, he saw the entire Church as responsible for the application of just principles to economic life. On the whole, Leo was content to establish the proposition of the primacy of man. The human person derives his dignity from his creation in God's image, from the role assigned him in creation, and from the fact that he was destined to become a son of God who would share God's own life. Since this dignity stems from a divine source, it must be reflected in human society. A society which does not place man in its center fails to regard his nature. Economic arrangements must be at the service of man. Production, profits, and institutions must be subordinated to his moral needs.

By locating the root of the industrial evils in the moral sector Leo could argue that what was bad in the existing system came from human failure. It was a disorientation that had to be cured by co-operative activity, not an inherently evil system that had to be destroyed by class war. There is a consistency in the whole analysis which leads to the conclusion of the need of an awakening of conscience to the imperatives of justice and charity. While modifications of institutions may be desirable, it is vital to modify human conduct in the direction of responsibility, self-sacrifice, love of neighbor, and devotion to the common good.

Some social historians have dismissed this as moralistic. But Leo did not intend that his principles remain on the level of abstraction. His whole purpose was to move men to action.[31] Against the claims of Leo's critics, it could be urged with equal validity that any practical program will remain a paper plan if it ignores the motive power of moral appeal.

Leo does not fail to recommend practical proposals for the mitigation of the social crisis. One of these was the intervention of the State, which the Pope saw not only as the legal protector of the propertied but the protector of the common good. He cut the Gordian knot of laissez-faire theory by placing the claims of justice above those of contracts.[32] With that step taken, he could claim that the workers, the weakest group in the community, were entitled to special protection from society. They must be safeguarded "from the cruelty of greedy speculators who use human beings as mere instruments for money-making."[33] It is the State that must remove the causes of social unrest.

The other means for the amelioration of the social crisis was the workers' associations of many types.[34] These exist by natural right and must be protected by the state. But governments must not choke their vitality by interference in their internal affairs. It is apparent that the Pope prefers confessional unions, but does not exclude the neutral type if they pursue legitimate purposes. He does eschew all violence in the pursuit of their ends.

It can be stated without exaggeration that Pope Leo XIII deserves the title "the Pope of the Workers." A half century later, Pius XII defined *Rerum Novarum* as "the fruitful germ from which has developed a social Catholicism which offers to the sons of the Church, both priests and laymen, the plan and the means for a reconstruction of society."[35]

This is a fair summary. Negatively, the encyclical helped dissipate some of the Catholic indifference to the social crisis. Positively, it encouraged existing social movements and stimulated the creation of new ones.[36] Primarily, it reasserted the position of the Church as a teacher of mankind and placed her authority firmly on the side of justice to industrial labor.[37] Nor did it block further development. Its firmness on moral principle and flexibility on means made it possible for subsequent popes to meet the ever-changing social situation fashioned by modern technology. As a minimum, we can say that we have never had to apologize for *Rerum Novarum*. More accurately, we can state that we owe it a profound debt. As its grateful beneficiaries, we should strive to grasp its relevance to our own time.

NOTES

1. For this reason I prefer the older English title for *Rerum Novarum, On the Condition of the Working Class,* to the more descriptive *Rights and Duties of Capital and Labor* employed by Étienne Gilson in *The Church Speaks to the Modern World* (Garden City, Image Books, 1957), pp. 200–244. However, this seems the best English text. It will be used throughout this paper and noted as *RN*. As justification for the title, cf. *RN,* sec. 60, p. 238: "At the time being, the condition of the working class is the pressing question of the hour."
2. The author of this paper has dealt with the problem in "The Dechristianization of the French Working Class," *Review of Politics,* XX (January, 1958), pp. 46–69.

3. Cf. Peter Viereck, "The Revolution in Values; Roots of the European Catastrophe, 1870–1952," *Political Science Quarterly* (September, 1952), pp. 339–356.

4. Many of the Pope's deepest insights are not developed, e.g., *RN*, sec. 49, p. 232, where he describes his time as "an age of wider education, of different habits, and of far more numerous requirements in daily life."

5. It is interesting that the Left Wing of the British Labor Party has become worried by working-class indifference to socialist goals and satisfaction with postwar prosperity. It is calling for a renewal of spiritual values. Cf. *The New Statesman*, LVIII, No. 1503 (January 2, 1960), pp. 1–12.

6. Note also his phrase "the increased self-reliance and closer mutual combination of the working class"; cf. *RN*, sec. 1, p. 205.

7. Cf. Val R. Lorwin, *The French Labor Movement* (Cambridge, Harvard University Press, 1954), p. 37. The whole volume is most useful as background for this paper.

8. Michael P. Fogarty, *Christian Democracy in Western Europe, 1820–1953* (University of Notre Dame Press, 1957), pp. 186–231.

9. *RN*, sec. 47, p. 230.

10. *RN*, secs. 19–21, pp. 214–217, gives the papal position on class conflict.

11. J.-B. Duroselle, *Les Débuts du catholicisme social en France (1822–1870)* (Paris, Presses universitaires de France, 1951), p. 24.

12. Von Ketteler had detailed the impact of anticlerical concepts on the religious practice of industrial workers in *The Problem of the Workers and Christianity* (1864).

13. Georges Jarlot, S.J., *Historia documentorum Ecclesiae de re sociale a Leone XIII ad Pium XII* (Roma, Pontificia Università Gregoriana, 1955–6), p. 12.

14. *The Church and Civilization, a Pastoral Letter for Lent, 1877,* by Cardinal Pecci, now Leo XIII, trans. by Henry J. Gill (Dublin, M. H. Gill and Son, 1878).

15. The reconciliation of Catholics to the "Republic of the Republicans" in France appears as the major concern of Leo. It is remarkable that *Rerum Novarum* appeared between two major steps in his *Ralliement* policy, the "toast of Algiers," and the publication of *Au milieu des solicitudes*. Even in *Rerum Novarum* his thoughts were never far from France. Cf. *RN*, sec. 53, p. 233.

16. One of his earliest encyclicals, *Quod Apostolici,* December 28, 1878, was on socialism.

17. In a conversation with M. Decurtins, the Pope called Von Ketteler "his great predecessor." Reported in *Association catholique* (organ of the French Social Catholics), Paris, October 15, 1893, p. 428. Ketteler's ideas became the common heritage of social-minded Catholics and thus found their way into *Rerum Novarum*.

18. Letter to Cardinal Gibbons, dated August 28, 1888.

19. Albert de Mun, June 6, 1892, in *Discours et Écrits divers*, Ch. Geoffroy de Grandmaison, ed. (Paris, 1893, *et seq.*), V, p. 179.

20. *L'Enciclia "Rerum Novarum." Testo authentico e redazioni preparatorie dai documenti originali*. A cura di Mons. Giovanni Antonazzi. Prefazione di S. E. Mons. Domenico Tradini. Roma, Ediz. di Storia e Letteratura, 1957, pp. 13 *et seq.*

21. Georges Jarlot, S. J., "Les Avant Projets de 'Rerum Novarum' et les 'Anciennes Corporations,' " *Nouvelle Revue Théologique*, Louvain, LXXXI (January, 1959), pp. 60–77. The author is professor in the Gregorian University and the most productive contemporary scholar in this field.

22. *RN*, sec. 49, p. 232.

23. This is the opinion of Père Jarlot in the article cited above. The substance of his other speculations is given in the following paragraphs. The discussion of Leo's method of working with his secretaries and aides in the text is found in Antonazzi, *op. cit.*, pp. 1–7.

24. Henry J. Browne, *The Catholic Church and the Knights of Labor* (Washington, Catholic University Press, 1949); John Tracy Ellis, *The Life of James Cardinal Gibbons* (Milwaukee, Bruce, 1952), p. 530. Both were written before Antonazzi's publication. They agree that there is "no clear proof."

25. Justification for this position can be found in the encyclical addressed to the American bishops a few years later, *Longinqua Oceani*, issued on January 6, 1895, in *Acta Sanctae Sedis*, Vol. 27, where Leo takes into account the special conditions in American trade unions.

26. Some still maintained a corporatist interpretation and traced its inclusion to the work of Cardinal Mermillod. Cf. Massard, *L'Oeuvre social du Cardinal Mermillod et l'union de Fribourg* (Louvain, Librairie Universitaire, 1914), p. 261. The issue would cease to be academic after the rise of Italian fascism.

27. Henri Rollet, *L'Action sociale des catholiques en France (1871–1901)* (Paris, Boivin, n.d.), p. 20 *et passim*.

28. Eduardo Soderini, *Il Pontificato di Leone XIII* (Milan, Mondari, 1932), I. p. 420. Trans. by Barbara B. Carter as *The Pontificate of Leo XIII* (London, Burns, Oates, and Washbourne, 1934), 2 vols.

29. With the fundamental equality in nature and dignity as sons of God and as citizens before the law, Leo saw differences in natural gifts and in social function as also of divine origin. Hence he saw social equality as an impossibility.

30. Leo would have approved the dictum of Pius XII: "Without the Church the social question is insoluble; but of herself, the Church cannot solve it." Message to the Workers of Spain, March 11, 1951. But Leo did not omit specifics where necessary: cf. *RN,* sec. 20, p. 215; sec. 30, p. 225; sec. 42, p. 228.

31. *RN,* secs. 62–63, pp. 238–239.

32. *RN,* sec. 42, p. 228.

33. *RN,* secs. 31–37, pp. 222–226. This language is so strong that some Catholics who accepted the prevailing economic philosophy appealed to the thesis-hypothesis distinction to mitigate it. Cf. Leroy-Beaulieu, *La Papauté, le socialisme, et la démocratie* (Paris, 1892), pp. 115–118.

34. *Rerum Novarum,* as it has been observed, did not end the discussion among Catholics on this point. But Bishop Doutrelouz of Liége, in *Lettre pastorale sur la question oeuvrière* (Liége Dessain, 1894), p. 19, expressed the opinion of the majority of the commentators when he wrote that, thought the mixed union was not excluded, the genuine trade union was approved. He further argued that in large industry only the latter would be effective. This interpretation was endorsed by the Sacred Congregation of the Council in its decision in 1929 favoring the appeal of the Christian trade unions against the Textile Consortium of Roubaix-Tourcoing, and finally made official by *Quadragesimo Anno.* Cf. the excellent treatise, J.-Y. Calvez and J. Perrin, *Église et société économique* (Paris, Aubier, 1959), p. 479. Also J.-Y. Calvez, "Association et corporation chez les premiers commentateurs de *Rerum Novarum,*" *Chronique Sociale de France* (December 3, 1957), pp. 647 *et seq.*

35. Pentecost Message, 1941, *Acta Apostolicae Sedis,* Vol. 33 (1941), p. 127.

36. French examples were the "Semaines Sociales" and "Action Populaire." For a comprehensive world-wide list, cf. Max Turman, *Le Développement du catholicisme social depuis l'encyclique Rerum Novarum* (Paris, Felix Alcan, 1900), p. 12 *et passim.* For a good sketch of the American reaction, cf. Aaron Abell. "The Reception of Leo's Labor Encyclical in America, 1891–1919," *The Review of Politics,* VII (October, 1945), pp. 464–495; and Marc Karson, *American Labor Unions and Politics, 1900–1918* (Carbondale,

Southern University Press, 1958), pp. 212–284. For a good statement on the present status of papal teaching, cf. John F. Cronin, S.S., *Social Principles and Economic Life* (Milwaukee, Bruce, 1959).

37. The author of this paper is not impressed by the objection that Leo's objective was basically defensive—to resist the tide of socialism. Granting that it was in large part, as sketched in the opening pages of this paper, it transcended its immediate environment—the social crisis.

4 Leo XIII and the Problem of Human Liberty

MOST REV. EGIDIO VAGNOZZI
Apostolic Delegate to the United States

DURING THE LAST QUARTER of the nineteenth century, Pope Leo XIII, as Bishop of Rome and Sovereign Pontiff, presided over the Catholic Church. He was sixty-eight years old when he mounted the throne of Peter, and it was generally thought that he was destined for a brief regime, characterized by few deeds or pronouncements of outstanding merit. But, in God's providence, Pope Leo XIII was to be one of the greatest of the Roman pontiffs. From the day of his election in 1878 until the day of his death in 1903 he stood before the world as an intellectual genius, a man whose mind could penetrate into the depths of even the most abstruse problem and propose a clear and detailed solution based on the immutable principles of human reason and divine revelation.

Appointed Papal Nuncio to Belgium at thirty-three, Monsignor Pecci spent three years at Brussels; then, for thirty-two years, he was Bishop of Perugia in Italy. In Brussels he dealt with a liberal government, which in a predominantly Catholic country was striving mightily to deny and to impede the right of the Church to educate its youth. In Italy too, he was confronted with a similar situation; a liberal government was in control of the country. While loudly proclaiming "a free church in a free state," these governments were in actual fact seeking to imprison religion within the confining walls of the churches.

During the regime of Pope Pius IX, Cardinal Pecci did not see eye to eye with the policies of Cardinal Antonelli, who for twenty-one years was Papal Secretary of State. His experience in Belgium and his acceptance of the inevitable unity of the Italian nation made him realize that the strength of the Church could not be entrusted to the weak military power of the Papal States, nor to the unreliable game of international alliances. Rather, its strength was to be found essentially and fundamentally in its organization, the world-wide support of its faithful, the prestige of the Papacy among all people, and above all in the eternal promise of the Lord: " . . . and the gates of hell shall not prevail against it . . ." (Mt 16, 18). For this reason we can rightly say that Pope Leo XIII is the first of the modern popes who, completely detached from the care and trouble of temporal sovereignty, placed their position and mission at the sole service of the spiritual welfare of mankind. Once dispossessed of the exercise of civil power, the Papacy has grown tremendously in world importance and influence. In great part this is due to Pope Leo XIII.

To the accomplishment of his task Pope Leo brought a wide and penetrating vision of the problems of his time in every sphere of human activity and human behavior, a courageous determination to reaffirm traditional Catholic principles and doctrine, and the faculty for the prudent and tolerant application of these same principles to the contingencies of the historical moment.

In the course of his pontificate Leo XIII issued official pronouncements on a wide variety of topics—the Christian constitution of governments, philosophy, Holy Scripture, industrial reforms, marriage, the duties of citizens, among others. One of the problems that engaged the interest of this distinguished Churchman was human liberty. It was a timely topic, for, as we have seen, there was in his day a powerful movement throughout the world for what its proponents called liberalism—the doctrine that liberty consists in freedom from law, the doctrine that every man has the right to believe and to do what he pleases.

Viewing such a notion of liberty as dangerous both to individuals and to society, Leo XIII spoke out frequently on the subject of *true* liberty. His chief pronouncement on the subject is found in *Libertas Praestantissimum* (*Liberty, The Most Excellent Good of Nature*), which was promulgated on June 20, 1888. In this authoritative mes-

sage the Pope explained in scholarly fashion the precise nature of
true liberty. At first sight, the concept he proposes may seem contrary to the idea of freedom. For he defines true human liberty, not
as freedom from law, but as adherence to law—fundamentally, to
the law of God. He tells us that "the eternal law of God is the sole
standard and rule of human liberty, not only in each individual man,
but also in the community and civil society which men constitute
when united."[1] In other words, genuine freedom consists in conform-
ing one's belief and conduct to the infinite wisdom and infinite good-
ness of God. Similarly, in the civil sphere, true liberty consists not
in the ability to violate the laws of God or the just laws of the state,
but in the right to obey them; for the authority of the human legis-
lator is derived from the law of God. Pope Leo XIII states this
important truth in these words:

Therefore, the nature of human liberty, however it be considered,
whether in individuals or in society, whether in those who command or
in those who obey, supposes the necessity of obedience to some supreme
and eternal law, which is no other than the authority of God, commanding good and forbidding evil. And so far from this most just
authority of God over men diminishing or even destroying their liberty,
it protects and perfects it, for the real perfection of all creatures is
found in the prosecution and attainment of their respective ends; but
the supreme end to which human liberty must aspire is God.[2]

Truly, this is a glorious and sublime concept of true liberty, so
different from the superficial notion that would make liberty license,
immunity from all restraint, in a word, the right to be lawless. The
Pope stresses the principle that only those who recognize a Creator
whose laws must be obeyed are truly free. Genuine liberty is a gift
of God, and in return man must render Him love and service. How
clearly was this perceived by the Founding Fathers of the United
States, when they incorporated into the Declaration of Independence,
as a self-evident truth, the memorable words: "All men are endowed
by their Creator with certain inalienable rights, that among these
are life, liberty, and the pursuit of happiness." When a person sin-

cerely seeks what is true with his intellect and what is good with his will, he is striving to perfect himself in the proper way, for he is aiming at the end for which life has been given him—the attainment of God. On the contrary, to accept intellectually what is false or to will what is evil is not a manifestation of true liberty. If this takes place in good faith, there will indeed be no offense to Almighty God, the Creator; yet, an erroneous choice, even though honestly made, is something unfortunate. But when the choice of what is false or evil is fully deliberate, then indeed is freedom frustrated. In the words of Jesus Christ: "Everyone who commits sin is a slave to sin" (Jn 8, 34).

It is especially deplorable when the rulers of a nation reject the notion of God's law or act in defiance of any obligations they owe to the Creator. Under such a government, liberty is bound to die. This is surely exemplified today by what is taking place under Communist rule. Why the brutality, the crushing laws, the treatment of citizens as though they were but cogs in a machine? Simply and sadly, because those who rule are atheists and consequently behold in their subjects mere animals, devoid of all rights save those their rulers will to grant them—rights which can be withdrawn at the mere whim of those same rulers. Wisely did Pope Leo XIII denounce such tryanny seventy years ago, long before totalitarian governments were established: "The liberty of those who are in authority does not consist in the power to lay unreasonable and capricious commands upon their subjects, which would equally be criminal and would lead to the ruin of the commonwealth; but the binding force of human laws is this, that they are to be regarded as applications of the eternal law, and incapable of sanctioning anything which is not contained in the eternal law, as in the principle of all law."[3]

Sometimes, it is true, there appears to be peace under a Communist regime, but it is not a true peace. It springs from the helplessness of those who have been treated so inhumanly by their dictators that they no longer have the courage or the will to fight for liberty. Recently, President Eisenhower made use of an appropriate expression to describe the goal of the United States in the international

order as distinct from the objective of Communist governments. The
President declared that the aim of the United States is "peace with
freedom." And the tradition of the United States, manifested by the
signers of the Declaration of Independence, will permit us to enlarge
this phrase to "peace with freedom based on God's laws."

In the United States freedom has been justly regarded as the
basic principle of the nation's life. This is not to say that the citizens
of this country in general consider themselves at liberty to speak or
act as they please, or to disobey the laws of the land as often as they
can evade punishment. Rather, the doctrine on liberty as outlined
by Pope Leo XIII has been put into practice in the United States
from the very beginning. "Liberty under God" is an axiom that signifies American freedom as most Americans understand it. To this
sympathetic observer it appears that Americans recognize that obedience to the laws of the Creator is essential for true liberty; they
acknowledge that those who hold posts of civil authority represent
God Himself, in accordance with the words of Saint Paul: "There
exists no authority except from God, and those who exist have been
appointed by God" (Rom 13, 1). And as long as this understanding
of true liberty prevails, America will justly be acclaimed as "the
land of the free."

It is disturbing, however, to realize that there are today some who
seem bent on destroying true liberty—either the liberty of individual
citizens by inducing them to violate God's law through salacious
writings, obscene shows, the bad example of loose manners, or the
liberty of individual nations through dishonesty in political life or
even subversive activities against established freedom-loving governments—all this in the name of liberty! Entirely appropriate to such
persons are the words of Pope Leo XIII regarding the so-called liberals of his day: "They deny the existence of any divine authority to
which obedience is due, and proclaim that every man is the law to
himself."[4] And the Pope goes on to point out that whenever such
an attitude predominates, discord and tyranny inevitably follow.

In regard to freedom as applied to religious belief and worship,
Pope Leo held, consistently with his teaching on liberty in general,

that true liberty is exercised only when a person accepts and practices what is true about God and His law, according to the dictates of reason and divine revelation.

However, this does not mean that either the Catholic Church or a Catholic state may use any coercive measures to induce non-Catholics to become Catholics. In his encyclical on the Christian constitution of States, Pope Leo XIII stated emphatically: "The Church is wont to take earnest heed that no one shall be forced to embrace the Catholic faith against his will, for, as St. Augustine wisely reminds us, 'Man cannot believe otherwise than of his own free will.'"[5] More recently, Pope Pius XII repeated this same doctrine: "Therefore, whenever it happens, despite the invariable teaching of this Apostolic See that anyone against his will is compelled to embrace the Catholic faith, Our sense of duty demands that We condemn the act."[6]

Pope Leo XIII repeated with great clarity and firmness that only in the Catholic Church is to be found the full measure of religious truth and the divinely prescribed form of worship:

Civil society must acknowledge God as its Founder and Parent, and must obey and reverence His power and authority. Justice therefore forbids, and reason itself forbids, the State to be godless, or to adopt a line of action which would end in godlessness—namely, to treat the various religions alike, and to bestow upon them promiscuously equal rights and privileges. Since, then, the profession of one religion is necessary in the State, that religion must be professed which alone is true, and which can be recognized without difficulty, especially in Catholic States, because the marks of truth are, as it were, engraved upon it. This religion, therefore, the rulers of the State must preserve and protect if they would provide—as they should do—with prudence and usefulness for the good of the community.[7]

This quotation is often repeated to prove that the Catholic Church expects the State to be intolerant of religions other than the Catholic. However, those who argue along this line usually fail to quote these words of the same Pope Leo XIII: "The Church, indeed, deems it unlawful to place the various forms of divine worship on the same

footing as the true religion, but does not, on that account, condemn
those rulers who, for the sake of procuring some great good, or of
hindering some great evil, allow patiently custom or usage to be a
kind of sanction for each kind of religion having its place in the
State."[8]

Pope Pius XII developed the same idea with even greater clarity
in his address to the Union of Italian Catholic Jurists on December 6,
1953:

The affirmation: religious and moral error must be impeded when it
is possible, because toleration of them in itself is immoral, is not valid
absolutely and unconditionally. God has not given even to human
authority such an absolute and universal command in matters of faith
and morality. Such a command is unknown to the common convictions
of mankind, to Christian conscience, to the sources of Revelation and
to the practice of the Church . . . the duty of repressing moral and
religious error cannot therefore be an ultimate norm of action. It must
be subordinate to higher and more general norms, which in some circumstances permit, and even perhaps seem to indicate as the better
policy, toleration of error in order to promote a greater good.[9]

Later on in the same address Pope Pius says: "The Concordats
are for her (the Catholic Church) an expression of the collaboration
between the Church and the State." And then the same Pontiff adds
the following significant words: "In principle, that is, in theory, she
(the Catholic Church) cannot approve complete separation of the
two powers."[10] Thus, in practice the Church will not interfere, and
has not interfered, in local situations where the separation between
Church and State may be considered the greater and more general
good.

In considering freedom as applied to religious belief and worship,
it is well to remind ourselves that the very concept of complete separation between Church and State is a relatively modern idea. Even
some of the largest Protestant denominations were born out of a
stricter and more nationalistic interpretation of a close relationship
between religion and the civil power.

In the practical field of relations with civil powers, the Catholic

Church shows, with reciprocal international agreements called concordats, a considerable variety of provisions in particular questions,
depending on local traditions, customs, and practices. In fact, it is
extremely difficult to define the neat line of demarcation between the
domain of the Church and that of the State. Actually, even in some
traditionally and predominantly Catholic countries, no preferential
juridical recognition is granted to the Catholic Church.

As far as the United States is concerned, I feel that it is a true
interpretation of the feelings of the hierarchy and of American Catholics in general to say that they are well-satisfied with their Constitution and pleased with the fundamental freedom enjoyed by their
Church; in fact, they believe that this freedom is to a large extent
responsible for the expansion and consolidation of the Church in this
great country. Whether they remain a minority or become a majority,
I am sure that American Catholics will not jeopardize their cherished
religious freedom in exchange for a privileged position.

Thus, in brief, we have considered the teaching on the important
subject of human liberty propounded by one of the great popes
of the Catholic Church, who was known as "Lumen de Coelo"—
"Light from Heaven." His message, as we have seen, was not contingent on the particular time in which he lived. It was the logical
conclusion from fundamental truths of reason and faith, applicable
to every generation. If we would ask an understanding of the true
nature of liberty, a subject so pertinent to the events of the present-
day world, we can find no better guide than the brilliant Roman
Pontiff who contributed so much to the progress of mankind in the
fields of religion, culture, and science—Leo XIII.

NOTES

1. *Libertas Praestantissimum,* in *The Great Encyclical Letters of Leo
   XIII* with a preface by Rev. John J. Wynne, S.J. (New York, 1903),
   p. 142.

2. *Op. cit.*, p. 143.
3. *Idem.*, p. 142.
4. *Idem.*, p. 145.
5. *Immortale Dei*, in *op. cit.*, p. 127.
6. *Mystici Corporis*, National Catholic Welfare Conference, No. 104, p. 40.
7. *Libertas Praestantissimum*, in *op. cit.*, pp. 150–151.
8. *Immortale Die*, in *op. cit.*, p. 127.
9. *Ci Riesce, American Educational Review*, CXXX (1954), p. 385.
10. *Op. cit.*, p. 137.

5 Leo XIII and the Roman Question

S. WILLIAM HALPERIN
University of Chicago

It is impossible to understand Leo XIII without keeping Pius IX constantly in mind. Leo could never divorce himself from the political legacy of his predecessor. That legacy was a fierce but unfinished battle. Actually, the pontificate of Pius IX knew hardly a moment of peace. The factors that were responsible for this lay both outside and inside the man who occupied the throne of St. Peter. Outside, two daggers were aimed at the heart of the Roman Catholic Church. One was a rampant and ethnocentric nationalism that threatened Catholic universalism as well as the territorial sovereignty of the Holy See. The other was liberalism, which in its passionate dedication to the ideology of secularism declared war to the bitter end against the Church and ecclesiasticism. Inside, there was a restlessness that sprang from several things. These included a volatile temperament; a deep-seated distrust of others that collided with an instinctive warmth and generosity; a hypersensitivity, a readiness to take offense, coupled with a rather extraordinary toughness; a yearning for popular acclaim that found itself thwarted by the fact that it was absolutely impossible for a man in Pius' position to come to terms with the popular forces of the times; a desire to innovate, to strike out in fresh directions, together with a fanatical determination to preserve intact the heritage of the past. The upshot could not fail to be a highly explosive mixture.

No single event disturbed Pius more deeply than the loss of his temporal power. The spoliation began in 1859–1860, when more than two-thirds of the States of the Church, the Papacy's ancient and vast domain in central Italy, came under the rule of King Victor Emmanuel II. It ended with the breach of Porta Pia and the Italian occupation of Rome on September 20, 1870.[1] Pius reacted with the fury of a man betrayed. At the beginning of his pontificate he had carried on an ardent flirtation with Italian nationalists and liberals. Conservatives had been scandalized and aghast. For them Pius represented the embodiment of a nightmare come true: a revolutionary Pope. By the same token, nationalists and liberals had acclaimed him. Within his realm he had relaxed the theocratic absolutism so often denounced by liberals throughout the peninsula and indeed outside it; without, he had given a fillip to the national movement by bearding the Austrian lion and by supporting the neo-Guelf dream of a confederation of Italian states. He had even gone so far as to take the lead in sponsoring the formation of a customs union between the Italian states. Such a union, which was reminiscent of the German *Zollverein,* might well have heralded a political federation. The papal initiative had come to nought, mainly because of Austrian opposition, but the very fact that it had occurred at all bespoke the revolutionary tenor of Pius' ways.

However, he had abruptly reversed himself in April 1848, at the time of the so-called national crusade against Austria. The requirements of the Papacy and the Church had left him no other choice. Thereafter, he became embroiled in a bitter feud with his former allies. They were furious with him for his defection. Pius felt equally aggrieved. He accused the liberals and nationalists of requiting him ill. More than that, he charged them with planning to destroy not only the temporal power but the very foundations of Catholicism itself. They struck back by enacting a series of anticlerical measures. These were aimed at the religious orders, the right of mortmain, the system of courts maintained by the ecclesiastical hierarchy, and the teaching of religion in the public schools. Finally, Pius' enemies robbed him of his temporal power.

It was at this point that his anger became an obsession. Time and again he denounced the culprits and demanded the restitution of his territory. But the despoilers, enjoying immense popular backing, declared the seizure final and irrevocable. Invoking the sacred rights of nationality, they refused to give up even the smallest part of Italy's title to Rome and the rest of the former Papal States. Instead, they offered Pius a statutory substitute for the temporal power. They voted him a perpetual subsidy in place of the revenue formerly collected by the papal government. They also voted him indefinite use of, but not sovereignty over, the Vatican enclave in the heart of Rome where the Pope was currently residing and which was known as the Leonine City. Here, in the sanctuary thus marked out, there would be no intrusion by agents of the Italian state save with the authorization of the Holy See. The inviolability of the Pope's person would be respected. Offenses against him would be punished in the same manner as offenses against the king. As before, he would maintain diplomatic relations with chiefs of state. Thus, though denied sovereignty in the legal sense, the pontiff would retain much of its substance and virtually all of its trappings. Besides, as the head of Catholic Christendom, he would continue to enjoy, so far as it lay in the power of the Italian state to assure it, complete and untrammeled freedom of communication with the episcopacy and faithful of every land.

Such were the terms of the Law of Guarantees, which the Italian state enacted in May 1871.[2] Pius spurned these guarantees as worthless. In the light of what had just happened, he could hardly be blamed for doubting the word of the Italian government. In actuality, the guarantees were offered in a spirit of sincerity. But even if this had been plain to the Vatican at the time, it would not have regarded the sincerity of the offer as conclusive. After all, there was no assurance that some future Italian government, dominated by anticlerical extremists, might not cancel, emasculate, or simply disregard the guarantees. In any case, Pius insisted, there could be no satisfactory substitute for the temporal power. Without territorial sovereignty, without a physical domain over which it ruled in law as well as in fact, the Papacy would not be free.[3]

From the outset, the Italian state, mindful of how much was at stake, leaned over backward in an effort to make sure that the Pope's spiritual functions were in no way hampered or interfered with. Although the Law of Guarantees had been rejected by the Papacy, the government scrupulously enforced those of its provisions that did not depend on papal acceptance or co-operation. This began to be clear after 1871, but Pius attached no importance to it. He continued to insist that the restoration of the temporal power was absolutely indispensable. He also remained convinced that it was impossible to assume that future Italian governments would honor the promises of their predecessors. He became more distrustful than ever during the last years of his pontificate, for they witnessed a sharp increase in anticlerical sentiment despite the correctness of the government's attitude.[4] Pius needed no further proof that his intransigence was justified. To regain the temporal power, he fashioned an elaborate pattern of combat. He persisted in his refusal to recognize the Italian kingdom and would not hear of establishing diplomatic relations with it. He declared himself a prisoner within the walls of the Vatican and refrained from setting foot outside them in order to dramatize this self-imposed incarceration. He put heavy pressure on the Italian government by appealing for help to other Catholic countries, notably France and Austria. However, his most powerful weapon was the *non expedit,* which was designed to coerce the Italian monarchy into submission by threatening it with dissolution from within. It should not be forgotten that republicanism, recently triumphant in neighboring France, was by no means dead in Italy. To be sure, the Papacy feared and detested republicanism as a subversive, left-wing force. It used its influence to bolster the monarchist cause in various parts of Europe. But in Italy it did not hesitate to make things easier for the republicans by neutralizing the country's most conservative elements. How far was the Vatican willing to go in order to have its way on the question of the temporal power? The *non expedit* provided the answer. It was a recommendation that all Catholics should boycott national politics. Loyal sons of the Church were to abstain from seeking seats in the lower house of the Italian Parliament, the Chamber of Deputies; they were likewise to stay away from the polls when such elections were being held.

Thus, they were to act as if the Italian kingdom did not exist. The Holy See had first proclaimed the *non expedit* in 1868, before the total destruction of its temporal power. It emphatically reaffirmed the recommendation after the events of 1870.[5] Thus denied the nucleus of a potentially powerful conservative party, Italian political life fell by default under the undisputed sway of Church-hating liberals and radicals. But for the Vatican there was no turning back. The Roman Question overshadowed all else in Italo-papal relations.

Did Pius and his advisers believe they could recover all the territory which had belonged to the Papacy? Publicly, of course, they did not surrender their claims to any part of the former States of the Church that had stretched across central Italy from sea to sea. Privately, however, they had to acknowledge the impossiblity of getting everything back. As prospects for an early recovery dimmed, as the hope of foreign intervention turned into a cruel mockery and the Italian state, though harassed, showed no sign of imminent collapse, the Vatican was forced to think more and more in terms of a partial restoration. Although Pius and the members of his entourage disliked to admit this even to themselves, they gloomily concluded that sovereignty over the Leonine City was all they could reasonably expect. To regain full titular rights to this enclave where they now resided, where the use of buildings and grounds had been guaranteed them by the Law of Guarantees, but where Italy claimed exclusive sovereignty, became thenceforward their paramount if as yet unavowed aim. The intensity of their determination, coupled with the mounting fury of anticlerical agitation, gave the Italo-papal conflict the appearance of a remorseless civil war.

Pius and his strong-willed Secretary of State, Cardinal Antonelli, completely dominated the Sacred College after 1871. This meant that the cardinals, in whose hands lay the choice of Pius' successor, could scarcely be expected to press for a change of papal policy. However, some highly placed prelates did favor greater gentleness in the matter of means along with continued inflexibility in the matter of ends. They agreed that every effort must be made to recover the lost territorial sovereignty. But they believed that the Vatican, to gain its object, must shun unnecessary provocation while remaining firm and resolute. Gioacchino Pecci stood out among the champions of such a course.

Appointed Cardinal at forty-three, Pecci was too young to figure at once among the *papabili,* the roster of eligibles for the pontifical throne. But the spare and austere man from Carpineto moved toward the top of the list as the Papacy experienced a succession of painful crises. This rise he owed to the firm yet circumspect quality of his position on questions of capital importance. Thus, although he joined his fellow prelates in denouncing the spoliation of the Holy See, he showed himself to be temperate and wise as well as resolute. He never forgot that he was living in the nineteenth century and that the Church's methods of combat had to be adapted to the realities of the present. The Vatican, he readily agreed, had no choice but to strive indefatigably for the recovery of the temporal power. But on the question of tactics he dissociated himself from the intransigent party in the Sacred College. Yet, likewise for tactical reasons, he did not align himself with the so-called moderates. Although Pecci realized that a policy of thunderbolts would not work, he thought he detected a dangerous confusion in the opposite extreme. By taking up a middle position, he kept a foot in both camps without doing violence to his own settled convictions. He thus acquired a uniquely commanding position in the College of Cardinals.

Pius appreciated this. In November 1876, following the death of Antonelli, he summoned Pecci to Rome, and a year later named him papal camerlingo or chamberlain.[6] The holder of this office wielded great power during a papal interregnum. The appointment further enhanced Pecci's prestige and made him easily the foremost candidate for the succession to the pontifical throne. Pius died on February 7, 1878. As camerlingo, Pecci took charge of arrangements for the forthcoming conclave. In the ensuing and often heated discussion in the Sacred College over whether the conclave should be held in Rome as usual or transferred to some non-Italian city because of the abnormal situation created by the events of September 1870,

Pecci comported himself with his customary moderation and wisdom.[7] It was decided that the conclave would be held in Rome.[8] It
took place without any interference whatsoever on the part of the
Italian authorities. There was never a freer papal election in the
entire history of the Church.[9] And never did the Sacred College make
a better choice: on February 20 Pecci received the requisite majority
and assumed the name of Leo XIII.

In his public pronouncements Leo revealed both his goal and his
methods. His first allocution, delivered on March 28, 1878, contained only a passing allusion to the loss of the temporal power. In
addition to being brief, this allusion was couched in language so
casual that it seemed to have been inserted almost as an afterthought,
as if intended solely to appease the intransigents in the Sacred College, who fretted over the possibility that the new Pontiff might carry
his known moderation too far in the direction of accommodation.
Compared to the violent language of Pius IX, the passage in question was undoubtedly a model of restraint. No one, of course, expected Leo to renounce the Papacy's territorial claims, but his
manner of expressing them could hardly have been gentler.[10] Actually, he had taken great pains with this part of his allocution. In a few
carefully chosen words he did indeed make it crystal-clear that in
principle the position of the Holy See remained exactly what it had
been under his predecessor. He noted that the Papacy had been
forcibly divested of its temporal dominion. This had rendered it impossible for the head of Catholic Christendom to enjoy the full, free,
and undictated exercise of his spiritual powers.[11] The uncompromis-
ing attitude assumed by Pius was thus reaffirmed, even though the
terms Leo employed in stating it were far milder than those to which
the world had grown accustomed. But to some observers, at least,
what Leo failed to say on this occasion was much more important
than what he did say. Unlike Pius, he kept silent about his future
intentions. He omitted to announce that he would continue his predecessor's combat for the restoration of the temporal power.[12] This
silence could be interpreted as implying that satisfaction from Italy

on the all-important territorial question might conceivably be obtained without prolonging the struggle that so far had proved quite barren. To lament the result of Italy's misdeeds, which Leo had been most careful to do, did not necessarily mean a renewal of the all-out war against her. This distinction, to which considerable importance was attached at the time by those close to the arena of Italo-papal relations, was not fortuitous. It was definitely part and parcel of Leo's approach at the beginning of his pontificate. It reflected his wish to feel his way and to test the possiblities rather than to aggravate an already well-nigh hopeless situation by premature and categorical formulations of policy from which later there might be neither deviation nor retreat.

The contrast between the two pontiffs stood out even more palpably after Leo's first encyclical, which bore the date of April 21, 1878.[13] The key passage of the letter ran as follows: "It is not a vain desire for dominion and power that moves us to demand the restoration of the civil power. We demand it because our duty and the solemn promises made by us render it imperative, and because it is not only necessary for the protection and maintenance of the entire liberty of the spiritual power, but also because it is evident that when the temporal government of the Apostolic See is at stake, the security and well-being of the entire human family is also in jeopardy."[14] Leo went on to say that in accordance with his obligations, which decreed that he must protect the rights of the Church, he was herewith renewing and confirming all of Pius' remonstrances and protests.[15]

What is striking about this declaration is its almost apologetic tone, its implicitly *pro forma* character, its avoidance of anything that might have irritated the Italian government or rubbed salt into old wounds. The word *occupatio* was the strongest used by Leo in referring to the destruction of the temporal power. There was no trace or suggestion of such terms as *spolatio,* so frequently employed by Pius. Moreover, in distributing his emphasis Leo deliberately sought to convey the impression that the Roman Question by no means monopolized his attention. Actually, his allusion to it was sandwiched in between far more extensive remarks about two other subjects: the history of the Church and the duties of the episcopate.

To be sure, in a series of subsequent pronouncements stretching over the years and intended for the world at large, Leo reiterated the familar thesis that the situation created by the legions of King Victor Emmanuel II on September 20, 1870, was intolerable for the Papacy. He also criticized those advocates of an Italo-papal reconciliation who failed at the same time to underscore the absolute necessity of restoring the temporal power. He was not free, he kept insisting, just as Pius had done; in the last analysis, he was dependent on the arbitrary will of others. He warned, too, that he would never leave off claiming what had been taken from the Holy See and what rightfully still belonged to it. But—and here Leo parted company with his predecessor—he persistently injected an accommodating note into his utterances. Time and again he voiced his desire for a satisfactory settlement of the Italo-papal dispute and on occasion even evinced a patriotic concern for the fate of Italy.

What were Leo's conditions for an acceptable solution of the Roman Question? He stated them clearly enough in 1879, a little over a year after his election. They could hardly be described as excessive. The Holy See, he let it be known, needed only so much territory as would suffice to make it completely free. Put another way, he explained, the Holy See must be so endowed as to be spared the cares of a large state, which would distract it from the discharge of its spiritual functions.[16] Leo thus served notice on Italy and the world that he was ready to renounce the former States of the Church and to content himself instead with something approximating the Leonine City.[17] What he was proposing, therefore, was to convert the existing *de facto* situation into a *de jure* one, to substitute full titular ownership for the Vatican's mere possession of the papal enclave in the heart of Rome. Under such an arrangement neither a single acre of land nor a single edifice would change hands. The right of unrestricted and unhampered use, which the Papacy already enjoyed, and which for all practical purposes was equivalent to sovereignty, would be confirmed. The gain, of course, would be the juridical separation of the Leonine City from the Italian kingdom. Thereafter, any intrusion by Italian agents would be not a breach of promise but a violation of international law. As I noted earlier, even Pius had come to see that this was the best the Papacy could hope for. But as the victim of spoliation, as the Pontiff who had lost the vast States of the Church, he had been understandably reluctant to admit this to himself, let alone to the world at large. Leo did not hesitate to say so publicly because he was prepared to sign such an agreement.

Unfortunately, nothing came of Leo's reasonable suggestion, which had to wait fifty-one years before it was converted into the keystone of an enduring accord between the Papacy and Italy. In the meanwhile, the failure of the bid for a territorial settlement left Leo no choice but to hold on to his most powerful weapon, the *non expedit*. Here, however, he found himself in an unavoidable quandary. He was worried by the spread of radical movements, especially republicanism with its secular, anticlerical, and even atheistic overtones. Indeed, so deep was his anxiety on this score that it frequently moved him to urge a rallying of all conservative forces in the face of the common threat. In Italy as elsewhere the cause of conservatism was, of course, bound up with that of the monarchy. This could hardly be minimized. But yet to aid the House of Savoy or even to acquiesce in a truce with it was unthinkable so long as the Roman Question remained unresolved.

But it was likewise unthinkable that the Holy See should do anything to increase the chances of a republican revolution. But this was precisely what it was doing. The Catholic boycott was pushing the Italian kingdom dangerously close to the precipice. This being so, should not the *non expedit* be lifted at once, before it was too late? Many clericals argued in favor of such a step. It would facilitate the election of deputies acceptable to the Church. By the same token, it would erect a stronger barrier against the danger of republicanism.

After much debate pro and con that was marked by increasing intensity, the matter came to a head in April 1880. As the Chamber of Deputies had just been dissolved, a number of prominent Catholics demanded papal authorization to participate in the forthcoming elections.[18] Leo, who seemed of two minds, did not say no. Instead, he hurriedly convoked a committee of cardinals to consider the question. These deliberations did not take long. When they were over, Leo announced that it would be neither advantageous nor useful from the standpoint of the Church to have the faithful take part in the elections. To be sure, he specified that it was not *now* expedient to effect a change of policy; he thus implied that this newly issued *nunc non expedit* might be revoked at any time.[19]

Spurred by the hope that such action would come soon, clerical adversaries of the *non expedit* kept up their agitation. They contended that Catholics would be more effective in their efforts to assure the freedom and independence of the Papacy if they made their numerical weight felt in the outcome of political elections. The ban against voting, these clericals insisted, reposed in the last analysis on considerations of opportuneness. The *non expedit* had been conceived as a temporary device. It must be reconsidered in the light of changing circumstances. Actually, the political conditions that now prevailed in Italy had made it obsolete and even harmful. Seen in this light, mass voting by Catholics had become imperative.[20] To influence the results of parliamentary elections represented a duty which had to be fulfilled by all loyal sons of the Church.[21] The defenders of the *non expedit* answered these arguments by falling back on the reasoning that had silenced dissenters during the last years of Pius IX. Participation in elections, so ran their rejoinder, could not be sanctioned. If it were, it would signify acquiescence in the exercise of sovereign power by a kingdom that had despoiled the Pope of his temporal domain.[22]

The prospects for a suspension or relaxation of the *non expedit* had meanwhile darkened as a consequence of a whole series of anticlerical incidents in Italy. The disgraceful happenings in July 1881, when the remains of Pius IX were being transferred to their final resting place in the Church of San Lorenzo Outside the Walls of Rome, scandalized the civilized world, nonbelievers and believers alike.[23] Leo himself was so upset that he seriously considered the idea of leaving the Eternal City.[24] Under these circumstances the adversaries of the *non expedit* could scarcely expect to get anywhere. Rather, they received a sharp rebuke. It came in the form of a categorical statement by the Vatican to the effect that the ban against voting in political elections was still in force.[25]

Nevertheless, the issue refused to die. It came up once more in May 1886, when the dissolution of the Chamber of Deputies again set the stage for nationwide parliamentary contests. On this occasion leading clericals renewed their attempt to persuade Leo to lift the ban in order that Catholic voting strength might help to turn the scales against the radicals, who were becoming bolder and ever more threatening. But now, as before, Leo's reply was in the negative.[26] This time the Italian government, which hitherto had discreetly kept out of it, decided to intervene. Through the devious channels of communication it ordinarily used in such cases, it conveyed to the Vatican its anxiety about the future, in which the Church as well as the State had a paramount stake. It asked that Catholics should be permitted to vote for candidates of the ministerial party, which faced a rather serious battle. The government warned that if a sizable number of ministerial candidates were defeated, the new majority in the Chamber would probably go on an anticlerical spree. It would in all likelihood abrogate the Law of Guarantees, curb religious freedom, and institute other measures against the Church.[27] But confidential conversations between the representative of the government and a member of the papal entourage proved fruitless.[28] Worse, they were followed by a strengthening of the ban. On July 30, 1886, the *non expedit,* in its wording a recommendation that left decisions to the discretion of the faithful, was converted into a prohibition by the Holy See.[29]

Although Leo's attitude could no longer be in doubt, the agitation which the question had provoked did not subside. On the contrary, more and more Catholic laymen maintained that the issue was a secular one and hence outside the Pope's jurisdiction. Accordingly, they not only continued to urge a change of policy but even defied the prohibition by going to the polls. In justification of their attitude they could point to the growing strength of Marxian socialism in Italy

and to the danger which this portended for the Roman Catholic
Church. As if to prove the legitimacy of this alarm, the 1890's turned
out to be a turbulent decade. A showdown between the coalition of
conservatives and liberals, now banded together in defense of the
economic and social *status quo,* and the left-wing elements who
made collectivism as well as secularism a primary goal, began to
take shape in the national arena. The climax of the struggle was
heralded by a series of spectacular crises that continued unabated
into 1900. The spring of that year witnessed some very disorderly
scenes in the Chamber of Deputies. These were followed by the dissolution of the Chamber and the decreeing of new elections for June
3. Amid signs that the Socialists would gain at the expense of the
ministerial party, Leo was once again implored to suspend the *non
expedit.* He was impressed with the arguments of the Catholic
spokesmen who presented the case for a prompt scrapping of the
ban. He did not have to be reminded of the gravity of the situation.
After all, nine years earlier he had promulgated his famous *Rerum
Novarum,* a deeply moving and perceptive encyclical on the condition of the working classes, precisely because he realized the
extent of the Marxian danger. Since then he had watched developments in Italy with vigilance and concern. The warnings conveyed
by the Catholic leaders therefore tallied closely with what he had
been telling himself. However, two things apparently kept him from
doing anything about the *non expedit:* bitterness over the shabby
treatment he felt he had received at the hands of the Italian government,[30] and the conviction that it was too late for him to execute
such a *volte-face.* To one of the pleaders for a change of policy Leo
is reported to have said: "As long as I live, the *non expedit* will be
maintained; my successor will see what is best to do afterwards."[31]
His belief that the policy would have to be re-examined and re-
assessed during the next pontificate seemed confirmed almost as
soon as he had spoken. An extraordinarily large number of Catholics
voted in June 1900. The Left Wingers also obtained heavier support
than before, with the result that they emerged with a greatly aug-
mented representation in the Chamber of Deputies. These two por-

tents had an unmistakable significance. As one writer has put it, by 1900 "the failure of the 'Non Expedit' was writ large upon the political sky."[32]

Leo's public pronouncements on the question of the temporal power and his prolongation of the *non expedit* were supplemented by an active diplomacy that never lost sight of the Papacy's territorial goal. The design here was to obtain foreign support of such power as to compel or induce the Italian government to acquiesce in a solution of the Roman Question on the Vatican's terms. The first decade of Leo's pontificate was dominated by the hope that it would be possible to secure the aid of Germany and Austria-Hungary in working toward a partial restoration of the temporal power. France, the traditional protector of the Holy See, could no longer be counted on because it had been taken over by republicans of an avowedly anticlerical complexion. The Kulturkampf which Bismarck had launched in the 1870's constituted the main obstacle to any rapprochement between the Vatican and the Germanic powers. Leo therefore lost little time in acquainting Berlin with his desire for an improvement in the relations between the Holy See and the new colossus in the heart of Europe. Austria-Hungary, which became Germany's firm ally in 1879, heartily approved the papal overture.[33] Emperor Francis Joseph had deplored the Kulturkampf. It embarrassed him no end. He needed Germany's friendship because of difficulties with Russia. But he also had to be on good terms with the spiritual head of the Church that commanded the devout allegiance of most of his subjects. Bismarck, for his part, likewise welcomed Leo's initiative. For a number of reasons, but mainly because the struggle had failed to go according to his expectations, he was more than ready to call it quits.

Nevertheless, success in the negotiations that followed did not prove easy,[34] but eventually it came, and relations between the Papacy and the Reich were normalized. However, neither Germany nor Austria-Hungary exhibited any eagerness to antagonize Italy by taking sides against her on the Roman Question. The unwillingness

of Emperor Francis Joseph to give effective aid when Italian anticlericals heaped scandalous insults upon the Papacy proved a cruel
and quite unexpected blow to Leo.[35] Far more devastating, however,
was Italy's success in concluding an alliance with Germany and
Austria-Hungary in 1882.[36] There could be little doubt that so long
as this alliance endured, the Central Powers would do nothing to
alienate or embarrass Italy.

Nevertheless, Leo did not write off Berlin and Vienna for the
simple reason that at this time he had nowhere else to look for
foreign assistance. He forced himself to hope that Germany and
Austria-Hungary might yet help, especially if something were to
happen to their alliance with Italy.[37] But in February 1887 that
alliance was renewed. In the summer of the same year Francesco
Crispi, archfoe of the Papacy, became Italy's Prime Minister, and
a few months later, in October, he visited Bismarck at Friedrichs-
ruhe. This visit, which received wide publicity, indicated that Italy's
relations with Germany were more cordial than ever. Although the
Vatican now began to evince a pro-French orientation, Leo himself
continued to cling to the hope that Bismarck might still be persuaded
to assist in the restoration of the temporal power. This is evident
from the instructions that Leo gave Cardinal Galimberti when the
latter left for Berlin in March 1888 to attend the funeral rites for
Emperor William I.[38] But the German Chancellor put a damper on
Leo's hopes. He told Galimberti that a solution of the Roman
Question would have to be deferred. If action were taken in the
immediate future, he warned, a republican revolution would occur
in Italy, and this would be followed by the conclusion of an alliance
between the French and Italian republics.[39]

Bismarck's language left little room for doubt and even less for
hope. Leo could hardly gainsay this. Nor could he overlook the fact
that the current intimacy between Italy and the Reich precluded
any change in Germany's attitude on the question which so interested the Vatican. Italy's possession of Rome was guaranteed by
her allies, Germany and Austria-Hungary. At least such was the
interpretation generally placed at the time on the treaty which united

the three powers. This being so, it seemed utterly unrealistic to expect anything at all from the German government. Conversely, there was ample reason to believe that at long last the Third Republic was not only able but willing to help. Spokesmen for the authorities in Paris stated without circumlocution that they wished to see the temporal power restored, provided of course that this involved no injury to the interests of their country.[40] They also undertook to assist Leo in attaining one of his favorite goals, the resumption of diplomatic relations with Russia.[41]

But even at this late date, although he was extremely resentful against the German and Austro-Hungarian governments because they had consented to renew their alliance with the despoilers of the Holy See, Leo apparently continued to repose confidence in Bismarck, the man with whom he had negotiated an end to the Kulturkampf.[42] But there was no trace of such confidence in the attitude of the new Papal Secretary of State, Cardinal Mariano Rampolla. Unlike Leo, Rampolla entertained no illusions whatsoever in regard to Germany and Austria-Hungary. Because they were Italy's friends, he decided that the Vatican must separate itself quite completely from them. By the same token, he favored a close liaison with France as the only course left open to the Papacy by the current conjuncture of circumstances.[43] Two things aided him in his efforts to persuade Leo that the policy he advocated must be followed boldly and resolutely to the exclusion of any other. One was the outbreak, on March 1, 1888, of a bitter tariff war between France and Italy that ushered in an international crisis of the utmost gravity. Enmity with a common foe, Italy, was to prove a powerful bond between France and the Vatican for several years, until the tariff war finally came to an end. It was in this context that Leo brought himself to adopt a revolutionary change of attitude toward the Third Republic that was to culminate in the policy of *Ralliement*.[44]

The second factor that aided Rampolla was a further deterioration of Italo-papal relations. The summer of 1888 saw a renewal of anticlerical demonstrations and a revival of rumors that Leo was contemplating flight from the Eternal City.[45] In October the announced intention of Emperor William II to call on the Pope so angered Crispi, who was afraid the question of the temporal power would be brought up, that he unleashed an aggressive propaganda campaign against the Vatican.[46] Matters reached a furious crescendo on June 9, 1889, when a statue was unveiled in Rome in commemoration of Giordano Bruno, the sixteenth-century philosopher who was burned at the stake by order of the Inquisition. Although the idea of staging the ceremony had originated with the Freemasons, Crispi gave it his wholehearted endorsement.[47] The principal speaker at the unveiling was Giovanni Bovio, an outspoken anticlerical and republican. He utilized the occasion to refer in glowing terms to the occupation of Rome and the extinction of the temporal power.[48] Leo reacted with undisguised bitterness. He denounced the ceremony as a declaration of war against the Catholic Church and, at the instigation of Rampolla, let it be known that he was thinking of leaving Rome to show how he felt.[49] Simultaneously, he warned the Italian government that if he was forced to go into exile, he would return to Rome as a temporal sovereign.[50] Crispi replied by threatening to bar Leo's re-entry if the city were abandoned. In addition, both Germany and Austria-Hungary, acting as Italy's good friends, made strong representations at the Vatican in an effort to dissuade Leo from leaving. He himself, as a matter of fact, was disposed to depart only if the current crisis in Franco-Italian relations developed into a shooting war and if the Italian government, in such an eventuality, proved either unwilling or unable to keep its oft-reiterated promise to protect the Papacy's freedom.[51] Leo stayed where he was. But the inevitable result of the Bruno incident and of the newest display of Germany's solidarity with Italy was to remove his residual resistance to the course advocated by Rampolla. Thereafter, until Leo's death in 1903, the pro-French orientation of papal policy remained virtually constant.

Thus, as we survey the politcal and diplomatic aspects of Leo's pontificate, we see how continuous and decisive was the role played by the Roman Question. Legitimacy was clearly on the side of the

Papacy; the apparently irresistible dynamism of nationalism buttressed the claims of Italy. But the territorial problem which thus arose was enormously complicated by the conflict between religion and science, ecclesiasticism and secularism. Until the passions generated by this conflict could begin to subside, prospects for a settlement of issues both small and large remained dishearteningly bleak.

During the second half of the nineteenth century, when Pius IX and Leo XIII presided over the destinies of Roman Catholicism, the passions that accompanied the struggle between science and religion, between ecclesiasticism and secularism, reached their highest point. Although still explosive, they began to recede somewhat in the early 1900's, during the pontificate of Leo's successor, Pius X. The first World War, which engendered a host of new preoccupations, dealt these passions a staggering blow, so much so that on the morrow of that struggle, the gap between clericals and anticlericals narrowed perceptibly. A solution of the Roman Question seemed to impend, and precisely along the lines envisaged by Leo. This period of rapprochement coincided with the pontificate of Benedict XV. The settlement finally came a few years later, when Pius XI sat on the papal throne. The role of Mussolini as a party to the Lateran Accords of 1929 shadowed them at the time of their signature. Actually, however, they responded to a profound historical need. They have survived the vicissitudes of the past thirty years. They should survive many more.

NOTES

1. For a discussion of the developments from 1860 to September 1870, see my *Italy and the Vatican at War* (Chicago, 1939), pp. xi–xvii, 1–65.
2. An analysis of the terms of the Law of Guarantees will be found in *ibid.*, pp. 117–120.
3. The Vatican's reaction to the Law of Guarantees is described in *ibid.*, pp. 130–132. As early as October 1870, its distrust was expressed as

follows by Cardinal Antonelli, the Papal Secretary of State, in the course of a conversation with a member of the Italian parliament: "I am loth to suspect the good intentions of your king or even of his Ministry, but how long are these men likely to remain in office? Who can answer for their successors? Was not the Government the first to promise us protection, and was it not the first to invade our territory? . . . Believe me, neither your Sovereign nor his Ministers are able to make us any promise on which we can rely. . . .Why should the Holy Father quit the basis of his rights, international as well as private, and enter into transactions, when he is sure he can only lose by them . . .? We had far better wait patiently till circumstances allow us to regain possession of what belongs to us, or till time shall have arranged matters" (reported in the London *Times* of October 11, 1870).

4. For convenient summaries of the period 1871–1878, see my articles, "Church and State in Italy during the Last Years of Pius IX," *Church History*, V (1936), pp. 71–84; "Italian Anticlericalism 1871–1914," *Journal of Modern History*, XIX (1947), pp. 23–24.

5. *Italy and the Vatican at War*, p. 377.

6. *Ibid.*, p. 458.

7. When Count Paar, the Austro-Hungarian ambassador to the Vatican, urged that the conclave be held in Rome, Pecci soothingly replied: "You may rest assured, Mr. Ambassador, that everything will be taken into account." See Friedrich Engel-Janosi, "L'Austria e il Vaticano durante la Prima Decade del Pontificato di Leone XIII (1878–1887)," *Rivista Storica Italiana*, LXVI (1954), p. 348.

8. On February 10, in a circular note addressed to the members of the diplomatic corps at the Vatican, the Sacred College announced its decision to hold the conclave in Rome. The text of this note is reproduced in *Archives Diplomatiques 1876–1877*, IV (Paris, n.d.), pp. 269–271, and in R. De Cesare, *Il Conclave di Leone XIII* (Città di Castello, 1888), pp. 183–185. Although the above-mentioned volume of the *Archives Diplomatiques* is dated 1876–1877, it contains many documents that originated during the year 1878.

9. On the conclave of 1878, see "Italian Anticlericalism 1871–1914," p. 24; De Cesare, pp. 61, 84, 305, and 309; Francesco Crispi, *Politica Interna* (Milan, 1924), pp. 82, 84, and 87; Camillo Manfroni, *Sulla Soglia del Vaticano* (Bologna, 1920), I, pp. 334–335; Pietro Vigo, *Storia degli Ultimi Trent'Anni del Secolo XIX* (Milan, 1908–1915), II, pp. 261 and 263; A. Leroy-Beaulieu, "Un Roi et un Pape—II— Pie IX et le Saint Siège," *Revue des Deux Mondes*, 3d ser., XXVII

(1878), p. 403; Eduardo Soderini, *Il Pontificato di Leone XIII* (Milan, 1932–1933), I, p. 46 and n. 2; André Danel, ed., *L'Année Politique 1878* (Paris, 1879), pp. 32–33.

10. Manfroni, I, p. 375.

11. The entire text of this allocution is reproduced in *Civiltà Cattolica,* 10th ser. (1878), VI, pp. 219–223, and in *Archives Diplomatiques 1876–1877,* IV, pp. 295–297.

12. This was noted by several contemporary observers, including Danel in *L'Année Politique 1878,* p. 34.

13. For the text of this encyclical, see *Civiltà Cattolica,* 10th ser., VI (1878), pp. 385–402, and *Archives Diplomatiques 1876–1877,* IV, pp. 299–307. The contrast between the two pontiffs was widely noted on this occasion. See, for example, H. Schulthess, ed., *Europäischer Geschichtskalender: 1878* (Nördlingen, 1879), p. 405.

14. *Civiltà Cattolica,* 10th ser. (1878), VI, p. 394; *Archives Diplomatiques 1876–1877,* IV, p. 303.

15. *Civiltà Cattolica,* 10th ser. (1878), VI, pp. 394–395; *Archives Diplomatiques 1876–1877,* IV, p. 303.

16. See the obviously inspired statement issued by the Papacy's newspaper organ, the *Osservatore Romano,* on March 22, 1879.

17. Manfroni, II, pp. 4–5. It is interesting to recall, in this connection, that late in August 1870, three weeks before the occupation of Rome, the Italian Cabinet addressed to the governments of Europe a memorandum listing possible terms of an Italo-papal understanding. The memorandum proposed, among other things, that the Leonine City should remain subject to the authority of the pope. For the text of this memorandum, see *Archives Diplomatiques 1874* (Paris, n.d.), II, pp. 37–38. Pius IX was in no mood at the time to accept such an offer, and it was allowed to lapse. It had been made contingent on acquiescence by the Vatican in a reconciliation with Italy. See Alessandro Guiccioli, *Quintino Sella* (Rovigo, 1887), I, p. 304; Stefano Castagnola, *Da Firenze a Roma: Diario Storico-Politico del 1870–71* (Turin, 1896), p. 27 and note. Instead of renewing the offer, which was sharply criticized by those who felt that not a square inch of the national domain should be sacrificed, the Italian government compromised by guaranteeing the Vatican the use of the Leonine City.

18. Manfroni, II, p. 23.

19. *Ibid.,* p. 24.

20. This view was presented by a Catholic polemicist in an anonymous pamphlet entitled *Il Vaticano e le Elezioni Politiche* (Rome, 1882).

21. So argued Count Carlo del Pezzo in *Una Questione Mal Posta* (Naples, 1882).

22. A representative recapitulation of this contention will be found in the brochure by Baron Luigi de Matteis, *Non Expedit! Chiarimenti sul Non Intervento dei Cattolici Italiani alle Urne Politiche* (Naples, 1882).

23. For the shocking outrages perpetrated by anticlerical agitators on the night of July 12–13, 1881, see Vigo, III, pp. 270–275; Saverio Cilibrizzi, *Storia Parlamentare Politica e Diplomatica d'Italia da Novara a Vittorio Veneto* (Milan, 1925–1952), II, p. 225; H. Schulthess, ed., *Europäischer Geschichtskalender: 1881* (Nördlingen, 1882), pp. 478–479; Hubert Bastgen, *Die Römische Frage* (Freiburg, 1917–1919), III, Part I, p. 200, note; *The Annual Register: 1881* (London, 1882), Part II, pp. 52–53; Humphrey Johnson, *The Papacy and the Kingdom of Italy* (London, 1926), pp. 45–46. The *Osservatore Romano,* commenting on the disgraceful incidents, bitterly declared: "Rome then is not free to render to the pope even the last sad funeral honors. It has not been possible peacefully and without molestation to carry the body of the dead pope to its sepulchre, and yet they talk of the living pope being free! What would happen if the Holy Father were to come out from the Vatican?" (issue of July 14, 1881).

24. In a note which Cardinal Jacobini, the Papal Secretary of State, dispatched on July 21, 1881 to the members of the diplomatic corps at the Holy See, Leo was described as filled with apprehension regarding the future. This state of mind, the note continued, might induce the Pontiff to take certain decisions with an eye to safeguarding the honor of the Papacy as well as the liberty and independence of his person. For the text of this note, see Bastgen, III, Part I, pp. 201–202. Leo himself, in an allocution delivered on August 4, 1881, lashed out against the authors of the recent incidents. "This grievous and atrocious outrage," he declared, "has brought the deepest sorrow and distress upon our soul. And since our office constitutes us the avenger of every offense attempted against the majesty of the Roman pontificate and the venerable memory of our predecessors, we solemnly protest . . . against these deplorable excesses, and we loudly complain of this wrong, for which the entire blame falls on those who failed to protect both the claims of religion and the liberties of citizens against the rage of the ungodly. By this alone the Catholic world may judge how much security we enjoy in Rome. It was already well-known that we were reduced to a painful, difficult and,

in many ways, intolerable condition, but the recent events of which we speak have made this even more plain and evident. They have also demonstrated that if the present state of things is galling, the future is bound to be even more so. If the transfer of the ashes of Pius IX has given rise to disgraceful disorders and grave tumult, who can guarantee that the audacity of the wicked will not result in the same excesses if we should be seen passing through the streets of Rome in a manner befitting our dignity? . . . Hence it is more than ever manifest that under the present circumstances we can remain in Rome only as prisoners within the Vatican. Nay, more: whoever reflects on certain indications which have appeared here and there . . . may well reach the conclusion that more pernicious projects are being prepared against the Christian religion, the supreme pontiff, and the ancestral faith of the Roman people." The text of this allocution is reproduced in *Civiltà Cattolica,* 11th ser. (1881), VII, pp. 385–395. On Leo's consideration of the idea of flight, see Francesco Salata, *Per la Storia Diplomatica della Questione Romana* (Milan, 1929), I, pp. 135–137; Manfroni, II, pp. 50–53 and 60–61; Engel-Janosi, pp. 359–360; "Italian Anticlericalism 1871–1914," p. 25; Bastgen, III, Part I, p. 200, note.

25. This statement appeared in the *Osservatore Romano* on September 28, 1882.
26. Manfroni, II, p. 144.
27. *Ibid.,* p. 304.
28. *Ibid.,* pp. 308–310.
29. The Vatican issued the following statement for the guidance of the faithful: *"Non expedit prohibitionem importat."* See Johnson, p. 70.
30. *Ibid.,* p. 71.
31. Bolton King and Thomas Okey, *Italy Today* (London, 1901), p. 52.
32. Johnson, p. 71.
33. Engel-Janosi, p. 353.
34. *Ibid.,* p. 351; Erich Eyck, *Bismarck* (Erlenbach-Zurich, 1941–1944), III, p. 126; Georges Goyau, *Bismarck et l'Église: Le Culturkampf (1870–1887)* (Paris, 1911–1913), III, pp. 5 ff.; Soderini, III, Chaps. 2–6; J. Heckel, "Die Beilegung des Kulturkampfes in Preussen," *Zeitschrift der Savigny-Stiftung für Rechtsgeschichte. Kanonistische Abteilung* (1930),L, pp. 215–353.
35. About a month after the events of July 12–13, 1881, Leo wrote the Emperor a personal letter requesting Austria's help. Francis Joseph's reply disappointed Leo. He pronounced it "reserved, cold, evasive,"

and confessed that he had been grieved by it. See Salata, I, pp. 141 ff.; Engel-Janosi, p. 359.

36. When the Vatican first learned of the conclusion of the Triple Alliance treaty, it pressed the Austro-Hungarian government for precise information about its terms. The Austro-Hungarian government stated unequivocally that it had not given Italy a territorial guarantee and added that it had done nothing whatsoever to injure the rights of the Holy See. See Engel-Janosi, p. 361.

37. In September 1885 Bismarck invited Leo to serve as mediator and arbiter in the Spanish-German dispute over the Caroline Islands. The Chancellor's gesture gave rise to high but unwarranted hopes at the Vatican. See *ibid.*, p. 367 and note. This typified Leo's state of mind at the time. For the impression produced on the Curia by Bismarck's move, see also Cardinal Dominique Ferrata, *Mémoires* (Rome, 1920), I, pp. 347-354; Ulrich Stutz, *Die Päpstliche Diplomatie unter Leo XIII. Abhandlungen der Preussischen Akademie der Wissenschaften* (Berlin, 1926), p. 60.

38. On the instructions given to Galimberti, see Soderini, III, pp. 375–378; Crispolto Crispolti and Guido Aureli, *La Politica di Leone XIII da Luigi Galimberti a Mariano Rampolla* (Rome, 1912), p. 423; Kurd von Schlözer, *Letzte Römische Briefe 1882–1894* (Stuttgart, 1924), p. 123; E. L. Woodward, "The Diplomacy of the Vatican under Popes Pius IX and Leo XIII," *Journal of the British Institute of International Affairs* (May, 1924), p. 134.

39. Soderini, III, p. 389; Crispolti and Aureli, pp. 443 ff.; Schlözer, p. 123; Woodward, pp. 134–135.

40. Crispolti and Aureli, p. 375.

41. *Ibid.*, Chap. 9; A. A. di Pesaro, "La Diplomazia Vaticana e la Questione del Potere Temporale," *Rassegna Nazionale* (May 1, 1890), pp. 89, 114–118; Edmond Toutain, *Alexandre III et la République Française* (Paris, 1929), pp. 360 ff.

42. William L. Langer, *European Alliances and Alignments 1871–1890* (New York, 1931), p. 473. Leo's state of mind at this time is revealed in instructions he sent to his Nuncio at Vienna and in his subsequent conversations with the Austrian diplomat, Count Hübner. See Salata, I, pp. 180–226.

43. It was Rampolla's aim to tie France so closely to the Curia that she would be prepared, in the event of an Italo-papal collision, and despite the danger of a clash with the members of the Triple Alliance, to protect the rights of the Pope. For this a high price would have to be paid, and Rampolla was ready to pay it: papal support for the

republican regime in France. See Maxmilian Claar, "Kardinal Rampolla als Staatssekretär und Papstwerber 1887–1903." *Europäische Gespräche* (1929), VII, pp. 473–474.

44. *Ralliement* in support of the Third Republic was urged by Leo in his encyclical of February 16, 1892. For the text of this famous letter, see *Civiltà Cattolica*, 15th ser. (1892), I, pp. 608–619. Leo's policy toward France is discussed comprehensively by Stutz, pp. 62–72.

45. Manfroni, II, p. 167; "Italian Anticlericalism 1871–1914," p. 26.

46. Crispolti and Aureli, p. 262; Johnson, p. 53.

47. Cilibrizzi, II, p. 167: "Italian Anticlericalism 1871–1914," p. 27.

48. Cilibrizzi, II, p. 372; "Italian Anticlericalism 1871–1914," p. 27.

49. Claar, pp. 469–470; Soderini, II, p. 163.

50. This warning was issued on July 12, 1889 through the *Osservatore Romano*.

51. Francesco Crispi, *Memoirs* (London, 1912–1914), II, pp. 404–405: Italicus, *Italiens Dreibundpolitik* (Munich, 1928), p. 125; Manfroni, II, pp. 183–184; "Italian Anticlericalism 1871–1914," p. 28.

6 Leo XIII and England

REV. ERIC McDERMOTT, S.J.
Georgetown University

ON THE FEAST OF PENTECOST 1559 the English *Book of Common Prayer* superseded the ancient missal and the Mass was no longer a legally permissible service in England. For generations successive English governments sought to destroy Catholicism in England and the number of Catholics slowly dwindled. The vicissitudes of that sad and slow decline have only partially been related for the modern reader. A general sketch has been offered, but the detail is lacking. The slow attrition in the counties caused by official persecution, and even more by social ostracism, by the demands of Catholic morality, and by the lack of adequate instruction in the Faith does not recommend itself as an inspiring theme for the ambitious historian. The nadir of Catholic fortunes, however, in the eighteenth century was quickly followed by a number of legal emancipations. These were granted because, surely, Catholicism had sunk almost to insignificance. The banner year was 1829, and, though the Catholic Emancipation Act passed in that year seemed to be chiefly of Irish concern, it, all unexpectedly, prepared the way for a Catholic renaissance of increasingly impressive proportions. In a hundred and twenty years the obscure sect had a claim to be regarded as the largest active Christian body in the Kingdom.

The year 1850 saw the restoration of the hierarchy. The first Cardinal Archbishop of Westminster was Nicholas Wiseman. In the course of the archiepiscopate of his distinguished successor, Henry Edward Manning, Pope Leo XIII ascended the papal throne. By the time Leo began to reign in 1878 the revived English Catholic

Church was making encouraging progress. Three groups of Catholics were contributing to its life and attempting to achieve a reasonable unity. There were the old Catholic families who had endured the penal centuries; there were the Irish immigrants who yearly crowded the boats to England for work building the railways, filling the new factories, and fleeing from the unemployment, the poverty, and often the starvation of the Irish countryside. Most were Catholics, but a large proportion of them failed to live up to the demands of their religion in England. The third group consisted of converts, chiefly from the Church of England. This group, never large, was noted for its convert clergymen, all well-educated, some very well-known. The most famous names were those of John Henry Newman and Henry Edward Manning. By the time Pope Leo came to the throne the normal life of the Catholic Church was well-established in the populous parts of England. Churches and schools had been built and public money was being given to maintain Catholic schools. Religious orders and congregations had been established; and Cardinal Manning had already failed in his attempt to maintain a Catholic University in London. Nevertheless, the fact that such an institution of higher learning came into existence gives some indication of the aims and achievements of that body that hoped to support it.

Change, however, was not confined to Catholicism alone. The Church of England, torn by Evangelicalism and by Ritualism, had altered too. An acute observer, Cardinal Vaughan, Manning's successor at Westminster, gave a vivid contemporary picture when he addressed a Catholic conference in Preston in 1893.

Contrast the churches of the Establishment [the Church of England] of sixty or seventy years ago—closed from week-end to week-end, no daily service, no festivals and Saints' Days kept, the Communion Service read three or four times a year, everything dry, cold and formal— with the present churches, which are often distinguishable only with extreme difficulty from those belonging to the Church of Rome. The study of the patristic, of the theological, ascetical, devotional,

liturgical and rubrical writers of the Catholic Church has brought about
a change in the mind, feelings and tastes of an ever-increasing section
of the Anglican Church, which has been simply a revolution. The
doctrines of the Catholic Church, which had been rejected and condemned as blasphemous, superstitious, and fond inventions, have been
re-examined and taken back, one by one, until the Thirty-nine Articles
have been banished and buried as a rule of faith. The Real Presence, the
Sacrifice of the Mass offered for the living and the dead—sometimes even
in Latin—not unfrequent Reservation of the Sacrament, regular auricular
Confession, Extreme Unction, Purgatory, prayers for the dead, devotions
to Our Lady, to her Immaculate Conception, the use of her Rosary and
the Invocation of Saints are doctrines taught and accepted, with a growing
desire and relish for them, in the Church of England.

A celibate clergy, the institution of monks and nuns under vows,
retreats for the clergy, missions for the people, fasting and other pen-
itential exercises, candles, lamps, incense, crucifixes, images of the
Blessed Virgin and the Saints held in honour, stations of the cross,
cassocks, cottas, Roman collars, birettas, copes, dalmatics, vestments,
mitres, croziers, the adoption of an ornate Catholic ritual, and now recently an elaborate display of the whole ceremonial of the Catholic
Pontifical—all this speaks of a change and a movement towards the
Church that would have appeared absolutely incredible at the beginning
of this century. And what is still more remarkable is that the movement
has been stronger than the rankest Protestantism, stronger than the
Bishops, stronger than the lawyers and the Legislature. A spasmodic
protest, a useless prosecution, a Delphic judgment, and the movement
continues and spreads, lodging itself in Anglican homes and convents, in
schools, churches and even cathedrals, until it is rapidly covering the
country. Has there ever been a more marvellous change, and this
within half a century?[1]

Pope Leo XIII had been interested in England thirty-three years
before he became Pope. As Nuncio to Belgium, he had met a well-
known English convert, Father Ignatius Spencer, and had discussed
with him the prospects for the conversion of England to the Catholic
faith. A little later, about February 1846, Monsignor Pecci, having
been recalled from the Belgium nunciature, spent a month in England to study its political institutions. He dined with Queen Victoria
at St. James' Palace and met the Prince Consort, Lord Palmerston,

and Lord Aberdeen, who was then Foreign Secretary. Monsignor Pecci also attended a sitting of Parliament.

In the Conclave which chose Cardinal Pecci to be Pope, Cardinal Manning took an active part, indeed an overactive part according to the gossipmongers, for Manning complained that his part in the Conclave which elected Leo XIII had been libelously described by newspaper correspondents. "It will probably go down to history that I divided the Sacred College by vehement debates, that I opposed the election of Leo XIII and that I counselled the holding of the Conclave in Malta. It little matters that the reverse of all these three, now historic fables, is fact and truth."[2]

The circumstance preceding the election of Leo, however, had already been the subject of a long, contemporary memorandum by the Cardinal. From it are taken the extracts which follow:

Pius IX died on 7th February: from that day till we entered the Conclave, the Sacred College sat day by day in the Vatican. On the Wednesday in that week, 13th February, Cardinal Monaco said to me, that we ought to confer together as to whom we should propose in the election. It was then fixed that we should meet at Cardinal Bartolini's rooms on Friday evening, 15th. There were present Cardinals Bartolini, Franchi, Bilio, Monaco, Nina and myself.

Cardinal Bartolini proposed Cardinal Pecci's name, in which we all concurred as the first name.

He then said for the second there were Cardinals Franchi, Bilio and Monaco. . . . Bilio said that he held it necessary in the present conflict of the Church that the next Pope should be a foreigner, and then suggested myself. I then said that in my judgment, as they already knew, the next Pontiff must be an Italian in blood and speech . . . , that the election of a foreigner might lose Italy to the Holy See. . . .

When they pressed that I had been so domesticated in Rome as not to be a foreigner, I said that though I knew their language, I knew it well enough to know that I do not know it well enough to be responsible for government . . . that I believed no foreigner would know Rome sufficiently for such an office. Bilio said that proved too much, that there had been foreign Popes. . . .

We then agreed on Cardinal Pecci, and undertook to speak to other Cardinals. I undertook the foreign Cardinals with Cardinal Howard, and most of them were invited to vote for Cardinal Pecci.[3]

One of Pope Leo's earliest acts as Pontiff was to create John Henry Newman Cardinal, to the great satisfaction of many more people than the English Catholics alone. On December 9, 1886 the Pope endorsed the decree of the Congregation of Rites which confirmed the honors which had been paid for generations, since the time of Pope Gregory XIII, to fifty English martyrs who had been put to death during the reigns of Henry VIII and of Elizabeth I. Among these martyrs were Bishop John Fisher of Rochester and Sir Thomas More, one-time Chancellor of England. A few years later Leo showed his continued interest in England by approving the foundation of the Beda College in Rome for the training for the priesthood of those Englishmen who have found their vocation late in life. Shortly afterwards he honored its patron, the Venerable Bede, with the title of Doctor of the Universal Church. Finally, at the instance of the English hierarchy Leo XIII on April 2, 1895, gave his approval to Catholics attending the Universities of Oxford and Cambridge.

The most famous encyclical written by Pope Leo XIII was the one on the problem of the working classes, known as *Rerum Novarum*. It has been stated by Joseph Schmidlin, a German historian of the modern Church, that the labor principles discussed and propounded by Cardinal Manning and by Cardinal Gibbons of Baltimore were influential in the genesis of the encyclical. The distinguished biographer of Gibbons, however, has stated that "there can be advanced no clear proof that the Pope was directly influenced by Gibbons and his memorial on the Knights of Labor."[4]

The destruction of the organization of the Catholic Church in England during the reign of the first Elizabeth caused for the English Catholics who remained faithful problems of ecclesiastical jurisdiction which were not solved until the reign of Leo XIII. Into the tangled skein of this history historians have hesitated to enter; and very much of it still remains obscure, nor is it necessary here to discuss it. It is sufficient to state that in the absence of properly constituted dioceses problems of sacerdotal jurisdiction were involved. The privileges of the regular clergy to whom the maintenance of

English Catholicism owed so much success were eventually to sit ill with the rights claimed by the English bishops when the hierarchy was restored in 1850.

In 1873 Father Peter Gallwey, the Provincial Superior of the Society of Jesus in England, asked the approval of Herbert Vaughan, Bishop of Salford, to open a high school in Manchester. The Bishop refused his assent, but that did not end the matter because after some correspondence between the Bishop and the Provincial, it became clear that the latter had asked the leave for propriety's sake only, and that, in fact, he did not regard the matter as falling under episcopal control. The reason for this was the possession of a papal privilege by the Society of Jesus which gave them the right to establish a school wherever they had a house. Accordingly, their Church of the Holy Name in Manchester gave them the right to associate with it a high school, even though the bishop objected to it. However, Bishop Vaughan refused to acknowledge such a privilege and proceeded to take strong measures, first to oppose the establishment of such a school and secondly to destroy it when it had been set up. To him it seemed essential that a bishop should have control over the building of Catholic schools in his own diocese. This demand, however, was weakened by the obvious need for good high schools in his diocese and by the fact that the Bishop had a desire to found his own high school and apparently feared the competition of a Jesuit school. To the Jesuit Provincial, on the other hand, the episcopal refusal to acknowledge a papal privilege, one indeed which was interpreted as being essential to the work of the Society, was a usurpation of authority which must be resisted both in principle insofar as such action threatened the privileges of all religious orders, and also in practice insofar as it crippled the work of his own order.

Both parties refused the sacrifice of what seemed to them essential principle, and the matter was appealed to Rome. Bishop Vaughan, indeed, proved so obstinate in his conviction that he threatened to resign his see unless his judgment of the matter were vindicated at Rome. With the backing of Cardinal Manning, the Archbishop of Westminster, he won the day, after personally campaigning in

Rome in 1875. One consequence, however, of the struggle had been to ventilate the whole question of the privileges of the regular clergy against the English bishops and, hence, against all ordinaries. This fundamental problem was discussed by the English bishops at the Fifth Provincial Synod at Westminster in the Low Week of 1877. The assembled bishops resolved unanimously that the Pope be asked to frame a constitution regulating the rights and privileges of the regular clergy in the face of episcopal authority. They proposed twelve questions which can be summarized under six complaints:

1. The Jesuits claim to be able to open schools even against the will of the bishop of the diocese.

2. Bishops are prevented from inspecting parochial schools attached to parishes served by regular priests.

3. Bishops are prevented from dividing missions staffed by regular clergy.

4. Regulars refuse attendance at synods.

5. Bishops were refused any information about, or control of, moneys of the missions served by regulars.

6. Bishops were refused any say in the changes in mission staffs provided by regulars.

To Cardinal Manning, who had proved constantly hostile to the Society of Jesus and who steadily refused its members leave to open a school in his archdiocese, the prospect of this attack on religious orders was exhilarating. He modestly gave a summary in 1887 of his actions in this struggle:

My part in the contest of Bishops and Regulars was (1) That in Low Week of 1877 I proposed to avoid all local and personal contention—to draw up one complete statement, lay it before the Holy See, and ask for a Constitution . . . to regulate under the Hierarchy the questions which were in existence also before it was founded. This was unanimously adopted. (2) I went to Rome, then came the election of Leo XIII. I asked him to proceed by way of a Constitution as it was not a conflict, but a legislative matter affecting the divine order of the Church, and the whole Church on earth. This he promised to do. (3) Then, at Cardinal Bilio's suggestion, I asked for a special Commission of cardinals. This also he granted. These three points were my chief part in the affair; save only that I went to Rome again—in all three times—and urged the matter with the Cardinals and the Holy Father till they wished me out of Rome. I went gladly, sick of the heat and the intrigues.[5]

The English hierarchy entrusted much of the early negotiations to the Bishop of Clifton, and in May 1877 he was in Rome expounding his case to the authorities concerned, especially to those at the Congregation of Propaganda who had jurisdiction over England. He found that the Jesuits had already got to work to rebut his charges. The death of Pope Pius IX in February 1878 and the accession to the papal throne of Pope Leo XIII much delayed proceedings. The new Pope told Cardinal Manning that he was very interested in the *Relatio* of the English bishops, and that he would be glad to issue a constitution in the matter after adequate examination and consideration. In the summer of the same year the hierarchy of Scotland officially entered into the case as associates of the English bishops.

The rest of the year went by and little progress was made, on the Roman plea that the regulars needed ample time to prepare their case. It was in the hands of a well-known canonist, the Jesuit Father Ballerini. Cardinal Manning and the Bishop of Clifton, chafing at the delay, went to Rome early in 1879. They were suspicious of the impartiality of the cardinals at Propaganda since most of them were regulars. To counter this, Manning went to Pope Leo and asked him to appoint a special cardinalitial commission. Manning wrote to Clifton, April 19, 1879: "In my audience with the Holy Father I asked what I might say to our Bishops when assembled. He said, 'You may say that I have taken the matter out of Propaganda, and shall have it treated by ten Cardinals. And I hope they will receive the result with acquiescence.' "[6] Prompted by Manning, Leo, on July 11, ordered Father Ballerini to send in his reply to the Episcopal *Dubia* before September. But the canonist successfully pleaded for further time. But on May 5 of the following year the reply was still not handed in, and Leo sent a peremptory letter to the General Superior of the Society of Jesus ordering him to use his authority with

Father Ballerini. The latter, at length, gave in his reply on May 17, 1880. Concerning this delay and Manning's great impatience, a Roman Monsignor remarked to the Cardinal: "If we have to suffer this under the eyes of the Pope, we can understand what you may have to endure."[6]

Herbert Vaughan, Bishop of Salford, joined the English party in Rome, where he found that his former campaign against the Society of Jesus was still well-remembered. The Propaganda cardinals pressed him for a compromise which would meet the immediate demands of the English bishops, but which would not necessitate radical legislation. Manning and his colleagues, however, held out stubbornly against this. The persevering pressure of Manning on the Roman cardinals got him the nickname of *Il diplomatico,* while they called Clifton *Il avvocato* and Salford *Il diavolo* for his persistence. There can be no doubt of the strong emotions roused by the protracted case. One litigant was reported to have said: "That talking with Cardinals in Rome was like talking to owls at noonday"; and Manning wrote of the case: "For two years I was assailed by the *Standard, Daily Chronicle* and Society papers with a mendacious and insolent animosity which pointed to personal malice. It became so personal and brutal that at one time many of the clergy thought of presenting to me an Address of indignation. I thought it best to wait till Leo XIII had spoken. The *Romanos Pontifices* wiped out the lies."[7] Such bitterness makes sad reading, but it should be remembered that the full story of the negotiations has not been generally made available. What exists is the accounts in the lives of the two episcopal protagonists, Manning and Vaughan; but there is no balancing account from the side of the regulars. In the various archives of those concerned in the case remains an abundance of documents.

After Father Ballerini had presented his reply, the Bishop of Salford and the Bishop of Clifton decided to alternate their stays in Rome so that one of them would be always there to urge on the case until it was decided. During the summer of 1880 they campaigned vigorously to get the cardinals to give a verdict on Ballerini's reply.

Meanwhile, the other side was also active. Bishop Vaughan reported some of it:

> The stratagem is to frighten the Pope and Cardinals—to say that the Bishops were hostile to the Holy See and wish to destroy the privileges of Regulars. . . . The Jesuits attach great importance to this case because it will regulate America. And it is better to settle the case with the English Bishops than with the American Bishops who are Irish and more violent. Ballerini had told him that the Jesuits must win their case; that the Society had been employed by the Popes all over the world for three hundred years to contend against and control Bishops who were troublesome to the Holy See.[8]

Vaughan also reports Manning's effort to disturb Leo XIII: "Cardinal Manning rather frightened the Pope by saying the matter is very grave: it is a question whether the Society will not diminish the power of an authority higher than that of the Bishops as well as theirs."[9]

On June 1, 1880 Manning had another audience with Leo to press the matter and on November 5 Cardinal McCloskey wrote to Bishop Vaughan telling him how important the case was for America. Vaughan had the letter translated and distributed among the cardinals. At length, in January 1881 the Commission had its last sitting and it presented its report to the Pope. It was said the cardinals were unanimous and favored the bishops. From that time until the promulgation of the bull *Romanos Pontifices* on May 14 great efforts were made from all sides to influence the papal Curia on behalf of the regulars. It was known that Leo himself was the immediate recipient of much of this propaganda, but there is no evidence that his judgment was altered by it. The Bishop of Clifton recalled that "the Pope firmly resisted all pressure, and though he took time to make himself thoroughly acquainted with all the bearings of the case, he never altered his resolution or drew back from his determination to publish a Constitution which should not only settle the relations of Bishops and Regulars in England, but which should serve as a guide and precedent to the whole church."[10]

The bull was accepted with enthusiasm by the English bishops, who saw it as a vindication of the principles on which they had stood. A translation of the bull appeared in England in *The Tablet* for May 21, 1881, and, together with it, an article sent from Rome by Bishop Vaughan. He began as follows:

Pope Leo XIII has published a Bull which will be long known in history under the title *Romanos Pontifices.* . . . This famous Act sums up and ends a recent controversy on matters of discipline affecting the working of the Church in Great Britain. The Pope begins with a reference to the establishment of the Hierarchy in England by Pius IX, and lays down the doctrine of the Fathers as to the teaching and governing office of Bishops. He openly recognizes the fact that certain difficulties and disagreements which have arisen between the Bishops and the members of Religious Orders have been incidental to the commission given to the Bishops on the establishment of the Hierarchy, to labor to bring about the restoration in England of the common law of the Church. The controversy, which has now been set at rest by the Sovereign Pontiff, touched no point of faith or morals, but regarded certain questions of jurisdiction and discipline, which were inevitable in the course of transition from the abnormal condition of the Church under Vicars-Apostolic, and in the days of persecution, to the hierarchical form and the common law of the Church in times of peace.[11]

The happy settlement of these jurisdictional problems was not to end Pope Leo XIII's influence on English affairs. In the following decade there developed in England a concern for the unity of Christendom which was to lead to a notable encyclical from Leo on the unity of the Church and to have a great impact on the future of the High Anglican party in the Church of England.

In the year 1890 the Abbé Fernand Portal, sojourning in the island of Madeira, made the acquaintance of Lord Halifax. They discussed religion and what Halifax said, especially about the Church of England, made a very deep impression on the French priest. In the Englishman he discovered a man outstandingly religious and of great charm. Furthermore, he was notably Catholic in his religious views. Not merely did he believe in the divinity of Jesus Christ, but he seemed also to hold Catholic views on transubstantiation, the sacrifice of the Mass, auricular confession, prayers for the dead, invocation of the saints, the supreme jurisdiction of the Roman See, and the primacy of the Bishop of Rome. Moreover, the abbé learned that very many other Anglicans thought as Halifax did, and were working actively for a corporate reunion of the Church of England with the Church of Rome. Overwhelmed by this joyful news, the Frenchman felt that this state of opinion in the Church of England should be revealed to the Catholics of France and Italy, and that speedy measures should be taken at Rome to consummate this long-desired union of two great Churches. In their conversations the abbé and Halifax came to an agreement that some point of difference between the Churches should be promptly ventilated and that its discussion and resolution would bring the leaders of both Churches into communication and thus prepare the ground for frequent and intimate contacts. To this end the Abbé published a pamphlet, *Les Ordinations Anglicanes,* under the pseudonym of Fernand Dalbus.

The second Viscount Halifax was born in 1839 and was to live on until 1934. At Oxford he had been strongly influenced by the Oxford Movement. His interest in High Churchmanship became so pronounced that in 1865 he took part in the establishment of an Anglican religious order of men, the Society of St. John the Evangelist, later more popularly known as the Cowley Fathers, and seriously considered becoming a professed member himself. For the greater part of his life he was accustomed to make an annual retreat at their Oxford headquarters. His presidency of the English Church Union, however, which he accepted in 1868 and held until 1919 and later for a further seventeen years, enabled him to take a leading part in the religious controversies of his time. The English Church Union was formed to support and spread High Church principles and the Catholic practices which flowed from their adoption. Thus Halifax seemed eminently qualified to initiate talks aimed at bringing together the two Churches. To continental Catholics, however, his beliefs and religious standpoint were difficult to distinguish from Roman orthodoxy. Nor is it difficult to appreciate this when Halifax could write to the Cardinal Archbishop of Toledo in the following terms:

I venture to approach your Eminence in order to express, on behalf of the English Church Union, a society consisting of many thousands of members of the Church of England, the profound distress which has been caused to us by the recent action of the Archbishop of Dublin in having presumed, without the sanction of your Eminence and of the Bishops of your province of Toledo, to consecrate a certain schismatic named Cabrera at Madrid, to the Episcopate. We desire absolutely to disclaim any complicity with such action, believing it to be a most grievous violation of well-established and universally recognized principles of ecclesiastical jurisdiction and of Catholic order.

Halifax went on to show how the Archbishop of Canterbury and the bishops of that province had repudiated in their provincial synod the act of the Dublin Archbishop; and he concluded with these words: "We on our behalf believe it to be right as members of the Catholic Church which is the mother of us all, and as members of the Church of England in particular, thus solemnly to assure your Eminence and the Bishops, clergy and faithful of the ancient and illustrious Church of Spain of our repudiation of the encouragement which the action we deplore has given to those who have withdrawn themselves from the communion and authority of their lawful pastors."[12] Was it to be wondered at that on reading such language continental Catholics could see no reason why Lord Halifax and the "many thousands" who had similar beliefs should not forthwith be united to the Roman Catholic Church?

The Abbé Portal's pamphlet might not, however, have drawn much attention to itself if it had not been reviewed by an eminent ecclesiastical historian. The reputation of the author of the *Liber Pontificalis* was so great that his considered judgment on the facts advanced by the abbé needed only to be unequivocally stated: "The conclusion is that Anglican Orders may be regarded as valid."[13] The fact that the Abbé Duchesne thought these orders were valid, despite Rome's unbroken practice of reordaining Anglican ministers, was enough to ensure that the matter was eventually to be taken to

Rome. In no long time another French priest wrote a book in favor of Anglican orders and the Bishop of Rodez and Vabres, Cardinal Bourret, publicly encouraged the Abbé Portal's work. The Anglican Bishop of Salisbury published a defense and explanation of the problem of Anglican orders in a public letter to the Abbé Portal; and two Anglican clergymen, the Reverend T. A. Lacey, Vicar of Madingley, and the Reverend E. Denny, issued a more elaborate defence of the Anglican position in a book entitled *De Hierarchia Anglicana*. Latin was presumably chosen in order that the book might be influential both in France and in Rome.

In 1894 the Abbé Portal paid a visit to England and inspected many High Anglican churches. In them he was deeply impressed by their Romanism: the vestments, the Stations of the Cross, the Lady altars, the Holy Souls chapels, the solemn Masses, the Catholic literature used and recommended. Even more striking were the Anglican convents of nuns and above all the devotion and evangelical simplicity of the Cowley Fathers with whom the abbé spent a few memorable days. In addition, he met Archbishop Benson of Canterbury in the summer, but the latter, however, conducted himself with an enthusiastic caution that utterly failed to reduce the sanguine views which were bedeviling the picture. Insufficiently appreciated by the abbé were the facts that the High Anglicans were but a small part of the English Church and thus could not speak on behalf of that Church, that for many of the High Churchmen the nearer they approached to Rome in belief and ritual, the less need they felt for repudiating their own Church, and that the majority of the members of the Church of England, including most of her bishops, were thoroughly opposed to the Roman Church both in belief and in sentiment. The horror of Romish practices was abundantly alive in the England of the Abbé Portal's daydreams.

What was notably unfortunate and egregiously so was the abbé's failure to meet the Cardinal Archbishop of Westminster, Herbert Vaughan. The Cardinal could have given the abbé a picture of the Church of England which would have brought actuality to moderate his hopes and plans. It was not the Cardinal's fault. He had gone to the trouble of inviting him to lunch together with Abbot Gasquet and Edmund Bishop, but the abbé had been unable to be present. This was all the more unfortunate since Abbot Gasquet and Edmund Bishop were well-known Catholic scholars alike interested in Anglican problems. Francis Aidan Gasquet, who had been Prior of Downside, was an eminent Benedictine historian, whose *Henry VIII and The English Monasteries* had caused a great stir when it was published in 1888. Later he was created Cardinal and made Vatican Librarian. Edmund Bishop, a former civil servant and convert, had developed a passion for liturgical research. In 1891 he had published in association with Abbot Gasquet *Edward VI and The Book of Common Prayer*. These two scholars were thoroughly capable of dealing with the historical problems raised by the question of the validity of Anglican orders, and they were to have decisive influence on the later determination of the issue.

French interest in the matter of Anglican orders waxed mightily and had results in Rome. All the more was this so when Monsignor Gasparri, the well-known professor of canon law in the Catholic Institute of Paris, declared himself a supporter of the validity of the orders. The Papal Secretary of State, Cardinal Rampolla, thought it wise to take cognizance of the issue, and hinted that he would like to meet the Abbé Portal. The latter immediately set out for Rome where he met not only the Cardinal but also Pope Leo himself and communicated to them some of his interest and enthusiasm for the solution of the problem, and for the likely reunion of the Church of England with Rome. The rosy pictures of that national Church, ripe for reunion, caused astonishment and gratification in Roman circles. The sanguine words of the abbé seemed only to relay the true sentiments of the English when the report of Halifax's annual address to the English Church Union contained the statements that

We have never renounced communion with Rome. There is nothing in the formal teaching of the Church of England which in the least degree implies the existence or the desirability of such a separation; on the contrary, it is distinctly repudiated. Priests in Roman Orders may minister, members of the Roman Communion may communicate, at our altars. We desire from the bottom of our hearts to be allowed to make our confessions to and to receive our communions from the hands of the Roman clergy abroad.[14]

A Protestant reporter provided the following account of the Abbé Portal's reception in Rome. He

started for Rome, where he arrived on the 11th of this month (Sept), and had an interview the same evening with Cardinal Rampolla. He told him his impressions of the English Church, and at the end Cardinal Rampolla said, "You must by all means see the Pope." The next day he had an audience of the Pope which lasted an hour. The Pope made M. Portal tell him everything quite frankly. He told him what he had seen in England—that the Church was at the head of the intellectual movement, that in dealing with the English Clergy he was dealing with men of real learning; of our services and ritual, convents and other features of English Church life; that there was a great feeling for union, and that many were praying every day for it. The Pope . . . asked M. Portal what he could do. M. Portal said that if he were not prepared to make the utmost concessions that could possibly be made, it would be of no use to take any step at all. He suggested that the Pope should write a sympathetic letter to the Archbishops of Canterbury and York. . . .

The Pope asked him how such a letter would be received. M. Portal assured him that it would not meet with a rebuff. . . . The Pope said in an impassioned manner, "How gladly I would say my *Nunc Dimittis*, if I could make the smallest beginning of such a reunion." He said to M. Portal more than once, "You know I am 85 years old."

The Pope told M. Portal that he would write, and bade him come back to the Vatican in two days' time. When he returned on the third day he found that there had been a *mouvement de recul*. It had been felt that it would be incautious for the Pope to write at once in person; and other people had been giving him different accounts of our condition. It was now decided that instead of the Pope writing direct to the Archbishop, Cardinal Rampolla should write a letter to M. Portal which he was not to publish, but which he might show to those whom it concerned; he was told that the Pope intended to commission the Abbé Duchesne to examine at length the questions of our Orders and report on it. . . .

A day or two later he had a farewell audience with the Pope, who was as warm as ever on the subject, and . . . said that if Cardinal Rampolla's letter were well received, he would then write in person.[15]

Halifax was very satisfied with the abbé's progress in Rome, and, on his return, arranged an interview with the Archbishop of Canterbury. Unfortunately, Archbishop Benson thought he was only going to meet Halifax, and was unprepared to enter into a discussion with the Abbé Portal. The meeting was an uncomfortable one; the Archbishop remained uncooperative and even hostile. He thought Cardinal Rampolla's letter unacceptable. It seems clear that the abbé was made aware that he had but a very one-sided view of the Church of England.

Though the Cardinal Archbishop of Westminster was impressed by the great changes that had taken place in the Anglican Church in the last sixty years, he had little hope for a general reunion. However, he saw quite clearly that the Anglo-French discussions on the validity of Anglican orders needed a definitive settlement. Accordingly, the report of a move to have the Abbé Portal's book condemned caused him to do what he could to ensure that the matter of the orders should be thoroughly re-examined. On more than one occasion in the past these orders had been examined and had been refused recognition. Past practices, however, would no longer suffice as a guide; for the progress of historical and liturgical scholarship made it necessary to open the whole question anew. Nevertheless, there were many, both Catholic and Protestant, who deplored any such delving into the past and its consequent rekindling of long-dead issues. Not merely would the whole proceeding be useless, but it would quite possibly be dangerous and wholly inimical to the end for which it was instituted.

In the autumn of 1894 the affair of Bishop Cabrera in Spain, to which allusion has already been made, disturbed the English ecclesiastical scene. However, amidst much temporary exacerbation of feeling between Cardinal Vaughan and Lord Halifax, the exchanges of correspondence enabled the Cardinal to feel relieved at his blunt statement of important facts in the Anglican case, though at the cost of seeming unsympathetic to Anglican aspirations.

About November Wilfrid Ward urged Cardinal Vaughan to be prepared for a change of opinion in Rome on the validity of

Anglican orders. No such change, however, seemed conceivable to the Cardinal without the previous consultation of English experts. Indeed, it seemed impossible to him that any such one-sided decision, as it were, should be taken. In December he learnt from Abbot Gasquet that Pope Leo was quite possibly intending to write a personal letter to the Archbishops of Canterbury and York. Alarmed by this news—for the Cardinal feared such a move to be misconceived and unwise—he pressed the Abbot to hasten his proposed trip to Rome. Anxiety about the matter at length decided the Cardinal also to make the same journey. On January 19, 1895, he arrived at the English College, and on the following day he saw Leo himself. Vaughan was not left in doubt that the Pope knew that the Anglicans regarded the English Cardinal as an obstacle to their Roman plans. For his part Vaughan tried to deflate Leo's Anglican misapprehensions and he urged him not to write a personal letter. Apparently persuaded by the Cardinal's views, Leo said that, instead of such a letter, he would publish an encyclical on the Church and the Papacy in a few months' time. The Cardinal Archbishop thought this a good idea and urged the Pope to accompany this clear statement of teaching with a few paragraphs showing special kindness toward the Anglicans. As if to reinforce Vaughan's words about the state of the English Church, the Archbishop of Canterbury had written to Lord Halifax in the previous December emphasizing the latter's very partial ideas about the Church of England.

After seeing the Pope the Cardinal had an interview with Cardinal Rampolla, the Secretary of State, and complained that the latter's "civil letter" to Portal had given undue encouragement to Anglican hopes. With regard to the general atmosphere of opinion Vaughan wrote: "There are all sorts of wild ideas in Rome as to the proximate conversion of England."[16] Despite the Cardinal's emphatic words, however, neither Leo nor Rampolla was wholly convinced. In February, therefore, Abbot Gasquet, who had already been commissioned by the Pope to prepare a paper on the traditional attitude of the Holy See with regard to Anglican orders, had again in a personal interview with both prelates to reinforce Vaughan's views and to discourage the excessively roseate picture. Monsignor Merry del Val, who was present, and who had been educated in England, confirmed what the Abbot said.

In consultation with Edmund Bishop, Gasquet had come to realize that a major guide to the matter would be found in the views of Cardinal Pole, who as the last Catholic Archbishop of Canterbury had first had to deal officially with the problem of Anglican orders in the sixteenth century. After much investigation among the Vatican documents the Abbot discovered Pole's negotiations with Rome on the matter and Rome's response. Apparently Cardinal Pole had submitted questions to Rome and they had been answered in the bull *Praeclara Charissimi* of June 20, 1555. On October 30, 1555, Pope Paul IV issued a brief commenting on the bull and emphasizing the invalidity of Anglican orders. Gasquet made these discoveries in the spring of 1895 at Rome. A little later he was delighted to find that in the Archiepiscopal Register of Pole, which he discovered in the Douai civic library, there was a note to the effect that the Cardinal had received a copy of the bull.

Cardinal Vaughan had frequently chafed at the lack of realism in the approach to Anglican problems. While he supported the proposed reinvestigation into the validity of Anglican orders, he suspected that it would be of very doubtful help in any way to reunion. To his mind such a reunion quite transcended any decision about orders and was, in fact, unlikely to come about in the foreseeable future. The atmosphere in England was not favorable and, indeed, the passing of another sixty years has only seemed to show how rightly the Cardinal judged. But the Cardinal had a further dislike of the talk of corporate reunion because it was being used to restrain individual conversions. Accordingly, therefore, he was impatient that the investigation should be terminated as soon as possible, consistent with a thorough examination of all the evidence, that the verdict be given forthwith, and thus the whole matter disposed of as speedily as possible. Far more influential in Vaughan's mind would be a papal exhortation to a recourse to prayer and divine grace in meeting the problems of reunion. What was needed was not argument but a change of Anglican minds and hearts. In pursuit of this end the Cardinal wrote a long memorandum on putting emphasis on a supernatural approach to this matter, which he gave to Rampolla, who promised to submit it to the Pope. The work of Vaughan had its fruit in the papal letter *Ad Anglos* of April 22, 1895, and in the encyclical concerning unity, *Satis Cognitum,* of the following year. *The Tablet* of the time spoke of "the memorable appeal *Ad Anglos.* From end to end there is not an allusion to any of the ordinary means of bridging over differences. The whole world of diplomacy is left far away, and we are lifted into a purer and serener atmosphere—the atmosphere of prayer." Such was Pope Leo's first major influence on the Church of England.

In June 1895 Lord Halifax again addressed the annual meeting of the English Church Union. He reported that the Society of Jesus and the English hierarchy had tried to throw obstacles in the way of a Roman recognition of Anglican orders. And he went on further to declare that

the failure of these attempts, which is certainly due to the personal intervention of the Pope himself and of Cardinal Rampolla, is a sufficient proof of what the feelings and dispositions of the Vatican are. These are as friendly as possible, and if the letter addressed by the Pope to the English nation is well received, it is certain that Leo XIII is willing, and indeed, is already preparing to take other and more direct steps in the way of furthering a better understanding. Meanwhile a revolution is being effected in the way the whole question of English Orders is being considered by such foreign ecclesiastics as have had the opportunity of acquainting themselves with the *De Hierarchia Anglicana,* in which the argument for their validity has been admirably stated in Latin by the Rev. T. Lacey and the Rev. E. Denny. Hardly any one who has studied the book but admits how strong the case is for their validity. Great admiration has been excited by the preface prefixed to the treatise by the Bishop of Salisbury, and, if nothing is done to divert the present current of feeling, there is every reason to believe that the question will be put on such a footing that it will be safe from the danger of any fresh attack such as has been made within the last six months, and that the opinions published by the Abbé Duchesne, Monsignor Gasparri, etc., will remain in possession of the field.[17]

Such words alarmed Cardinal Vaughan and on August 7, 1895, he wrote to Gasquet:

I am writing a strong letter direct to the Holy Father confining myself to the point that mischief beyond words will be done if any decision as to Anglican Orders changinig the practice of the Church for 300 years, is made without the fullest investigation and without the co-operation of the representatives of the Catholic Church in England. I ask for a full investigation and a Decision, but protest against this being attempted behind our back. A letter from the Bishops may come later if needed. . . . In my letter I remind the Holy Father of his promise to me in this matter and say we are preparing to be ready for the winter.[18]

Leo XIII was being subjected to pressures from various sides, but he does not seem to have been ready to make a final judgment at this time. At any rate, at the annual conference of the Catholic Truth Society at Preston in September Vaughan was able to emphasize again that a reunion of the Churches completely transcended any solution of the problem of Anglican orders.

The kernel of the question of the reunion of Christendom consists in the admission of the Roman claim that the Pope has received, by Divine right, authority to teach and govern the whole Church, as defined, for instance, in the Councils of Florence, Trent and the Vatican, and as set forth by Thomas Arundell, Archbishop of Canterbury, in the formulary drawn up as a test of Catholic doctrine in 1413, and approved by the Convocation of Canterbury. Or all this may be briefly summed up in the famous axiom of St. Ambrose "Ubi Petrus ibi Ecclesia."[19]

The Cardinal announced at this meeting that a commission was to be set up in Rome to re-examine from the beginning the question of Anglican orders.

The Archbishop of Canterbury had been pressed by Lord Halifax to reply to Leo's encyclical. Archbishop Benson noted in his diary under April 22:

Halifax,very much agitated about the Pope's "Encyclical to the English," which appeared in our papers to-day—very anxious I should make an answer in the same spirit, and say nothing of difficulties—very determined in minimising every Roman error as if they were all matters of taste, pious opinion, or "allow a large liberty," and say nothing about it now! As if it were a matter of which the English ever could think yet lightly. These principles in which all Teutons *see* Latins bewildered. As if the Reformation did not rest on principles far beyond all he talks about. But he is a most saintly man of [*sic*] heart.[20]

A few days later the Archbishop wrote that he had given Halifax his plain views about reunion: "I have pointed out to him that I have always stated that Union could only be on Truth. That it was impossible to be united with Rome as it is, and that even if they recognised our Orders (I am quite sure they cannot so stultify their action) this would only be a preliminary to a Conference. That our Orders cannot be submitted to the decision of a conference with them, though we are willing to supply them with proofs. But that we sue for no recognition, as if our view, or anything else depended on their view."[21] The Archbishop admitted, however, that he was "truly touched by the tender Christian spirit of the late Encyclical."[22] But his general view on the letter seems to have been that he "thought the Pope was trying his best to be honest, that hereafter it might not be said that his letter had compromised doctrine or held out any hope of modification." The Archbishop also added "Signor X———, a leading banker here, has a brother who is one of the Pope's chaplains and secretaries, who says the Pope cannot be got to talk about or attend to anything except Union with England."[23]

Addressing the Diocesan Conference in the summer of 1895, the Archbishop of Canterbury publicly complained of Leo's letter *Ad Anglos* for ignoring the existence of the Church of England.

The representative of the Roman Communion had, in his desire for reunion, spoken to the English people as if they possessed no Church at all, apparently in total ignorance of the existence of any Church with any history or claims, and offered this reunion with a parade of methods of worship and of rewards of worship which was totally alien to the feelings of a nation which had become readers of the Bible, and who could never admit that such things had any attractions for them.[24]

Indeed the Anglican Communion was, in the Archbishop's view, more than worthy to stand comparison with the Roman Church, distinguished as the English Communion was by its "Apostolic Creed and constitution, by the primitive Scriptural standards of its doctrine and ritual, by its living catholicity and sober freedom, by its existence rooted in the past and on the whole identified with education and with progress, by its absolute abstention from foreign political action, by its immediate and intense responsibilities for the Christianity of its own spreading and multiplying race and of its subject races."[25]

At Rome a steady supporter of the Anglican claim to validity of orders was the Secretary of State, Cardinal Rampolla, and he was backed by Monsignor Gasparri and, of course, the fully committed backers, Monsignor Duchesne and the Abbé Portal. At times it seemed that Leo XIII would definitely commit himself to this group. Thus Monsignor Merry del Val wrote from Rome to Gasquet on July 29, 1895: "I go through moments of terrible anxiety at times when I see the ups and downs of impressions received and misleading actions of those who are quite strangers to the whole question and the situation in England." Again on August 20: "Things have taken a more favourable turn and, though there is some danger still, I think we are pretty sure of getting the question properly sifted when it does come on. My last interview with the Holy Father has been satisfactory; I think he quite reckons with you now. At all events he and I are most thankful you came to Rome, for this has been the corner of the wedge."[26]

On December 15 Monsignor Merry del Val again reported to Gasquet that Pope Leo was occupied with the Anglican question and again a vivid picture of the papal negotiations is provided.

The Holy Father is anxious to begin this week, though of course in spite of my unceasing efforts to counteract the impressions he receives from wild and foolish reports, he has only an imperfect grasp of the religious situation in England. You are quite right in saying that the mischief has been done here and is almost exclusively due to Cardinal Rampolla, who has acted without seeking and very often in spite of information and warnings received. It is all the more sad that it is difficult to speak too highly of his right intentions and high qualities. But facts are facts. Still I can assume that we have to be thankful that matters are not worse, for we have had some hairbreadth escapes in the last few months. I wonder that my hair has not turned white, for it has only been at the last minute and by speaking directly to the Holy Father that some things have been stopped.[27]

In the following month the problem was still on the Pope's mind. "The Holy Father asked me this morning," wrote Del Val to Gasquet on January 5, 1896,

whether you had seen Gasparri's work *De la Valeur des Ordinations Anglicanes* which has just been published. . . . He is evidently much impressed with it. He gave it to me yesterday and asked me to-day what I thought of it. . . . I pointed out some of the weak points which had struck me in Gasparri's historical acquaintance. . . . I have just read Halifax's letter to the *Guardian* on Primacy and Jurisdiction; I am going to translate it for the Holy Father. I hope he will be convinced I was right some months ago when I assured him that Cardinal Rampolla was mistaken in asserting that Halifax believed in the Primacy as we understand it.[28]

Again, on February 6 the same correspondence noted that "The Holy Father as yet is unprepared for a technical discussion, so that arguments fall rather flat. When he does go into the matter it will be different. It is important for many reasons however that he should be on his guard and be informed of the issues and that there is another side of the question."[29]

In March 1896 Pope Leo set up an international commission at Rome to consider the question of the validity of Anglican orders. Of the six members the three English, including Gasquet and Canon Moyes, were regarded as unfavorable to the Anglican view, and the three foreigners, including Monsignori Duchesne and Gasparri, were known to be favorable. The prolonged historical researches of Gasquet were related by him some years later during a lecture in an American seminary, and a report of them is given in his

Memoir by Sir Shane Leslie. (It is amusing to note on April 15, "A talk with De Augustinis the Jesuit [member of the Papal commission] who expected the result would let down the Anglicans easily by declaring the orders doubtful and give the *sub conditione* solution. He thought it would please everyone. Bishop noted, 'How S.J.!' When Gasquet told him nothing could be agreed to 'that could not be made to square with the facts,' Bishop added, 'How British!' "[30])

Lord Halifax and the Abbé Portal had hoped for a Leonine commission of a different character from the one actually set up; namely, one composed of Anglicans as well as Catholics, and one which would proceed by a series of conferences beginning with a discussion of Anglican orders for purposes of clarification only, and then proceeding gradually to wider issues. It was thought that this plan was not adopted at the instigation of Cardinal Vaughan, who was regarded as the leader and spokesman of an English Catholic hierarchy abidingly hostile to the Anglican position. However, in public, at least, Halifax thought that the choice of the three foreigners on the commission showed Leo's desire to favor the Anglicans.

A detailed account of the working of the commission was given by Canon Moyes.[31] On May 7 occurred the last session of the commission and its report was sent to the Pope. There then began a campaign to put pressure on the Pope either to decide that the orders were doubtfully valid or else to give no decision at all. An unfavorable decision would, in many Anglican eyes, be not only a catastrophe but also an absurdity. As Mr. Gladstone put it in his letter to the Archbishop of York in this same month (May 1896) commenting on their conviction that Leo would not condemn their orders:

It is to the last degree improbable that a ruler of known wisdom would at this time put in motion the machinery of the Curia for the purpose of widening the breach. . . . But the information which I have been allowed, through the kindness of Lord Halifax, to share altogether dispels from my mind every apprehension of this kind, and convinces me that, if the investigations of the Curia did not lead to a favourable result, wisdom and charity would in any case arrest them at such a point as to prevent their becoming an occasion and a means of embittering religious controversy.[32]

It was also confidentially reported to Cardinal Vaughan "that the other side are bringing a great deal of influence to bear upon the Pope, and that he has received letters from many quarters impressing on him that if he gave any decision against Anglican orders he would effectually close the door upon any hope of Reunion, not only now, but *for ever in the future.*"[33]

In June 1896 there circulated among the cardinals the Latin pamphlet written by the Reverend T. A. Lacey, the Anglican vicar of Madingley. It stressed the Catholicity of the Church of England, showed how its Puritan inclinations had steadily diminished in face of its Catholic sentiments, and that at last it was ready for reunion. Rejection of Anglican orders would lose the British Empire for Rome. Abbot Gasquet and Monsignor Moyes had written a reply within eight days. Among other things, their *Risposta* showed that the views of Halifax and Mr. Lacey were not held by the Anglican bishops. They showed that Anglican heterodoxy was widespread and that Mr. Gladstone had no thought of regarding the Anglican Church as in any way inferior or subordinate to the Church of Rome. Indeed, they stated that as the great Liberal Prime Minister had endeavored to nullify the work of the Vatican Council under Pius IX so also he hoped to make it wholly without consequence in the hands of Leo XIII. The two authors gave a copy of their *Risposta* to the Pope, with whom they had their final audience on June 18 before returning to England.

The weeks went by and the Pope made no public declaration. Rumor was rampant. Some protagonists in the matter continued to speak and the issues consequently became more widely understood. To Cardinal Vaughan, however, the delay was of great concern since it hindered individual conversions. The Abbé Portal was unfortunately lending the authority of his position to this as when in the course of a speech on July 14, 1896 to the Society for Promoting the Reunion of Christendom he said: "This method of Corporate Reunion . . . saves the individual from the torture of doubt and other risks incurred by a personal investigation of the faith."[34] Abbot Gasquet was told that some Anglicans were asked "what would happen were the Pope to take Lord Halifax's advice and Mr. Gladstone's letter seriously, and, in the event of not being able to satisfy Anglican claims as to Orders, to keep silent; they replied that of course all would declare that the Pope was quite convinced of the rectitude of their claim to Orders, but refrained from saying so for fear of stultifying the previous actions and declarations of the Church for three centuries."[35]

The encyclical *Satis Cognitum,* promulgated on June 29, 1896, was an unmistakably clear statement by Pope Leo on the terms of any reunion. The comment of *The Times* on the occasion of its publication gives its flavor:

Like the epistle *Ad Anglos,* which Leo XIII gave to the world about fifteen months ago, this declaration of Papal policy is dignified, temperate and charitable. But even more than the former utterance of the Roman Pontiff, it makes clear that in no single particular, either of doctrine or of discipline, will the claims of the Papal See be relaxed to meet the aspirations for what is known as Reunion among a section of those bred up in the faith of the Church of England. The Pope leaves those who persisted in misinterpreting his original letter no shadow of an excuse for their delusion. The terms on which alone reunion is declared to be possible are plain and simple. They are complete and unhesitating acceptance, not only of the primacy, but of the paramount and absolute predominance, of the Roman Pontiff over all professing to belong to the Christian Church, the entire submission of the heart and mind, the intelligence and conscience of Christendom to the decrees of the Papal See.

It is hardly necessary to say that Cardinal Vaughan welcomed this plain speaking, as he said: "It will, no doubt, dispel vague and hazy theories, which are rich only in delusive hopes, while, by God's grace, it will make clear the path to all who believe they ought to walk in it."

On July 16, 1896, the cardinals declared to the Pope that, in their opinion, Anglican orders were invalid and two months later, on September 13, came the definitive bull, *Apostolicae Curae*. Pope Leo XIII ruled that these orders were null and void on account of defects both in form and in intention. There was surprisingly little outcry in England at the Pope's decision. Even the comment in *The Times* was mild, if not indeed favorable to Rome, as at least one shrewd reader thought. But perhaps not enough consideration had been given to the consequences of a Roman approval. There could be no doubt that an official Roman declaration that Anglican clergymen were priests in the full Roman sense, with power to consecrate, to offer sacrifice, to hear and forgive sins, would, as a thoughtful writer has said, have caused grievous offence to a large number of devout members of the Church of England. The bull did nothing to disturb, outwardly at least, the Anglican bishops. As the Archbishop of Canterbury confidently wrote: "Our Holy Orders are identical with those of the whole Catholic Church. They are in origin, continuity, matter, form, intention and all that belongs to them identical accordingly with those of the Church of Rome, except in the one modern point of subjection to the Pope, on which point at the Reformation we deliberately resumed our ancient concurrence with the whole Catholic world besides."[36]

It is hard for the non-English mind to appreciate such thinking. To the Latins it was incomprehensible. No wonder that Abbot Gasquet and Cardinal Vaughan feared its effect in Rome. Perhaps it has a link with the thought underlying the old Cambridge squib:

> Coulton tells the Cambridge youth
> That Roman Catholics doctor truth:
> While Abbot Aidan Gasquet cries:
> Your English History's packed with lies!

But perhaps this is too secular for the grave subject under discussion. Since it has had much to do with the Oxford Movement, perhaps the irreverent Oxford undergraduate should have the final say, and, indeed, it gives the future in brief:

The rather, rathers, will go to the Cowley Fathers,
But the whole hoggers, to Ally Woggers.*

NOTES

1. J. G. Snead-Cox, *The Life of Cardinal Vaughan* (London, Burns and Oates, 1912), II, pp. 157–158.
2. E. S. Purcell, *Life of Cardinal Manning* (New York, Macmillan and Co., 1896), II, pp. 511-512.
3. Purcell, *op. cit.,* pp. 550–551.
4. John Tracy Ellis, *The Life of James Cardinal Gibbons* (Milwaukee, Bruce, 1952), I, p. 530.
5. Purcell, *op. cit.,* p. 507.
6. Snead-Cox, *op. cit.,* I, p. 330.
7. *Ibid.,* p. 508.
8. *Ibid.,* p. 337.
9. *Ibid.,* pp. 338–339.
10. *Ibid.,* pp. 345–346.
11. *Ibid.,* p. 350.
12. *Ibid.,* II, pp. 164–165.
13. *Ibid.,* p. 148.
14. *Ibid.,* p. 153.
15. A. C. Benson, *The Life of Edward White Benson* (London, Macmillan, 1899), II, pp. 597–598.
16. Snead-Cox, *op. cit.,* p. 178.
17. *Ibid.,* p. 187.
18. Shane Leslie, *Cardinal Gasquet* (London, Burns, Oates, 1953), p. 57.
19. Snead-Cox, *op. cit.,* pp. 189–190.
20. Benson, *op. cit.,* p. 615.
21. *Ibid.,* p. 616.
22. *Ibid.,* p. 617.
23. *Ibid.,* p. 616.
24. *Ibid.,* pp. 618–619.
25. *Ibid.,* pp. 619–620.
26. Leslie, *op. cit.,* p. 58.
27. *Ibid.,* pp. 59–60.

*I.e., to St. Aloysius Church, Oxford, in the charge of the Society of Jesus.

28. *Ibid.*, p. 60.
29. *Ibid.*
30. *Ibid.*, p. 61.
31. Snead-Cox, *op. cit.*, II, pp. 203–206.
32. *Ibid.*, p. 209.
33. *Ibid.*, p. 208.
34. *Ibid.*, p. 218.
35. Leslie, *op. cit.*, p. 68.
36. Benson, *op. cit.*, II, pp. 623–624.

7 Leo XIII and America

REV. THOMAS T. McAVOY, C.S.C.
University of Notre Dame

IN FEBRUARY 1878, when Pope Leo XIII ascended the papal throne, the Catholic Church in the United States was the most promising of all the mission lands in the English-speaking world.[1] As matter of fact, if one classified countries by their official church, which had been the practice in the Western World since the Reformation, the United States was the only country in the English-speaking world in which the Church really enjoyed full civil liberty. This American revival of Catholicism in the English-speaking world was made the subject of an article by J. A. Froude in *The North American Review* in December 1879, under the title "Romanism and the Irish Race in the United States." Froude wrote: "A prophet, who had foretold at the time of the Declaration of Independence that within a century the Roman Catholics would be the largest single religious community in the United States, would have deserved a place in a lunatic asylum, so absurd would such an anticipation have seemed." Yet he adds: "The Catholic revival is a fact, and it will serve, among other purposes, to clear our minds on the real meaning of modern self government."[2]

Froude was undoubtedly expressing the reaction of the English-speaking Protestant world to the growth of Catholicism in the United States, which the English and American Protestants attributed too completely to the Irish immigrant. The implications of his statement are quite clear because in both the English and the non-English world of that day English culture implied not only Protestantism, but also parliamentarian democracy. Froude explicitly said of

Catholicism: "If not incompatible with republican institutions it is uncongenial with them." Answering Froude, Bishop John Lancaster Spalding of Peoria wrote in the same magazine a few weeks later, pointing out glaring contradictions in Froude's statements, and adding, "that were Catholics nine-tenths of the total population they should no more think of interfering with the rights of those who differed with us in faith than do the Catholics of Belgium who are ninety-nine hundreths of the population of their country. Catholics accept the principles of American government as they take their wives, for better or worse, and until death. These are our professions, and these are our honest and heart-felt sentiments."[3]

Perhaps the charges of Froude do bring into focus the chief problems in the relationship between the Roman See and the fast-growing Catholic Church in the United States. The first handicap of American Catholicism was the tradition existing in western Europe for three hundred years that to be English was to be Protestant and to believe in democratic government, while to be Catholic was to be Latin and to believe in nondemocratic government. In the Western World only the English-speaking Catholic minorities in England and in America seemed to grasp the fact that one could accept English culture and democratic government with full participation in the life of the Catholic Church. It was to be the glory of the relationship between Pope Leo XIII and the Church in America that during his pontificate there existed for the first time an understanding of the great possibilities of the Catholic Church in the nineteenth and twentieth centuries in the English-speaking world, where it was not fettered with perfervid nationalism and dominated by an autocratic government.

The second handicap was the lack of set ecclesiastical laws adapted to the American scene. It would be a mistake to think that the new Pope was particularly concerned about Catholicism in North America. Had Joachim Pecci, the Cardinal Bishop of Perugia, had a great familiarity with the Church in the United States, he would have had to acquire that familiarity by extraordinary and personal effort. To Europe, the United States was an infant country

REV. THOMAS T. MACAVOY, C.S.C.

which had survived a bitter Civil War but which played a very minor part in the political battles of western Europe. Culturally the United States had even less influence. On the contrary, the material wealth and the technical progress of America was becoming a legend which was drawing away millions of the less fortunate peoples from Europe to the opportunities of the New World. Actually, it was by the immigration of millions of the less fortunate peoples of Europe that the Church in the United States had grown so fast during the second and third quarters of the century. At Rome the Catholic organization in the United States was under the direction of the missionary arm of the Church, the Congregation for the Propagation of the Faith and its Cardinal Prefect—for many years, Cardinal Barnabo, then Franchi, and later Simeoni and Ledochowski. The sending of ministers from the United States to the Papal States in the 1850's had lasted only a short time and had really changed nothing in the relations between Rome and the United States. There was in 1878 no official representative of the Pope living in the United States, and there was no longer any minister of the United States accredited to the Holy See. As a matter of fact, the chief representative of the Catholics of the United States in Rome, outside of an occasional episcopal visitor, was the rector of the American College, Monsignor Louis Hostelot. There was no American of even monsignor rank on any of the Congregations of the papal government in Rome. Even allowing for the distance and the means of travel and the unsettled condition since the Italian occupation of the Papal States, the exchanges between Rome and the Catholics in the United States were quite meager.

Roman officials had witnessed the activities of the American prelates in the Vatican Council, in which some had stood out strongly against the declaration of papal infallibility until the promulgation, although all the American bishops had eventually given their adherence to the papal doctrine. The fidelity and loyalty of the American Catholics to the papal throne had little bearing on this controversy because personal loyalty to the Holy Father, with or without infallibility, had always been a strong feature of American

Catholicity. But the rapid increase of Catholics and dioceses in the
United States had made it imperative that the Roman officials become better acquainted with the American Catholic organization.
The Sacred Congregations had begun this inquiry during the last
years of Pope Pius IX chiefly on two delicate questions: the provision of Catholic education for the children of the immigrants and
the organization of proper discipline between the bishops and their
clergy. The existence for the first time since the Reformation of a
large body of English-speaking Catholics without governmental
support and adhering to democratic notions of government created
new problems for the Roman officials.

Catholics in the United States had grown in number within a
century from about 30,000 to approximately six million. The one
bishop of 1789 was multiplied to one cardinal, 12 archbishops, 51
bishops, and 5,050 priests in 1878. These were organized into 63
dioceses or vicariates.[4] Had this large number been gathered together into a small region in which they were the predominant group,
the application of European Church law and customs would have
been comparatively easy. But in only a few regions in the United
States, in what had once been Spanish or French territory, or in
some small colonization projects, were the Catholics predominant
in number or social prestige. The United States was in fact a
dominantly Protestant country. In many regions Catholics were very
few or unknown, and even where they were numerous they were
chiefly impoverished immigrants without social position or economic
wealth. Their political power in some communities was only by
reason of the concentration of voting numbers—usually of one
national origin—not by their devotion to any political or religious
ideal.

Catholicism in the present region of the United States had begun
in the seventeenth century with the English Catholics in Maryland,
and, while these English were soon joined by Irish, German, and
French immigrants, for a few decades after the founding of the
Republic until approximately the 1840's the Catholic group in the
United States could be considered an English-speaking Catholic

minority, probably the most important in the world. But the later growth of the Church in the United States after 1840 had been chiefly by immigration of non-English Catholics. First in large number came the Irish fleeing from persecution and famine, and then the Germans in even larger numbers, and eventually the Slavic peoples and the Italians. By 1850 the greater part of the American hierarchy was Irish-born or of Irish descent; there were a few German, French, and Belgian prelates. The Irish immigrants either spoke English or quickly learned it but were not thereby accepted by the American of English descent. Where whole communities of Catholic immigrants were of a non-English-speaking origin, the community, its priest, and usually its social institutions clung to the language and traditions of the country of their origin. Eventually, the vast majority of the Catholic population of the United States, even when English-speaking, was non-English in descent and culture. Thus, there were two important developments taking place among the Catholics in the United States when Pope Leo XIII was elected. There was first the gradual Anglicization, or better named the Americanization, of the immigrant Catholics. The second, from Rome, was the imposition on these haphazard immigrant communities of the traditional canonical organization of the Church.

This imposition of the traditional canon law of the Church had already begun under the cardinals of the Propaganda before Pope Leo XIII came to the throne. The Instruction of 1875 on the schools and that of 1878 on the handling of ecclesiastical discipline were but the beginning. There were still not enough exchanges between Rome and the United States. Bishop Bernard McQuaid of Rochester, on his return from Rome in May 1879, said; "There in Rome are high ecclesiastics not of our nationality, who are anxious to know about America, its churches, schools, and institutions. They want to know of our young, growing and already grand Church of America."[5] Other American clergymen were suggesting that the American bishops appoint some American of episcopal rank to reside in Rome to give information to the Holy See at the opportune time. Rome in its turn was trying to establish in the United

States its own observer, either as a nuncio or apostolic delegate. Unfortunately, neither idea seemed acceptable to the other side. Rome did not accept any Americans into its Curia, and the American bishops were unfriendly to a Roman resident delegate whom they felt would interfere with their own jurisdiction. Rome did send an Apostolic Delegate to Canada, Archbishop George Conroy, who made a visit to the United States to install the new Archbishop of Baltimore, James Gibbons, in 1878, and toured even to California. He died in August that year, before he had an opportunity to return to Rome, but not before he sent to the Roman authorities a critical estimate of American Catholicism. In the United States some Bishops, especially of the new dioceses of the West, desired to hold a national council of bishops to discuss the problems that had arisen in the American Church since the Second Plenary Council of 1866. The Roman cardinals and Pope Leo heeded the requests of those who wanted a council and called certain American archbishops and bishops to Rome in October 1883, to decide on the problems to be discussed at a national council to be held the next year.[6] Leading the group to Rome was the new Archbishop of Baltimore, James Gibbons, and the older Archbishops, Peter Richard Kenrick of Saint Louis and John Baptist Purcell of Cincinnati. Although Pope Leo approved this action, the meeting of the bishops was directly under the supervision of the Sacred Congregations and the cardinals.

When the American prelates reached Rome, they found prepared for them a program of disciplinary regulations which the officers of the Sacred Congregation of the Propaganda said should be enacted into law for the United States. These regulations covered such problems as the erection of seminaries and vacation villas for training candidates for the priesthood, the establishment of cathedral chapters and of irremovable pastorships, the regulation of the episcopal visitations and the organization of ecclesiastical courts for the clergy, clerical garb, the participation of Catholics in non-Catholic organizations, the provision of Catholic education, the care of the Italian immigrants, and the Negro and Indian missions. The American bishops opposed some of the proposals. They succeeded in limiting the proposed decrees about seminaries and in substituting the American council of episcopal consultors for the cathedral chapters, which they did not believe suitable for the United States. The American bishops opposed also the sending of an Italian archbishop to preside over the council, and obtained the appointment of Archbishop Gibbons instead.

Between December 1883 and the following November these proposals were discussed by committees of Bishops in the United States and, when the Council met in November 1884, the decrees of the Council conformed very closely to the program agreed upon in Rome. The body of these decrees was subsequently approved almost entirely by Rome and became the official rule of the Church in the United States. Thus under the direction of Pope Leo and his Curia the major work of imposing Roman law on the American Church was accomplished. There remained only the additional step of establishing a resident delegate of the Pope to provide the necessary information to Rome for the proper working of these decrees. The American bishops did not desire a delegate, but the divisions within the American hierarchy hastened the decision of Pope Leo XIII to send a resident representative to America to promote unity.

Very early in the pontificate of Pope Leo XIII there appeared a feeling of sympathy between Pope Leo and American Catholics. The *Freeman's Journal*[7] of New York, the chief conservative Catholic newspaper of the day, was shocked when the liberal press greeted Pope Leo XIII as a friend but felt consoled when the new Pontiff asserted his adherence to the principles of his predecessor. The same newspaper[8] immediately published the Lenten pastorals of the new Pope, as Bishop of Perugia in 1877 and 1878—the second written even after the death of Pius IX—in which he had discussed the relations between the Church and civilization. In these pastorals, besides defending the rights of the working people, the Cardinal Bishop of Perugia had said that the article of the Syllabus condemning reconciliation of the Church with modern civilization meant by modern civilization only that kind which would do away with the Church. On the contrary, he insisted on the great role of the Church in the process of civilization. As Pope, Leo showed no inclination to accept any notion of civilization which would not recognize the unique role of the Church, but he did find it possible to deal diplomatically with those countries, such as Russia and Turkey, in which the Church was in an unfavorable position. His re-establishment of the Scottish hierarchy and his elevation of Father John Henry Newman to the College of Cardinals were events that seemed to make the Holy Father personally closer to American Catholics. In the meantime, the problems of American Catholicism were being carried to the papal throne. Some of these problems were merely the disciplinary growing pains of a young Church organization, but some involved the adaptation of Catholicism to the American way of life.

The Americanization of the Church in the United States was not the main subject discussed in the meetings of the Third Plenary Council of Baltimore, which was chiefly concerned with Romanization; but Americanization was more than hinted at in the public sermons preached by various members of the hierarchy in the Baltimore Cathedral during the Council. With the exception of a few recommendations about caring for immigrants and the reference of the question of secret societies to the Council of Archbishops, there was little evidence in the decrees of the Council of the growing internal struggle among the members of the American Church concerning the adaptation of an almost overwhelming mass of non-English Catholic immigrants to the American milieu. The question of Americanization was not primarily a religious one, but because of the centuries-old tradition of union of Church and State in the countries of western Europe many social, economic, and even some political problems of the faithful had become intertwined with religion. J. A. Froude was not the only one who felt that there was a conflict between the reviving Catholicism of the New World and the principles of English-speaking democracy. As the years passed some American bishops were a bit unenthusiastic about American life. Many other Americans began to see in Pope Leo XIII one who understood and sympathized with their efforts to reconcile Roman

Catholicism with the American spirit. Among these were several of the younger members of the American hierarchy.

It is not without significance that Archbishop Gibbons was installed in Baltimore just before Leo was elected and that the bulls for Bishop John J. Keane as Bishop of Richmond were in transit at the same time. Bishop John Ireland, who was to be their close associate in later years, had been consecrated coadjutor of Saint Paul just three years before. These and several other clergymen of Irish descent who held most of the episcopal sees of the United States were the leaders in adapting Catholicism to the American scene. The major factor in this dominance of the Irish in the American hierarchy was probably the method of nomination of candidates for these sees which, besides allowing the local clergy to express a preference, permitted those already in office to nominate those from whom the Holy See usually chose the new bishop. Nevertheless, it also was natural that the Irish, who spoke English and joined most readily in the customs of English-speaking America, should rise to a position of influence in the Church of the United States. But because of the cultural poverty and the lack of a special language of the Irish when contrasted with the strong nationalisms which the other immigrants had brought from Europe, the Irish were not regarded by others as having any cultural or national supremacy. In effect, the Irish were respected neither by the native Americans nor by the non-English immigrant. In some regions of the Middle West, chiefly in Wisconsin, Illinois, and Missouri where there had been a concentration of German immigration, the clergy were also predominantly German and the German language persisted in the parish church and school. In the larger cities national parishes were erected in which foreign-born clergy preached, confessed, and conducted schools in the foreign language of the neighborhood. Since foreign language parishes usually lacked territorial jurisdiction, their pastors and flocks felt that they were being discriminated against. Some clergymen filled with German nationalism insisted that they had the right to preserve the German language in their schools and churches, and to make the children of German immigrants attend them. Failing to get a hearing with the

Irish-led American episcopate and feeling that Rome would give them redress, a group of German priests sent a petition in 1886 through Father P. M. Abbelen, the vicar general of Milwaukee, to the Roman Congregations.[9] The American bishops, when they were warned of this petition by Bishops Ireland and Keane, then in Rome, met in Philadelphia and protested against the petition. Keane and Ireland also wrote an answer to the petition. The Sacred Congregation gave an answer in 1887 and, while urging the American bishops to aid the foreign language immigrants, rejected the petition for forced membership in the foreign language parishes and the demand that there be a German representative in the hierarchy. Unfortunately, a German merchant, Peter Paul Cahensly, and representatives of German, Italian, and other European societies for the protection of the European migrants, meeting in Lucerne in 1891, renewed the petition to Rome for foreign representation in the American hierarchy and for greater protection of the foreign language immigrants in America. Again the American bishops protested, and through the instrumentality of Archbishop John Ireland the action of the European petitioners was condemned as European imperialism on the floor of the United States Senate. Again Pope Leo XIII and his counselors recognized the legitimacy of a distinct American nationality and rejected the petition.

Archbishop John Ireland[10] of Saint Paul by his activity against the Germans had attracted their hostility. He was indeed preaching the Americanization of the Catholic immigrant and saw a great future for the Church in the United States if the Catholics entered fully into the liberty and social reform of the age. In his speech at the Plenary Council, and especially in his sermon at the silver jubilee of Cardinal Gibbons, he called on Americans to grasp their opportunities in this new intellectual and democratic age. Earlier, however, when the state legislature of Wisconsin had passed the Bennett Law requiring the use of English in all schools and the German bishops of that state had fought the law, they accused him of supporting the legislation. Again, in 1890, while speaking to the National Educational Association in Saint Paul, Ireland had regretted the necessity of the expense of the separate Catholic parochial school, and the following year he had instituted in two communities of his diocese, Faribault and Stillwater, agreements whereby the schools were supported by the state while the teaching was done by Catholic teachers. This arrangement was not a new idea, but by reason of his speech it aroused much discussion. Ireland was accused by his opponents of trying to destroy the Catholic parochial school which had been commanded by the Third Plenary Council. Although the Minnesota agreement did not last long, Ireland defended himself in December 1891 in Saint Louis before the Council of Archbishops and then decided to go to Rome to make sure that his side of the argument was understood. Against him and Cardinal Gibbons, who had similar ideas, Archbishop Corrigan had sent to Rome a criticism of Ireland's school policy. Corrigan was supported in his attack by the German bishops and by Bishop Mc-Quaid of Rochester, who was an outstanding defender of Catholic parochial schools.

When John Ireland went to Rome in 1891, he was not a stranger to Pope Leo.[11] In 1886 he and Bishop John Keane had gone to Rome to prepare the way for the foundation of the Catholic University of America. Pope Leo, himself a scholar of superior ability, embraced the idea of the Catholic University as one of his own projects, which would be one of the chief institutions of Catholicism in the United States. Ireland, moreover, was still in Rome in 1887 when his friend Cardinal James Gibbons came to Rome to receive his red hat, and incidentally had helped the Cardinal defend the Knights of Labor from the condemnation urged by Cardinal Taschereau of Quebec. Also, many of Ireland's speeches had been translated and published in the French press, and along with Gibbons he was regarded by the French as the chief representative of that portion of the American Church which was co-operating so successfully with American institutions. On his return from Rome he had agreed to visit Paris. The Pope had meanwhile in February 1892 issued his encyclical to the French which called for French unity and for co-operation of the French Catholics with the Third Republic. Far from uniting the French clergy, the letter made the division even sharper. Such were the circumstances of Archbishop Ireland's public visit to Paris. Ireland, who had had several interviews with the Pope, seemed to represent the ideas of Leo when he praised the relations between Church and State in democratic America, urged the clergy to participate more actively in public social reform, and praised the Church in America for adopting modern methods. After Paris, Ireland continued on to the United States, and his hopes for a reconciliation between Catholicism and American life were very high.

Scarcely had Ireland returned to America when a move was made to have the Vatican send some Columbus maps and documents to the Columbian Exposition in Chicago in 1893. Secretary of State John W. Foster opened correspondence with Cardinal Rampolla with the result that the Pope sent not only the desired Columbus documents but also his personal delegate to the Fair. As that delegate he chose Francisco Satolli, Archbishop of Lepanto, who had been his delegate in 1889 to the celebration of the centennial of the American hierarchy at Baltimore and who had also defended Archbishop Ireland in his 1891 controversy about the school question in the German papers. Through Monsignor Denis O'Connell, the rector of the North American College and the close friend of Gibbons, Ireland, and Keane, Satolli was committed to the care of Ireland and Gibbons, to the almost total exclusion of Archbishop Corrigan and the conservative critics of Ireland. Satolli hurried through New York to Washington and then to Chicago, where he attended the dedication of the Columbian Exposition building, then visited Ireland in Saint Paul. Later, while awaiting the opening of the Fair, he attended the annual meeting of the archbishops, held that November 1892 in New York. To the consternation of many bishops he offered the assembled prelates a program on the school question which seemed very close to the policies of Archbishop Ireland, and also suggested the establishment of a permanent Apostolic Delegation. The bishops by majority vote rejected both ideas. To the consternation of the conservatives Satolli went on to Washington and after an examination restored Father Edward McGlynn, the follower of Henry George, an excommunicated priest of the New York Archdiocese, and an opponent of Archbishop Corrigan, to his priestly functions. The Delegate then announced on January 14 that he had a letter from Pope Leo XIII establishing a permanent Delegation with himself as the first Apostolic Delegate. Undoubtedly this had been the plan of Pope Leo all the time. By establishing the Delegation and the appointment of Satolli as Delegate, Pope Leo hoped to heal the breach between the liberal and the conservative groups of bishops and at the same time to provide for quicker access to the Holy See in matters requiring an appeal to the Pope. For a while Satolli lived at the Catholic University and seemed to follow the advice of the rector, Bishop Keane, but after he established his own residence in Washington he followed a more independent path.

From the correspondence Count Eduardo Soderini found in the archives of the Papal Secretary of State, it is evident that Pope Leo XIII's principal purpose in sending Archbishop Satolli was to establish a papal source of information on the Church in the United States in the country itself. Up to that time he had observed two main groups in the Church in America. One group, described as progressive, led by Ireland, Gibbons, Keane, and their friends, insisted that the future of the world lay with the Anglo-Saxon and democratic nations and that the prospects of the Catholic Church in that world were good. Ireland and his friends were also urging the Pope and the papal court to learn and adopt American approaches to this modern world. With Satolli, Ireland's friend, established as the Apostolic Delegate in Washington, with his friend Bishop Keane as the rector of the Pope's special project, the Catholic University of America, and with Cardinal Gibbons, also Ireland's friend, in the Baltimore see, it seemed that the liberal or progressive bishops would soon dominate the American Church and even have influence in Rome and Europe.

The conservative group was not so well-united. It was led by Archbishop Corrigan, Bishop McQuaid of Rochester, and the German bishops of Wisconsin. They had not been idle. They never ceased making charges that Ireland was opposed to the Catholic parochial schools, and that through him and Keane the Catholic University had likewise opposed these Catholic schools. They also accused him and his friends of a too close association with non-Catholics and of religious minimism and liberalism. Small incidents of awkward co-operation between these bishops and non-Catholics were publicized, and their opposition to the condemnation of the Knights of Labor and of the fraternal secret societies was given a sinister meaning. Further, the conservatives reproached the progressives for their participation in the Parliament of Religions held in 1893 during the Columbian Exposition. In this World Parliament of Religions all religions were presented on an equal basis. Although the Catholic participants in the meeting, Gibbons, Keane, Ireland and some other clergymen, tried to protect themselves from seeming to treat other religions as equal, their critics felt that they had endangered the unique position of Catholicism.

As the correspondence between the new Apostolic Delegate and Rome progressed, the public exchanges between the Holy See and the American bishops became more frequent. In May 1893 the Holy Father wrote to the American bishops defending the statement of Satolli on the schools, but insisting also that the decrees of the Council of Baltimore be enforced. Then in June 1894 the Congregation of the Holy Office issued a decree against Catholic membership in certain American secret societies, especially the Odd Fellows, the Sons of Temperance, and the Knights of Pythias. Gibbons and Ireland tried to prevent the public promulgation of the decrees, but Rome insisted and overruled the American bishops.

In September 1895 Pope Leo XIII wrote his first great encyclical to American Catholics. There had been, as has been mentioned, exchanges of letters between the Pope and the American bishops in connection with the Plenary Council, on the school question, on the occasions of the assembly of Bishops to celebrate the centenary of the hierarchy, and during the Columbus celebration, but this was the first formal encyclical to the American Church. The encyclical *Longinqua Oceani*[12] marked the fact that in the eyes of Pope Leo XIII the American Church had come of age.

In the encyclical the Holy Father praised the progress and the prosperity of the Church in the United States. He admitted that this progress was possible chiefly because of the tolerance of religion in the American Constitution and laws, but admonished the faithful not to think that this was the ideal solution of the relationship between Church and State for everywhere. His special interests in the Church in the United States were twofold. The first was the advancement of learning, and for that purpose he had established the Catholic University in Washington, first as a center of theological and philosophical learning and then as time passed to be the center of the other sciences, and also the North American College in Rome for the advanced training of American clergy. His second interest was the perfection of the management of the affairs of the Church, and for that purpose he had established the Apostolic Delegation in Washington. He praised the decrees of the Council of Baltimore and insisted that the Apostolic Delegation was not intended to interfere with the carrying out of its decrees but to bring the American people closer to the Holy See. He warned American Catholics especially against divorce and other conditions which tended to destroy the family. He warned the faithful against civil disobedience and against membership in societies dedicated to violence. Finally, he urged more of the faithful to dedicate themselves to writing. For those who write he also gave a warning to be respectful of those in authority and especially of the authority of the bishops. He finally urged them to pray and work for those not of the Faith and to be mindful of their duties to the Negroes and Indians.

In the spring of 1895 Cardinal Gibbons made a trip to Rome to assure the Holy Father that all was well in American Catholicism, but the trip was comparatively uneventful. There were, however, some events at this time that caused gloom for the progressive bishops. In June 1895 Monsignor Denis O'Connell was forced to resign from the rectorship of the North American College. O'Connell remained as rector of Cardinal Gibbons' church in Rome, but the resignation was unpleasant. In September of that same year, at the urging of Archbishop Satolli,[13] the Pope sent a letter to Satolli forbidding the co-operation of Catholics in interdenominational congresses such as the Parliament of Religions. While praising the activity of the Paulist Fathers in their practice of holding conferences for non-Catholics, the Pope insisted that Catholics hold their congresses apart. Although the urgency of the document arose from attempts in France to organize a similar parliament of religions at the Paris Exhibition of 1900, the letter had a disturbing effect on the progressive bishops. Ireland was a bit upset by this decree, although he insisted at first that the document did not actually prevent Catholic participation in such congresses.

Within a year other effects of the presence of Archbishop Satolli in the United States became evident. At the end of the year Satolli was made a Cardinal, and Gibbons conferred the red hat on him in January 1896. He remained for awhile as pro-Delegate and seems to have been the chief agent in the decision from Rome the following September to remove Bishop Keane from the rectorship of the Catholic University. The removal of Keane was heralded by the critics of the progressive bishops as an indication that the progressives were no longer in favor in Rome. To the progressives this and Satolli's public praise of the German Catholics indicated that they had lost the friendship of the Delegate.

In 1891 there had been published in the United States a biography of Father Isaac Hecker, the convert founder of the Paulist Fathers. For the volume, Archbishop Ireland had written an introduction in which he praised Hecker as the kind of priest needed in the modern world. There had been no great excitement aroused by the book in this country. In France the group working for the collaboration of Catholics with the French Republic arranged to have the biography translated and then adapted by Abbé Felix Klein of the Institut Catholique, who added a preface which was even more laudatory than the introduction by Ireland. By a clever campaign of advertising, in the spring of 1897 the book became the talk of Catholic France and soon went into many printings.

That summer Monsignor Denis O'Connell made a speech at the International Congress at Fribourg in Switzerland in which he urged the theme of the progressive American bishops about the success of the American Catholic solution of the problem of the

Church's relation to democracy and reform. Taking advantage of the popularity of the Hecker biography, he found in Hecker an exemplification of his favorite theme—the reconciliation of the Church and the age and of the Church and democracy. There was some criticism of his theme in the Congress and further criticism when the speech was printed in French periodicals.

In November 1897 this criticism became public in a series of sermons in prominent Paris pulpits, in which the heresy of Americanism was tied in with other evils which were said to threaten the Church. In March 1898, in *La Verité,* the organ of those opposed to the reconciliation of the Church with the French government, a series of articles signed "Martel" but written by Abbé Charles Maignen, began to appear. They attacked Americanism and the Hecker biography. Soon the controversy over Americanism reached a fever peak in the French Catholic press. When Abbé Maignen was refused an imprimatur for the *La Verité* articles in book form, he took the volume to Rome for publication and obtained the imprimatur from the Master of the Sacred Palace. The controversy had also involved the Roman press, and the imprimatur seemed to some to give papal approval to the attack on the American Church. In the meantime, the Spanish-American War broke out, despite the unsuccessful attempts of Archbishop Ireland to prevent it. The feeling against the United States among conservative and Latin circles became intense. Demands reached the Holy Father for the condemnation of the biography of Hecker and of Americanism. Pope Leo XIII listened to his American friends and to the cardinals who were friendly to the United States. He stopped the effort to place the biography on the Index and appointed a commission of cardinals to examine the question of Americanism. The report of the cardinals, however, was against Americanism. Cardinal Gibbons, hearing of an impending letter of condemnation, sent a cable to Rome asking for a delay. Archbishop Ireland hastened to Rome in January 1899, only to be told that the letter had already been issued.

The papal letter to Gibbons, *Testem Benevolentiae,* dated January 22, 1899, condemned certain doctrines said to have arisen on the

occasion of the publication of the translation of the biography of
Hecker. These doctrines, called "Americanism," advocated a new
apologetics to fit the modern day with less insistence on dogmas, a
new approach to spiritual direction with more emphasis on natural
and active virtues, and less external direction, and placed less emphasis on the vows of the religious life. The Holy Father added to
the condemnation of these doctrines, however, the assurance that
the American bishops would not hold such doctrines and that
the reprobation was in no sense to be applied to American political
and social customs.[14]

Archbishop Ireland, who was still in Rome, immediately accepted
the letter, insisting that he did not hold the erroneous doctrines,
and Cardinal Gibbons later in his letter insisted that no educated
American Catholic held such ideas. But the letter was a crushing
blow to Ireland, Keane, and O'Connell. The concluding paragraphs
allowed these bishops to say that they did not hold the condemned
ideas and at the same time kept their critics and opponents from
claiming a complete victory. However, Archbishop Corrigan of New
York, Bishop Ignatius Horstmann of Cleveland, and the German
bishops of Wisconsin wrote letters thanking the Pope for saving
American Catholics from these erroneous ideas. The Wisconsin
bishops and the *Civiltà Cattolica* even accused the progressive bishops of being insincere in their denials. Quickly the controversy sub-
sided. Stories were told that some time later the Holy Father insisted
that he had written the letter chiefly to stop the controversy in Europe and that the Americans should not worry about it affecting them.

The Pope was now in his twenty-fifth year as Pope, and the
American bishops sent a letter of praise and fealty to him. In answer,
on April 15, 1902, the ninety-two-year-old pontiff acknowledged the
joint letter of the American hierarchy. He insisted that he had always
cherished the devotion of American Catholics to the Holy See and
was happy to see the great growth of the Church in America, to
which he gave a special paternal blessing. The next year, after the
celebration of his jubilee, he died.

The age of Pope Leo XIII was one of the most exciting periods in the history of the Catholic Church in America. Under his benign care the Church in the United States, from being a mere mission organization, had become one of the most important groups of the world-wide Church. Not only did Pope Leo recognize the importance of the Church in the United States and regularize its canonical organization, he showed that he looked to the Americans as loyal sons at a time when he was being opposed by the more autocratic and illiberal governments of Europe. In his paternal wisdom he also saw that the Church in the United States needed unity and that it must be American. When others thought they found essential heresies in this Americanism, he gave a paternal rebuke to anyone who might hold these errors, but at the same time he uttered no condemnation or penalties against individuals in this country. He accepted the letters of those prelates who were most persistent in desiring Catholicism to lead in America and who supported his grand plan for a great Catholic University. Certainly not all the problems of the Church in America were solved during his regime, but he could at the end write a letter of love and praise for his sons in the United States who were working hard to reconcile the Church and the age. The Church in the United States has increased in numbers and wealth since 1903, but the best achievements had their origin in the golden era of Pope Leo XIII.

NOTES

1. Any definite account of the relations between Pope Leo XIII and the United States will have to await the opening of the pertinent Vatican archives, possibly until 2003. The present writer had the privilege of seeing the notes on these matters taken by Count Eduardo Soderini from the papers of Cardinal Rampolla as well as his unpublished manuscript, "Leone XIII e gli Stati Uniti di America." Published accounts contain little more than published official documents and statistical summaries.
2. J. A. Froude, "Romanism and the Irish Race in the United States,"

North American Review, 129 (December, 1879), pp. 519–536; 130 (January, 1880), pp. 31–50; especially pp. 520, 533.

3. John Lancaster Spalding, "Mr. Froude's Historical Method," *North American Review,* 130 (March, 1880), pp. 280–299; especially pp. 287–288.

4. These statistics are drawn from *Sadlier's Catholic Directory Almanac and Ordo for the year of Our Lord 1879,* etc. (New York, 1879). These statistics were changing so rapidly by death, birth, and migration that one can at best use them as an approximation.

5. *New York Freeman's Journal and Catholic Register,* May 10, 1879.

6. John T. Ellis, *The Life of James Cardinal Gibbons, Archbishop of Baltimore, 1834–1921* (Milwaukee, 1952), 2 vols., is the best account of the activities of Gibbons in this regime. Cf. Chap. VI, as the most complete account of the Third Plenary Council.

7. *New York Freeman's Journal and Catholic Register,* March 2, 1879.

8. *Ibid.,* March 23, 1879 and following.

9. Cf. Rev. Colman Barry, O.S.B., *The Catholic Church and German Americans* (Milwaukee, 1953), pp. 62–69, discusses this petition. Father Colman has a well-balanced discussion of the German-American Catholics.

10. James H. Moynihan, *The Life of Archbishop John Ireland* (New York, 1953), is the only full-length biography yet published.

11. Cf. T. T. McAvoy, C.S.C., *The Great Crisis in American Catholic History, 1895–1900* (Chicago, 1957), for a more detailed account of the Americanist controversy.

12. The encyclical was published in most of the Catholic press of the day. Cf. *The Great Encyclicals of Pope Leo XIII,* with a preface by Rev. John J. Wynne, S.J. (New York, 1903), pp. 321–335.

13. Soderini manuscript and notes.

14. *Great Encyclicals of Pope Leo XIII,* pp. 513–516.

8 Leo XIII and the Philosophical Approach to Modernity

JAMES COLLINS
Saint Louis University

AT ANY COMMEMORATION of the life and teaching of Pope Leo XIII we must give major recognition to his labors in behalf of sound philosophy. Both in his pastoral letters as the Bishop of Perugia and more especially in the steady flow of documents issued during his long pontificate, he displayed a marked concern for the condition of philosophy and its bearing upon Catholic life. His teachings and practical decisions in this area were not only decisive during his own lifetime but also helped to shape the course of Catholic philosophical studies during the twentieth century. Indirectly, this influence extended far beyond the Catholic community to count as one of the great intellectual forces shaping our time. Hence it is only right that we should give separate consideration to this portion of Leo's achievement or, at least, to one of its important aspects.

When a Christian philosopher sets out to deal with the encyclicals and other relevant materials of Leo XIII pertaining to his own discipline, he does not presume to invade the theologian's domain or to render the latter's professional office superfluous. But the documents in question do bear upon the work and the ideals of the philosopher, so that to this extent he is being specially addressed and must render back his own kind of response. This is not an easy task, and neither is it one that has already been accomplished so thoroughly that further investigation is unnecessary. There is a strenuously demanding quality about all of Leo's writings, since they combine a finely balanced literary form with an intense compression and precision of thought. They present a real challenge to the philosopher who is willing to read them carefully and take instruction from them, even though his approach does not exhaust their significance. What he can attempt is to relate the papal teaching as closely as possible to his own experience of philosophical thinking and its concrete conditions. In this way he can hope to capture at least some aspects of Leo's abiding significance for those whose vocation it is to respond both to the life of Christian faith and the intrinsic requirements of philosophy.

There are many facets in Pope Leo's relationship with philosophy. We are familiar with what his successor, Pope Pius XI, did not hesitate to call his greatest service to the Church and civil society, namely, the strong impetus which Leo gave to the renewal of Christian philosophy, mainly in its Thomistic form, but with due regard for the doctrines of the Fathers and the other Schoolmen. This is the main theme of *Aeterni Patris,* the key encyclical which has served since 1879 as the guiding stimulus toward recovering the sources of Christian philosophical ideas.[1] But Pope Leo's encouragement of this vast work of historical investigation does not exhaust his significance for philosophical studies. Both in *Aeterni Patris* itself and in most other Leonine pronouncements bearing upon philosophy there is another intention, closely related with that of restoration but nevertheless sufficiently distinct from it to permit a separate analysis. This is the theme of making a proper appraisal of modern philosophy, determining the philosophical relevance of the advances made in the modern arts and sciences, and thereby enriching the whole body of Christian philosophical wisdom. This other concern of Leo did not escape the attention of his successors, particularly Pius XII, so that it can be said to define the most authentic Catholic position on the study of modern and contemporary tendencies in philosophy.

It is this latter side of Pope Leo's mind which we intend to examine here and to link up with the more familiar aspects of his attitude on philosophy. We will try to bring out how the study of modern philosophy is bound up intimately with three major Leonine teachings: on the best way in which the Christian can philosophize, on the method for recapturing the wisdom of St. Thomas, and on the policy of continuous building rather than destroying in philosophical discussions. Combining these three themes, we will then be in a position to see that Leo XIII is pre-eminently the Pope of *the open tradition in philosophy,* which joins a firm rooting in our Christian philosophical heritage with a critical yet generous response to modern thought.

To discover why Leo included the study of modern philosophy in most of his general counsels on philosophical matters, we have to keep in mind the conception of philosophy underlying his teaching. His attitude toward the philosophical enterprise as a whole helped to determine his remarks on how a Christian thinker should relate himself to postmedieval philosophies. This connection has to be made clear.

One characteristic note running through all of Pope Leo's treatments of philosophy is that the Church has a stake in the issue and hence has the right to speak with authority about at least some aspects of philosophy. In maintaining that there is a real basis for this relationship, he establishes his continuity with the views of Pope Pius IX. Some of Leo's contemporaries were puzzled by his remark about wanting people to understand and be reconciled to his predecessor's Syllabus of Errors, but on many crucial matters this is indeed the case. It is likely that, as the Bishop of Perugia, he had been influential in urging Pius IX to draw up the 1864 Syllabus and in suggesting some of the doctrines to be condemned. Prominent in the official list are two closely related propositions taken from a previous letter of Pius IX to the Archbishop of Munich. Among the errors of rationalism are these two statements: "Philosophy is to be treated without taking any account of supernatural revelation," and therefore "the Church not only ought never to pass judgment on philosophy, but ought to tolerate the errors of philosophy, leaving it to correct itself."[2] A cognate proposition holds that, whereas the philosopher as an individual ought to submit to Church authority, philosophy itself cannot and should never do so. These propositions are the speculative counterparts of other ones which advocate the total separation of the Church from all the vital interests of modern man in social and religious affairs. Hence their net effect is to recommend the isolation of the Church from all of our living concerns, both in the order of ideas and in practical life.

To appreciate why Leo XIII regarded his position as being essentially one with that of his immediate predecessor, we have to watch him develop the positive conception of philosophy with respect to which the above condemned propositions are shown to be untenable. At the very outset of *Aeterni Patris* he touches the core of the issue by noting some hard facts about man which we cannot ignore or legislate away. Since the Christian faith involves an act of the understanding and an intellectually determinate content, its relation to our minds is concretely affected by what we think. Not only what we think in an informal way but also the formal elements contained in the arts and sciences, especially in philosophy, exert a deep influence over the integrity of faith as entertained by the minds of living men. Under the actual conditions of human existence, our integrity of faith tends to be either safeguarded or else corrupted by our philosophical convictions. A man who accepts the philosophical notion that God is a projective compensatory myth, that all our actions are determined by impersonal natural laws, and that our little life is wholly snuffed out at bodily death, is apt to be ill-disposed for accepting or remaining loyal to the Christian faith. Furthermore, the influence of philosophical ideas is practical as well as speculative and, within the practical order, spills out far beyond one's individual conduct to the whole shape and direction of social life.

On the wide and observable social repercussions of philosophical doctrines, Leo speaks incisively and out of the fullness of his own varied experiences.

Whoso turns his attention to the bitter strifes of these days and seeks a reason for the troubles that vex public and private life must come to the conclusion that a fruitful cause of the evils which now afflict, as well as those which threaten, us lies in this: that false conclusions concerning divine and human things, which originated in the schools of philosophy, have now crept into all the orders of the State, and have been accepted by the common consent of the masses.[3]

On the basis of our present forms of social knowledge and our experience of the domestic effects of naturalism and the international effects of communist ideas, we have good grounds for reaffirming this connection as a very potent one. Little wonder, then, that Leo's great social encyclicals are distinguished by their persistent care to analyze the philosophical principles which help to shape modern social life and which have to be critically revised in order to open up new possibilities.

Leo grants that there are major areas in philosophical discussion which do not have a traceable bond with issues of faith and morals, and hence where the Church cannot and should not make any authoritative pronouncements affecting the field of speculation. Yet the fact that there are other large areas where such a link is present between philosophical ideas and the attitudes of men toward revelation and moral law means that the Church cannot remain entirely indifferent to such ideas. That is why the total separatism mentioned in the 1864 Syllabus is both unrealistic for the Christian mind and undiscerning from the philosophical standpoint.

Let us now consider the sense in which doctrinaire separation is at once unrealistic and undiscerning. It is unrealistic, once we grant that philosophy has a very important set of human functions to perform. Both Leo XIII and Pius XII correlate the Church's concern about some aspects of philosophy with their high conception of the office and power of philosophical thought. Operating at its peak, philosophy can bring out and safeguard the natural evidence supporting our confidence in the human mind and its ability to reach some real truths concerning God, human reality, and moral law.[4] One's philosophical position on these issues profoundly affects one's growth as an intellectual inquirer, a man of faith, and a shaping agent in the moral community of men. Leo's favorite image for expressing the function of philosophy is that of the bridge. Philosophical activity provides the bridge for joining together our secular concerns and our religious beliefs, our intellectual interests and the practical arts of life. Because of this unifying work within its own sphere, philosophy does actually affect the relation of men to the practical organizing of society and the order of grace.

Were it not for this rather exalted notion of the philosopher's vocation, the problem of a sound philosophy capable of working effectively in the modern world would not be nearly so acute in Leo's estimation. And were it not for this same conception, his interpretation of philosophy would be much less relevant for our own intellectual climate than in point of fact it is. We can feel the sting behind his contention that any lower evaluation of philosophical work is undiscerning, when we compare the functions specified by him with some current opinions on the job of the philosopher. Outside of the naturalists and Marxists, the phenomenologists and existentialists, it is presently fashionable for philosophers to disclaim any burning interest in the grand problems of human destiny and any definite responsibility for the practical consequences of their theoretical analyses. Making a careful analysis of the linguistic and conceptual structures would presumably exhaust the philosopher's task, and would leave him professionally unaccountable for how people may use the results in deciding what to believe and how to act as individuals and groups. But historical experience shows that this disavowal does not tell the whole story and that it cannot sustain itself over a long period and with respect to all the main issues. Usually, the policy of abstention from inquiring beyond the language system or the conceptual structure contains an implicit assumption about the range of the human mind and about the accessibility of human nature, the moral law, and the truth about God to our human intelligence. When this latent element is eventually brought to open statement, it usually does affect the concrete attitudes of men toward these matters.

Another provocative aspect of Pope Leo's general conception of philosophy comes in view when we pay careful attention to the language he customarily uses to describe it. It is quite noticeable that he often prefers to speak about "philosophizing" rather than "philosophy," especially when there is question of the optimum functions and the relationship with faith. This preference for the verbal form is not accidental, and neither is it merely an adornment of style. It is a significant, deliberately chosen usage which recurs in many different contexts. Leo likes to speak about the *ratio philosophandi* and the *forma philosophandi,* the *optima ratio philosophandi,* and the *optima forma philosophandi.*[5] He secures several advantages in thus approaching philosophy as an operation having a form and a pattern. This usage helps to undercut the proposition in the 1864 Syllabus which advocates a divorcement between the philosopher as an individual agent and his philosophy taken as a separate entity, molded by purely impersonal laws. Leo suggests, on the one hand, that philosophy lives and flourishes as a habit and mode of activity in the human mind and, on the other, that the activity itself is of a reasonable sort which respects the intelligible structures of things. Philosophizing constitutes this conjunction between the personal activity of living minds and the reasonable pattern of beings, and only in such a meeting does philosophy achieve its perfection as a human discipline.

To show the essential modernity as well as traditional character of Leo's thought on this issue, we do not have to attempt any strained comparison with the elaboration of the theme of philosophizing in Dewey, Husserl, Jaspers, and other twentieth-century thinkers.[6] It is sufficient to note that the Pope is responding to some definite intellectual needs of our age and also is responding to them precisely in the manner appropriate for the chief teacher in the Church. His conception of effective philosophizing as a union between the living intelligence and the patterns of being points out the way of overcoming what we may call that estrangement of mind from nature and God which underlies our psychic and social disorders. When we engage in philosophical work, we should retain a basic openness both to the significance of things within our experience and to the initiative of the revealing God. Once we learn to place the accent upon philosophizing, we will be disinclined to regard philosophy any longer as a closed universe in which there are no pathways leading from the analytic scheme to the significance of natural things and the traces of God which they bear.

Speaking not as a philosopher but as the supreme teacher of revealed truth to whom the religious renewal of all things human is a prime concern, Leo XIII compresses into a pregnant sentence his view of the best way to philosophize: "Those, therefore, who to the study of philosophy unite obedience to the Christian faith, are philosophizing in the best possible way; for the splendor of the divine truths, received into the mind, helps the understanding, and not only detracts in nowise from its dignity, but adds greatly to its nobility, keenness, and stability."[7] In a word, the Christian mind's mode of philosophizing offers the best prospects of obtaining humanly valuable results, provided that it is careful to unite professional competence of the highest order with a meditative grasp of the truths of faith.

Leo's teaching on this score is sharply critical of the widespread modern assumption that one can best philosophize by keeping the mind isolated from any sort of influence of religious faith. This premise has been the working law for philosophers who have come in the wake of Machiavelli and Bruno, Descartes and Locke. The Pope is well aware, however, of the depth of his challenge and its connection with considerations joining philosophy to a wider context of thought. He often associates the estrangement between faith and philosophical activity with his broader theme about the historical stages in the dismemberment of human intelligence.[8] The sixteenth-century revolt took a decisive step by contrasting the sphere of Christian faith with all our secular interests, among which was counted the whole human interest in philosophy. This contrast between the domains of faith and philosophical reason was solidified and extended systematically by the key modern philosophers to the point where one's religious faith came to be regarded as an alien intruder and as a hindrance to speculative work. But Leo XIII makes the bold suggestion that the time has now come to review critically this conventional assumption and to move ahead to a more positive and fruitful conception of the influence which one's assent to revealed truth can have upon philosophical inquiry, provided that the professional standpoint is also operative.

Throughout this discussion the Pope shows much more concern about the philosopher's general attitude than about this or that particular idea he may entertain. Here perhaps is the ultimate reason prompting Leo XIII to emphasize the theme of philosophizing. The root of the matter reaches down to the philosopher's personal conviction about how he ought to do his work and what constitutes an aid or a hindrance to it. A transformation in our view of how best to philosophize is the most reliable path for achieving a radical improvement both in the intellectual sphere and in the political and social order, insofar as the latter reflects the philosophical separation between religious and philosophical truths. The Christian philosopher cannot cut himself off from a direct and careful study of modern philosophical ideas, since such an attitude of separatism would be only compounding that mutual estrangement between Christian faith and human inquiry which Leo seeks to overcome on both sides.

Both in the text just quoted and in other crucial places the Pope is quite careful in designating the component factors in the best way of philosophizing. He speaks not simply about Christian faith but about obedience or service to the Christian faith: *obsequium fidei christianae;* and similarly, he refers not simply to philosophy but to the study of philosophy: *studium philosophiae.* This language underlines once more the cardinal role of the living human mind in achieving a genuine restoration of Christian philosophy. The latter cannot spring into being through decree, through curricular shifts, or through descriptive praise from the outside. Although these conditions may help to provide an atmosphere in which Christian philosophizing can go on, that activity itself has to grow out of the mind's own acts and habits of studying philosophy and serving the truths of faith. Provided that there is no methodological withdrawal of philosophical intelligence from the influence of faith, Leo XIII and Pius XI regard it as only just that a Christian philosopher should adhere carefully to the method, principles, and arguments proper to his own discipline.[9] Philosophy must inquire into those truths which can be shown from a close study of natural things, and hence it has an order and a set of tasks distinctively its own. The Christian philosopher enjoys the guiding and illuminating influence of his faith, and he shows in practice its consonance with the truths established from his philosophical investigation of nature. His responsiveness to the truths of faith helps him to stabilize, sharpen, and ennoble within its own order the philosophical inquiry which seeks to move from a strenuous analysis of natural things and human reality to their bond with God. The relation of friendship and fidelity to distinct offices which Pope Leo envisages between faith and philosophical intelligence can only lead to the enrichment of the Christian philosophical life within the modern context.

In outlining the main functions for the Christian philosopher today, the Pope usually specifies three areas of work. One task is to reread and revivify the wisdom of the ancient Greek and Roman sources. Another is to feed upon and develop the Christian wisdom slowly elaborated by the Fathers and Scholastic doctors, especially St. Thomas. And finally, one must make a careful study of the fruits of modern research in the physical, psychological, social, and historical fields, especially for the relevant light they may cast on philosophical issues. We should not be surprised to find this latter duty assigned to the Christian philosopher. There is a sharply practical note in all the papal teachings during the past eighty years on the subject of Christian philosophy.[10] Its practical growth and influence can occur only within the actual conditons of modern thought as well as modern social circumstances. The Christian philosopher must preserve his roots in the great sources of the past, but he has to carry on his own work within the field defined by the modern centuries of inquiry and discovery. This threefold function has become embodied in the curriculum requirements of Catholic universities and seminaries, but at the level of advanced original work it is not always realized even now that such an integration constitutes the best way of philosophizing on a long-term basis.

One reason for Pope Leo's admiration of St. Thomas is that the latter made an adequate preparation for approaching the questions prominent in his own day. The Common Doctor set the example of making a comprehensive and continuing study of his intellectual heritage and reorganizing the materials under firm principles of order

and future growth. In turn, our own personal reading of St. Thomas
should be a liberating experience in the sense of inducing us to examine the intellectual riches of the ancient and medieval worlds,
providing us with some lasting truths of being which still have a yield
to give, and inviting us to do some creative work of critical evaluation
and assimilation within our own philosophical environment. Here
we must confine our attention to one aspect in recent papal recommendations of the study of St. Thomas, namely, that it should lead us
eventually to make an internal and constructive study of the scientific
and philosophical evidences and difficulties developed since the
Middle Ages.

No one was better aware of the need for this new dimension of
awareness on the part of Thomists themselves than was Leo XIII.
During the full generation preceding *Aeterni Patris* he was a keen
observer and promoter of the Italian developments leading up to the
full revival of Thomistic doctrine. As the Bishop of Perugia, he took
definite measures to have this doctrine taught in his seminary and
to have it discussed and developed with respect to modern ideas,
during the sessions of his Academy of St. Thomas. Through the wide
contacts of his brother, Cardinal Joseph Pecci, he continued throughout his lifetime to keep abreast of the men and writings in the Thomistic field. Through this fund of first-hand information about the
state of Thomistic studies, he acquired a deep conviction that at
least one condition for the full restoration and growth of the Christian philosophy of St. Thomas lay in securing a profound and sustained engagement of that philosophy with all the tendencies in
modern philosophy. Moreover, the Pope held that it was essential for
the Thomists of today to realize just how far they were already
involved in modern problems and methods, with the aim of getting
a better grasp on the authentic doctrine of Aquinas and also of making a more reflective and adequate approach to the issues of our age
in philosophy.

It is only by keeping in mind this broad experience of Leo XIII
with respect to the quality and predicament of Thomism in his own
day that we can understand why *Aeterni Patris* calls for the restora-

tion, not precisely of Thomism, but of "the wisdom of St. Thomas"—
Sapientia Sancti Thomae. These words do not have a purely eulogistic
sense but convey a normative and critical meaning. Their intent is
to urge us both to study the writings of St. Thomas himself without
remaining content with the Thomistic manuals and schools, and also
to take due account of later advances in human knowledge so that
what we accept from St. Thomas are the permanently sound and wise
foundations.

On the need for making a direct reading of St. Thomas the controlling factor in forming our conception of his teaching, the results
of historical research have fully confirmed Pope Leo's caution. Our
historical work is putting us in a better position for comparing
Aquinas with the leading Thomists of Leo XIII's day. In connection
with many specific issues in methodology, metaphysics, theory of
knowledge, and social ethics, we can see how deeply these Thomists
were already involved in modern philosophy. Men such as Sanseve-
rino and Taparelli, Liberatore and Kleutgen, were originally
grounded in an eclectic position combining some Scholastic elements
with Cartesian, Lockean, and Wolffian borrowings.[11] When such
writers made a shift toward the medieval sources after the social up-
heavals of 1848, they did not simply slough off their eclectic modern
background. Nor did they feel that they could do so and still fulfill
their responsibility to students in their own generation. Even after the
turning point of 1879, many Thomistic manuals continued to employ
the modern rationalist framework in terminology, statement of principles, division and organization of materials, and mode of inference.

We cannot treat these pioneers in a patronizing or satirical fashion,
for they responded as promptly and completely to their intellectual
challenge as it was possible for men in that transitional time to do.
But Leo XIII had the further responsibility of promoting the long-
range welfare of Christian philosophy, and this he saw to consist in a
double policy. One side of it was to encourage an accurate and ex-
haustive study of the sources of Christian philosophy such as would
live up to the high critical and historical standards of our time. Even
in asking researchers to return to the pristine sources of Thomism

in the writings of the Common Doctor himself, the Pope was inviting a revolutionary approach to the sources of Christian thought which would meet the requirements of rigor in our historical references in philosophy. His general conviction that careful historical studies can only advance the cause of truth found particular application here in his encouragement of exact research into the mind of St. Thomas and the other doctors.

The second part of the Leonine policy in this matter was to direct that there be a conscientious and sustained comparison made between St. Thomas and the modern philosophers. The Pope did not disapprove of the fact that Thomists in his day were concerned about modern problems and were trying their best to deal with them. His point of criticism was that many men who called themselves Thomists were nevertheless lacking in a precise textual and contextual understanding of both the thought of St. Thomas and the thought of modern philosophers. To have an unsteady and nonrigorous grasp upon both poles of the comparison was an invitation to confusion and easy criticism. This was a dangerous condition for the intrinsic development of Christian philosophy, as well as for all the educational activities and practical policies dependent upon this philosophy. Perhaps the peculiar genius of Leo XIII in this area lay in his ability to distinguish clearly between the historical work in St. Thomas and other doctors and the careful investigation of modern philosophical and scientific theories, and yet to insist on the need for both tasks as being related phases in the Christian mode of philosophizing at its best. He did not conceive of the restoration of the philosophy of St. Thomas as a flight from the modern scene, but rather as a process of recovering the sound origins and foundation which will enable us to philosophize more effectively and stably within our present field of resources and problems.

The word "wisdom" was also employed in an evaluative way in the program of restoring and rethinking the teaching of St. Thomas. Leo XIII made this unmistakably evident in a paragraph toward the end of *Aeterni Patris* where he looked forward to the practical use and influence of the doctrine he was recommending.

While, therefore, We hold that every word of wisdom, every useful thing by whomsoever discovered or planned, ought to be received with a willing and grateful mind, We exhort you, venerable brethren, in all earnestness to restore the golden wisdom of St. Thomas, and to spread it far and wide for the defense and beauty of the Catholic faith, for the good of society, and for the advantage of all the sciences. The wisdom of St. Thomas, We say; for if anything is taken up with too great subtlety by the Scholastic doctors, or too carelessly stated—if there be anything that ill agrees with the discoveries of a later age, or, in a word, improbable in whatever way —it does not enter Our mind to propose that for imitation to Our age.[12]

In the Pope's mind, then, even the success of revitalizing the philosophical and theological doctrines of Aquinas was indissolubly bound up with a careful critical weighing of it in the light of modern findings, so that we could be sure that we would be building upon what is genuinely wise and tested in his thought. Restoration of the wisdom of St. Thomas was to be a discriminating task involving our speculative judgment as well as our historical recall, and involving that speculative judgment precisely as being well informed about the subsequent work done in modern philosophy and science. To underline the importance of Leo's statement and to insure its force even during the confusing period of Modernist activities, Pope St. Pius X incorporated it in full into the 1907 encyclical *Pascendi.* He added that the truth of his predecessor's position is obvious and does not need insisting upon. However, we can now see that the Modernists themselves were instances of overhasty apologists who had not followed Leo's counsel of making a detailed and patient study of both the great Christian sources and the background in modern philosophy for the issues they sought to resolve so rapidly.

The finely balanced text of Leo which we have just given will repay a closer examination from our center of interest in philosophy. It concerns three aspects of philosophical wisdom. The first is the fact that the seeds of wisdom have been widely scattered under God's providence. Corresponding to this fact is the attitude it demands in us of remaining open to and grateful for any ray of illumination we can find, without being predisposed against the source and context in which it may actually be imbedded. We do not have the right or the power of predetermining where the words of wisdom are to be found, but we do have the duty to remain on the alert for them and to cultivate a prudent frame of mind for recognizing and incorporating them, whether they have been spoken by the ancient Greeks or by the modern authors. Secondly, Leo directs our study specially to St. Thomas as providing a unification of many scattered themes of philosophical and theological truth broached elsewhere and as forming the mind with principles for continuing the search after philosophical wisdom.

But along with the fact of fragmented pieces of wisdom and the counsel to base oneself upon the principles in Aquinas, the Pope asks us to consider a third facet of wisdom under its human, philosophical form: this wisdom must continue to do its work in the world, to profit by the findings of the human mind in modern history, and thus to grow and perfect itself even in our own era. This open-ended character of philosophical wisdom is specially important in Leo's view, since without it a Christian philosophy cannot perform its proper functions of defending the faith, consolidating and ordering the sciences, and enlightening our social decisions. The sciences do not stand still, and society does not freeze itself into a single mold forever. Moreover, the new forms they take, the new methods they use, the new problems they uncover—all these factors are philosophically significant and hence affect the sound development and presentation of Christian philosophical wisdom. That wisdom cannot rightly be proposed for imitation in our own age unless it shows that it has assimilated the findings of our age, tussled with its problems, and thus proved itself in fact as well as profession to be a wisdom in and for our time.

In making this last point as concrete as possible, without pretending to do the philosopher's work for him, Pope Leo mentions four specific ways in which we must become critical of our heritage and willing to add to the store of wisdom. Here he extends his view to the body of doctrines received from all the Scholastic doctors, without confining the analysis to St. Thomas. He asks workers in the field of philosophy to make good use of their modernity by being on guard against excessive subtlety, carelessness, conflict with sound modern discoveries, and improbabilities of any sort. These four avenues for improvement are not carelessly chosen, since they can be correlated with some of the constructive trends in modern philosophy with which Kleutgen and other advisers of Leo XIII were quite familiar. To reflect upon this correlation from a philosopher's standpoint is helpful to us even today, when the intellectual situation has changed so vastly in some respects.

(a) One of the strongest forces aiding the early growth of modern philosophy in the time of Bacon and Descartes was the revulsion people experienced when they tried to enter into discussion with the representatives of Scholasticism. The Scholastics gave the strong impression of being more interested in perpetuating their school disputes and in outrivaling each other in subtle distinctions and terminology than in reaching the truth and conveying it to men. Hence the moderns took drastic measures in simplifying their approach and in seeking to make a fresh start closer to what we can all experience. Whatever their particular failures, they did teach the lesson that in the modern period a philosophy cannot long survive unless it pares down on the subtleties and develops in an intelligible, straightforward, relatively public fashion. We do not want to lose this lesson, even now that we have entered an age of analysis which sometimes outbids the older Scholasticism for its involuted discussions. One of the marks of identity and attraction on the part of a Christian philosophy today should be its sense of primary concern for the significance of being as it manifests itself in the human persons and things of our ordinary experience.

(b) Even a well-substantiated body of wisdom can fail to win the mind's assent, if it is presented in a careless way or if it fails to take full advantage of modern means of attaining rigor of proof and statement. One great modern objection against the late medievals was that they were being subtle to no good purpose. We now know through the resources of symbolic logic that some of these medievals were striving, somewhat cumbersomely, to attain to a new exactness of thought. But this was the case mostly in the logical treatises, and even there the mathematical means were not available for a more economical expression of their ideal of precision. In large areas of natural philosophy, even in areas touching on man and God, however, subtlety of expression was combined with considerable carelessness in the description of evidence, the analysis of structures, and the proof of implications. This is always a fateful sort of combination, since it can easily convince the reader that truth is not seriously being sought and that it is not likely to be found in the direction indicated by the careless thinkers. The modern stress upon methodology, analytic techniques, and symbolic logic has led to the acceptance of a high standard of rigor in philosophical thinking. Every advantage should be taken of these instruments. But as Husserl once pointed out, this still leaves unsettled the question of the pluralism of modes of rigorous investigation and hence the question of which type of rigor is best suited to a particular line of study. The Christian philosopher must be concerned to show that he respects the requirements of rigor and also that he is employing that sort of rigorous method which is best adapted to his kind of inquiry.

(c) That the discoveries of the modern age do have a significance for the Christian philosopher and do impose on him the obligation to revise his positions against any ill-considered disagreements, is one of Pope Leo's strongest convictions. It underlies his repeated affirmation that the Church is not opposed to genuine intellectual progress, in the sense of the human effort at obtaining always a better understanding of our own nature and capacities and always more efficient means of controlling our world.[13] This is not a piece of fatuous optimism, since the recognition of a slow elaboration of methods and insights is combined by Pope Leo with the acknowledgement that they bring in their wake a whole new set of problems to be considered. Apart from a few exceptions among Scholastics who took the restoration of Christian philosophy to mean a simple repetition of previous ideas, most of the nineteenth-century Christian philosophers were quite sensitive to the difficulties raised by modern views of method and knowledge, by Newtonian physics, and by the infant sciences of laboratory psychology and psychiatry. Leo characterized the advances made in the sciences of nature and man as being so many sparks coming from the Creator and bearing witness to the dignity of our human vocation. But the sparks of new understanding embodied in the work of various kinds of modern scientists and artists are relevant for the philosopher's own interpretation of the natural and human universe.

The ultimate unity of all truths in their divine source should not have a lulling effect upon our minds. Instead, this conviction should operate in two ways to prevent a complacent quiescence of intellectual outlook. For one thing, it means that the steady advances made in the other sciences and the arts do have some bearing upon philosophy: growth in one part of the body of truth tends to affect the other parts and to require a careful review and often an advance in philosophical insight itself. In the second place, the perfect harmony and unity of various kinds of knowledge are assured from God's standpoint, but have to be worked out in actual steps by our human minds. We can draw comfort and encouragement from accepting the ultimate unity of all truths in God, but the encouragement is intended to sustain us in a difficult task rather than to dispense us from actually carrying it out. We have to traverse the long and sometimes rocky path between the plural condition of knowledges at our human level of vision and their ultimate unification, which for us always remains somewhat in the status of a continuing program of work still to be undertaken.

That process is one of growth on the basis of solid foundations, so that the permanent truths of Christian philosophy remain fully operative throughout the work of assessing and assimilating relevant findings from the physical and psychological, social and methodological, sciences of our day. Only it is necessary to keep these principles in working order and to display their critical and assimilative power in the detailed cases of difficulty. Precisely how this continuous relating of philosophy to modern discoveries should go on does not belong within the province of the Pope, but he does regard it as part of his office to remind philosophers that it must go on as an indispensable phase in the restoration of Christian philosophy, in its Thomistic form as well as any other form.

(d) All of these previous notes of counsel add up to the warning to avoid any semblance of improbability in the program of restoring, enriching, and spreading our Christian philosophical wisdom. Not to avoid it would be doing an injustice to St. Augustine, St. Thomas, and the other great men in this tradition, and it would also be placing an unnecessary hindrance in the way of a ready acceptance on the part of our contemporaries. Here we are touching upon the springs of assent and upon the subjective conditions required for a firm adherence to philosophical truths. One of the great lines of modern exploration reaches into the domain of the human subject and his interiority. Philosophers are keenly interested in this domain, both as a way of access to human reality and as a means for understanding why some ideas win our ready assent and others leave us doubtful or indifferent.

A philosophy displays the look of improbability about it when it fails to establish meaningful links with the problems of greatest concern to a particular age or when it ignores the sources of evidence and method made available in that age. When it fails in these two ways, it also disconnects itself from the framework of positions which are taken seriously as relevant interpretations and aids for the reflective minds of the time. It then appears to be a philosophy belonging to another era, an antiquated set of doctrines which have seen their day and which can no longer have a real claim upon our interest and assent. In such a situation it is not enough to maintain that truths are permanently valid for every age of man. This is indeed the case, but those who are not already convinced of its correctness are not likely to be moved by the mere assertion itself. The relevance of the doctrines has to be shown in actual instances, where they come to grips with current problems and prove in action their capacity to illuminate, to criticize, and to grow. If one remains content with a general affirmation of perennial truths and then refrains from making those truths visibly operative within the intellectual context of our time, one is responsible for the air of improbability and remoteness surrounding so many presentations of Christian philosophies. One of the aspects in the restoration of this tradition is the restoring of it to a real, functional role within the range of teachings which the modern mind regards as urgently significant and worthy of acceptance.

The precept of avoiding the appearance of unlikelihood and of earning the right to be treated as a challenging, pertinently true body of philosophical wisdom is consonant with Leo XIII's stress upon the Christian way of philosophizing. So that this philosophizing may be more widely shared, it must be related closely with all the other areas where our contemporary evidence and concerns lie. This synthesis between well-tested doctrines and respect for the peculiar concrete conditions affecting modern man's assent to the doctrines helps to explain Cardinal Newman's enthusiastic reception of *Aeterni Patris*. Although he could not claim to be a Thomist, he did see a likeness between his conception of how philosophy should be carried on today and the recommendations made by Leo XIII on the spirit of Christian philosophizing in the modern world. In a letter drafted to congratulate the Pope upon the occasion of the encyclical, he observed firmly that creative Christian work of an intellectual sort "should be grafted on the Catholic tradition of philosophy, and should not start from a novel and simply original tradition."[14] In his own way the English Cardinal was striving to achieve a living balance between the wisdom of the classical philosophers and Christian doctors and the concrete way of philosophizing which can address and move our contemporary intelligence.

It is noteworthy that Pope Leo, in turn, should have included his counsel about philosophizing within the modern context in his encyclical asking for the restoration of the wisdom of St. Thomas. He continued to join these themes in the later practical acts which carried out his intention. In his letters concerning the Roman Academy of St. Thomas Aquinas, the establishment of the chair of Thomistic philosophy and the school of philosophy at Louvain, and the founding of the Catholic University of America, Pope Leo asked that responsible scholars undertake the twofold labor of studying St. Thomas in his own writings and comparing his doctrine with the teachings of ancient and modern philosophers.[15] He specified that the comparison be made not only to show in actual detail the basic integrity of the Thomistic position but also to enrich the general body of wisdom. We should expect to find some new teachings which bear the marks of industry, knowledge, and wisdom, and we should be quick to praise and incorporate whatever stands up under critical scrutiny. This same generous and constructive spirit in philosophical work was reaffirmed in *Humani Generis,* when Pius XII remarked that the study of modern and contemporary philosophies is not simply a cataloguing of errors but also a mining of sound nuggets, and hence an instrument for the internal perfecting of Christian philosophy itself.

We can now appreciate the striking convergence which has been gradually made between our first theme of philosophizing in the best way and our second theme of studying the modern thinkers. The Pope's basic advice is that our philosophizing should combine a permanent fidelity to the traditional sources of wisdom with a reflective study of the new paths in human scientific and philosophical knowledge. His pithy phrase, "strengthen and complete the old by aid of the new,"[16] furnishes the guiding motto for those who are trying to work effectively as Christian philosophers under present intellectual conditions.

The Leonine ideal for the contemporary Christian philosopher is, then, that he should build upon the tested heritage of doctrines rather than reject the foundation and destroy the continuity in philosophical thought. He should strive to complete the old by the aid of the new, while carefully avoiding the two extremes of standing still with a napkin-wrapped treasure or eliminating the solid work of the past. The precise way in which this organic growth is to be accomplished is properly left to the Christian philosophers themselves. There is leeway for legitimate differences among them, for specialized interests leading in many diverse directions, and even for errors which must be expected in new work and for which they have to develop the methods of detecting and correcting. The responsibility for the actual state of Christian philosophizing at a given time lies squarely with the men whose professional vocation leads them to devote their lives to this work.

In this final section it may be useful to ask whether Pope Leo's counsel and direction have started to yield any definite fruit in our century, always bearing in mind that progress in philosophy is never sensationally rapid. Although it would be invidious to pretend to make any definitive selection, the people whom we will mention are generally recognized as having done competent work lying chiefly in the modern field, and having done it in the spirit of building upon their Christian philosophical heritage.

The decisive breakthrough was the handiwork of Cardinal Mercier at Louvain.[17] Even his insistence upon teaching some philosophy courses in the vernacular helped to bring the Scholastic mind within closer hailing distance of modern philosophers and their distinctive problems. For it gradually forced the men in the field to rethink the older doctrines in modern terms, to take account of new evidence on the perennial issues, and thus to engage in the kind of restoration of Christian philosophy which Pope Leo had in mind. Mercier's own study of psychological findings and the new field of psychiatry helped to open up one avenue to a deepening grasp of man and the life of affections, desires, and imagery. And it was Mercier's example in taking Descartes and the problem of knowledge seriously which gave the lead to the intense epistemological investigations of the first four decades of our century.

Many early efforts in this field were hampered by a faulty knowledge of the critical problem as it was formulated by Kant. One of Father Maréchal's major services was to provide us with a precise historical understanding of the Kantian system. Furthermore, he tried to make the Kantian problem more accessible by linking it up with the centuries-long speculation of Greek, medieval, and early modern thinkers on the nature of knowledge, its relation with the real, and the basis for metaphysics.[18] By rethinking some Thomistic sentences on the relation of being and action, the desirability of knowledge, and the basic search of man for God, Maréchal provided a powerful example of what it means to use one's philosophical heritage in an original way to meet the problems of modern criticism. His psychological studies of mysticism show this same exploratory spirit. In his wake there has been a re-examination of the implications of physical science, along with a renewed study of the role of love in constituting the human person and leading him to God.

For a better grasp of the general history of modern philosophy, we are indebted to the studies of Monsignor Olgiati and Father Copleston.[19] The former has brought out how difficult it is to make any comprehensive generalization about the modern thinkers. He has worked out a minimal interpretation of the various modern movements around the principle of phenomenalism. By calling attention to the scientific line which stems from Galileo and the empiricist line from Hobbes and Locke to the positivists, he has helped to overcome a tendency of Catholic authors to emphasize only the rationalists. In his works on Descartes and Berkeley, Olgiati shows in detail the fundamental phenomenalist assumptions held in common by rationalists and empiricists. From Copleston's writings we learn to connect the modern thinkers with their predecessors through the presence of recurrent problems. Perhaps even more helpful is the example he gives of dealing with analytic philosophy on its own terms and with full command of its techniques. He is doing a cautious, professional work of reviving the central metaphysical questions within the analytic context and only so far as that context permits.

Jacques Maritain's arresting quality springs from his sensitivity to what is specifically new in our world, as combined with his fidelity to St. Thomas and some commentators.[20] This cross-graining of old and new underlies his approach to natural philosophy and modern science. He sees no need to sacrifice the essential points in either standpoint, provided that we recognize them to be distinct types of knowledge. He refuses to reduce the modern scientific analysis to an already anticipated subdivision of the Aristotelian philosophy of nature, just as he finds no good grounds for eliminating that philosophy itself in the line of ontological explanation. To observe Maritain's mind working on the testimony of the French poets or on the data of social scientists is to learn how a philosopher proceeds at the very frontier of research. There, the modern esthetic and social discoveries of the human spirit retain their freshness without being cut off from all relationship with the Thomistic metaphysics of knowledge and theory of society.

Many younger Catholics today are engaged in studying the existentialisms of Marcel and Heidegger, as well as the phenomenological movement from Husserl to his German and French descendants. For many young people, this experience induces an intellectual crisis. They become so keenly aware of the significance of existentialist and phenomenological concepts for penetrating into the perceptual, ontological, and historical dimensions of man that they sometimes wonder whether such concepts and techniques must not simply replace the older doctrines.[21] There is no easy solution here, any more than there is in the question of how to reconcile recent analytic theories with metaphysical inferences. But that a patient wrestling with this complex issue is better than a simplistic choice of only one side is the import of Edith Stein's efforts. In philosophy she never achieved that close integration of things which marked her religious life. Yet she did embody that most precious virtue of the modern Christian philosopher: *stabilitas*. For hers was the method of tenaciously confronting the traditional positions with new methods of description and argument and then, in turn, submitting the newer problems to analysis in the light of the permanent principles of act and potency. And it must be added that Edith Stein deliberately posed the question of Husserl and Thomas at the most crucial point of the relation between finite and eternal being, between the

structures of our experienced world and the transcendent God. She
spelled out for our instruction the meaning of a lifelong, unevasive
inquiry into the problem of Christian philosophizing in a phenomenological milieu.

It is appropriate for us to bring our study to a close with two
texts taken from *Aeterni Patris*. The first is a piece of salutary advice
from Leo XIII addressed to those Christian philosophers whose
main work lies in the modern field.

We have no intention of discountenancing the learned and able men who
bring their industry and erudition, and, what is more, the wealth of new
discoveries, to the service of philosophy; for, of course, We understand
that this tends to the development of learning. But one should be very
careful lest all of his chief labor be exhausted in these pursuits and in
mere erudition.[22]

All our research stands rightly in an instrumental relationship with
the chief task of the philosopher which is to achieve true acts of
judging concerning the natural things in the world, the being of
man, and our common rootedness in God. The philosopher has to
work constantly to bring his erudition to bear on questions, and to
stay alert to all the findings of the human spirit in his own age, as
well as the past. Yet these are ministerial functions, not the ends
of his activity. They minister to his most characteristic act for which
he is personally and chiefly responsible, namely, the act of true
judging about beings and especially about God, wherein wisdom
lies. The second text is a quotation from Scripture itself which
Pope Leo offers us as a final encouragement in our labors:

If any of you want wisdom, let him ask of God, who giveth to all men
abundantly, and upbraideth not: and it shall be given him.[23]

Today, as well as in the former ages, the Christian philosopher is
impelled both by his faith and by the ultimate reaches of his philosophical inquiry to ask for this wisdom from God Himself and to
remain confident that it will be given him in proper measure.

NOTES

1. The most durable commentary continues to be by F. Ehrle, S.J., *Zur Enzyklika "Aeterni Patris"; Text und Kommentar,* newly edited by F. Pelster, S.J. (Rome, Edizioni di storia e letteratura, 1954). On pp. 110–13, Ehrle observes that the encyclical seeks not a reproduction of the past, but a repristination of Christian philosophy as supplying a fresh response to modern questions.

2. Propositions 11 and 14 in the Syllabus of Errors, appended to Pius IX's encyclical *Quanta Cura.* There is a convenient translation in *The Papal Encyclicals in Their Historical Context,* edited by A. Fremantle (New York, Putnam, 1956), pp. 144–45. Compare Proposition 10, p. 144. B. O'Reilly's old-fashioned *Life of Leo XIII* (rev. ed., Philadelphia, Winston, 1903), pp. 226–35, gives excerpts from Archbishop Pecci's 1864 Lenten pastoral on current errors.

3. The translation of *Aeterni Patris* annotated by E. Gilson is used here. Page references are made to the translation as printed in J. Maritain, *St. Thomas Aquinas* (rev. 2d English ed., New York, Meridian Books, 1958), because Appendix III (pp. 179–266) of this book contains the major recent papal documents on St. Thomas and Christian philosophy. For the quoted text, see *Aeterni Patris,* paragraph 2 (Maritain, pp. 184–85). Also, Pope Leo's Letter "Dum vitiatae," *Acta Sanctae Sedis,* 13 (1880–81), p. 3. On the recent influence of philosophical ideas in India and China, cf. E. Vagnozzi, "The University and the Truth that Will Prevail," *The Catholic University of America Bulletin,* 27 (1959), pp. 7–8.

4. *Aeterni Patris,* par. 29 (Maritain, pp. 206–207). See also, Leo XIII, Motu Proprio "Ut mysticam Sponsam," *A. S. S.,* 23 (1890–91), p. 523; Pius XII, *Humani Generis,* par. 29 (text in Maritain, *St. Thomas Aquinas,* pp. 257–58).

5. Along with the texts cited below in notes 7 and 16, see the Allocution "Pergratus Nobis," *A. S. S.,* 12 (1879–80), p. 487; the Letter "Quod in novissimo," *Acta Leonis XIII,* 2 (1883–87), p. 263.

6. This recent development is explained in J. Collins, *The Existentialists: A Critical Study* (Chicago, Regnery Gateway Edition, 1959), pp. 212–20.

7. *Aeterni Patris,* par. 9 (Maritain, p. 192). It should be noted that Pope Leo is relating the act of philosophizing with the influence of the Christian faith, without requiring the use of the theological order of development. For a different reading of the text and its implica-

tions, consult E. Gilson, "What Is Christian Philosophy?" in *A Gilson Reader,* edited by A. C. Pegis (Garden City, Hanover House, 1957), pp. 185–87.

8. *Aeterni Patris,* par. 24 (Maritain, pp. 203–204); *Immortale Dei,* par. 10, translation in J. Husslein, S.J., *Social Wellsprings,* Vol. I: *Fourteen Epochal Documents by Pope Leo XIII* (Milwaukee, Bruce, 1940), p. 76. Apart from *Aeterni Patris,* Leo's translated encyclicals are cited from Husslein's volume.

9. *Aeterni Patris,* par. 8, 29–30 (Maritain, pp. 191, 207–208); Pius XI, *Studiorum Ducem* (text in Maritain, *St. Thomas Aquinas,* pp. 231–32). See the Apostolic Letter "Cum hoc sit" (in the form of a Brief signed by Cardinal Mertel), which establishes St. Thomas as patron of all Catholic schools. There (*A. S. S.,* 13 [1880–81], pp. 57–58), we are assured that St. Thomas's way of relating reason and the Christian faith results in a noble service of philosophical intelligence rather than a demeaning servitude, since he retains the distinction of offices between philosophical demonstration of truths from a study of natural things and faith as an acceptance of truths coming from God as their author. The contrast between *servitus* and *obsequium* is reminiscent of the views of M. Liberatore, S.J.

10. Read, for instance, the Letter "Susceptum a Nobis," reprinted conveniently along with Pope Leo's other letters on the Thomistic chair and Institute of Philosophy at Louvain in the Appendices to L. de Raeymaeker, *Le Cardinal Mercier et l'Institut Supérieur de Louvain* (Louvain, Publications universitaires, 1952), pp. 241–43.

11. This is brought out in three historical studies devoted, respectively, to epistemology, metaphysics, and ethics: G. Van Riet, *L'épistémologie thomiste* (Louvain, Éditions de l'Institut Supérieur, 1946), pp. 32–133; J. Gurr, S.J., *The Principle of Sufficient Reason in Some Scholastic Systems, 1750–1900* (Milwaukee, Marquette University Press, 1959), pp. 121–58; R. Jacquin, *Taparelli* (Paris, Lethielleux, 1943), pp. 51–57, 168–74. The decisive influence of Leo XIII and *Aeterni Patris* is recognized by all three scholars. B. Bonansea, O.F.M., "Pioneers of the Nineteenth-century Scholastic Revival in Italy," *The New Scholasticism,* 28 (1954), pp. 1–37, is mainly a summary of Van Riet. For the theological side of the same story, see E. Hocedez, S.J., *Histoire de la théologie au XIXe siècle,* 3 vols. (Paris, Desclée De Brouwer, 1947–52), I, pp. 49–60; II, pp. 347–64; III, pp. 41–52, 351–94.

12. *Aeterni Patris,* par. 31 (Maritain, p. 208). See the interpretative remarks of E. Soderini, *The Pontificate of Leo XIII* (London, Burns,

Oates, and Washbourne, 1934), I, pp. 129–30. The passage in
Pascendi where Pius X quotes this text of his predecessor is presented
in Maritain, *St. Thomas Aquinas*, p. 136. In the same tradition Pius
XII mentions the ways in which Christian philosophy can be en-
riched today, even in regard to fundamental doctrines: *Humani
Generis,* par. 30 (Maritain, pp. 258–59).

13. *Immortale Dei,* par. 19 (Husslein, p. 85); *Libertas Praestantissimum,* par. 20 (Husslein, p. 132). See R. Fülöp-Miller, *Leo XIII and
Our Times* (New York, Longmans, Green, 1937), p. 41.

14. Text in W. Ward, *The Life of John Henry Cardinal Newman,* 2 vols.
(New York, Longmans, Green, 1912), II, pp. 501–502.

15. Letter "Iampridem," *A. S. S.,* 12 (1879–80), p. 227; Letters "Insti-
tuto" and "Per alias literas," reprinted in De Raeymaeker, *op. cit.,* pp.
231, 237 (especially the second sentence in each letter); Letter
"Quod in novissimo," *Acta Leonis XIII,* 2 (1883–87), pp. 262–63.
Also, Pius XII, *Humani Generis,* par. 9–10 (Maritain, p. 248).

16. *Aeterni Patris,* par. 24 (Maritain, p. 204). Cf. Letter "Quod opera,"
Acta Leonis XIII, 3 (1887–89), p. 292.

17. De Raeymaeker, *op. cit.,* gives the record of Mercier's achievements
at Louvain.

18. A ready introduction to Maréchal is provided in *Mélanges Joseph
Maréchal,* 2 vols. (Paris, Desclée De Brouwer, 1950), I, pp. 3–101,
containing a sketch of his work, a genetic essay, a bibliography, and
Maréchal's own summary of the argument in his chief work, *Le
Point de départ de la métaphysique.*

19. See J. Collins, "Olgiati's Conception of Modern Philosophy,"
Thought, 18 (1943), pp. 478–504. Beginning with the third volume
of his *History of Philosophy* (Westminster, Md., Newman Press),
F. C. Copleston, S. J., treats of Renaissance and modern thinkers.
His *Contemporary Philosophy* (Westminster, Md., Newman Press,
1956) deals critically and constructively with logical positivism and
existentialism. Copleston's noteworthy series of articles on "Man
and Metaphysics," in the first volume of *The Heythrop Journal*
(1960), provides a modern defense of metaphysical inference.

20. Maritain's range of thought is described in two co-operative volumes
of essays: *The Maritain Volume* of *The Thomist,* 5 (1943), and *The
Social and Political Philosophy of Jacques Maritain,* edited by J. W.
Evans and Leo R. Ward (New York, Scribner, 1955).

21. This problem is explored particularly in respect to existential
phenomenology by A. Dondeyne, *Contemporary European Thought
and Christian Faith* (Pittsburgh, Duquesne University, 1958). A

sampling from Edith Stein is furnished in *Writings of Edith Stein,* translated by H. Graef (Westminster, Md., Newman Press, 1956).

22. *Aeterni Patris,* par. 24 (Maritain, p. 204).

23. *James* 1, 5; quoted in *Aeterni Patris,* par. 32 (Maritain, p. 209). In his study of *La Philosophie catholique en France au XIXe siècle avant la renaissance thomiste et dans son rapport avec elle (1800–1880)* (Paris, Vrin, 1955), especially pp. 237–68, L. Foucher suggests that the issuance of *Aeterni Patris* corresponded with the view of tradition-minded French Catholic philosophers of the nineteenth century that the spiritual authority of the Church should provide some decisive guidance in unifying Christian intellectual life around a sound, enduring philosophy of a nonrationalistic kind and open to the wisdom of the faith.

9 Leo XIII and Contemporary Theology

REV. GUSTAVE WEIGEL, S.J.
Woodstock College

THE LITERARY LEGACY of Leo XIII is quite vast. Among the elements therein contained some will sound almost antediluvian to men of our time. He left a volume of Latin verse—an accomplishment still esteemed in Leo's day but somewhat *démodé* in 1960. Among his pontifical directives there were decrees concerning duels. Dueling is not entirely dead in this generation but then neither is the duckbilled platypus. On the other hand, Leo's concern with the social problem and the functions of the State are altogether resonant with our worries in the second half of the twentieth century.

This double facet of Leo's efforts gives us the key to the significance of the man. He had one foot in the past and the other in the present. The revolutionary movement in Europe consequent on the Napoleonic Era turned Europe toward a new form of society and it has not yet taken its definitive shape. The popes prior to Leo tried to withstand the flood action of revolution but they had failed, and their failure was most conspicuous in the loss of the Papal States. Leo, without really accepting the new order, did seek to make peace with it. He was the first pope to do so. He did not wholly understand what was going on, but he was shrewd enough to see that it was revolutionary. The title for his encyclical on social justice used the Latin words for revolution: *rerum novarum.*

Much has been written about Leo's approach to sociology, politics, and economics. Not so much has been said about his contribution to theology, and yet in this field his influence has been significant and lasting. He did not define any new dogmas nor did he open up new lines of doctrine, but he opened the door to a new spirit in theology which has been very fruitful.

The nineteenth century before Leo had its meritorious theologians. The names of Gazzaniga, Rossi, Zigliara, González, Perrone, Franzelin, Schrader, and Kleutgen were ornaments of the tradition which had begun in the thirteenth century and passed through the molding action of the Baroque period. Somewhat out of this tradition, other nineteenth-century theologians were outstanding. We need only mention names like Johann Adam Möhler and Matthias Scheeben in Germany, Cardinal Victor Dechamps of Belgium, and Cardinal John Henry Newman in England. Yet none of these men individually, nor all of them collectively, made a deep impact on the thought of their century. Catholic theology was not an element in the main stream of the intellectual life of the West. Hegel, the German historicists, the French empiricists, Darwin, and Marx gave the tone to nineteenth-century thinking.

Since Leo's time Catholic theology is different. It is hardly dominant in the intellectual life of our day, but it can be identified as a well-defined vision which does have something to say to our generation. The glowing introduction of the empiricist Sir Julian Huxley to Teilhard de Chardin's *The Phenomenon of Man* (New York, Harper, 1959) is something that his grandfather Thomas Huxley could never have done a hundred years ago. Nor would a nineteenth-century Jesuit have written a book like Chardin's.

Leo XIII had something to do with the new look in Catholic theology. He was not a great theologian himself, but he was deeply interested in the discipline and had great affection for it. He influenced it in various ways.

Any intellectual discipline has as one of its functions the transmission of the findings of the past. Sometimes a discipline concentrates almost entirely on this chore. When this happens the discipline becomes irrelevant to its own time. There may be fervor in the study, but it will engage the energies of relatively few men, and these men stand in the backwaters of the current stream of thought. The Talmudic rabbis of the late Middle Ages are good examples of such scholarship. The situation becomes worse if the masters of the discipline communicate only a schematic reduction of former thought. In such a process not even the vital thinking of past masters as embodied in their own writings will reach the present generation. The only movement of the discipline is toward an ever briefer synopsis and to greater clarity, achieved at the cost of dropping out all the complications which history injects into questions. The end term is an algebraic formula, succinct, logical and clear, but with no understanding of the historical values of the x, y, z terms in the equations. This is formalism, valid indeed in mathematics, but deadly in a discipline which deals with existential realities.

Much of nineteenth-century Catholic theology was done in this fashion. Whether Leo explicitly recognized this condition in the theology of his time is not evident, but implicitly he had some awareness of it. The corrective of formalism is historical research. The meaning of terms can only be found in the history of the terms. A lexicographic definition of a sign must be derived from the historical usage of the sign. The mathematician has a much easier job. He stipulates the meaning of the symbol by his own fiat, but other forms of scholarship cannot use this device. A phrase like the Real Presence of Christ in the Eucharist must take on the meaning which ecclesiastical documents of the past gave to the word. Unless we achieve this meaning we cannot read the documents correctly. Changing the meaning of the term, we may draw wrong conclusions from ancient pronouncements.

Historical research, therefore, is necessary for theology. Without it theology becomes stagnant. In spite of the extravagances of nineteenth-century historicism Leo realized the importance of historical investigation. No one who writes or speaks of Leo omits to tell us that he opened the Vatican archives in 1881 to all competent scholars. Some commentators think that this showed Leo's liberal spirit, but such an interpretation is not in place. What Leo realized was that the communication of truth demanded familiarity with truth, which in its turn demanded accessibility to evidence. The Church has as one of its essential tasks the communication of Christ's truth as made available in the Church.

Leo was not making a gesture of deference to the spirit of his time. He was anxious to fulfill the perennial function of the Church to communicate the gospel. Opening the Vatican archives was a recognition of the importance of scholarship as an aid to the magisterium in its task of transmitting a message received continuously from the past.

Historians took advantage of Leo's action, and theologians soon found themselves confronted with the need to look at their formulas in the light of history. Leo probably did not think of this effect on theology when he made the written monuments of the Vatican available to scholars. Yet his decision did much to bring back Catholic theologians to the sources. This return gradually overcame the then current style of doing theology schematically. From Leo's time onward Catholic theologians are deep in history and realize today more than ever that research and investigation are the very foundation of their theologizing. Perhaps never before in the life of the Church is so much attention being paid to the historical setting of ecclesiastical pronouncements. The theologians are digging into the past and shedding light on what have been obscure corners in the transmission of the gospel. Fathers of the Church and medieval masters, little known in the past, are being studied and their contributions made public. The story of the Councils of the Church is being told with great detail. All this has given a freshness and depth to theological affirmations. Today the theologian knows that it is not enough to give off the glib definition of hypostatic union as found in a manual. He must go back to the days of Athanasius, Nestorius, and Cyril of Alexandria to see what they understood by the word and how the Church accepted the term at the Councils of Ephesus and Chalcedon. This is not at all easy, but it is stimulating and enriching. Now we know that theology can never be done once and for all; it is a never-ending doing. No formula remains static; it is ever-evolving into fuller expression of some great Christian truth. What was affirmed is not lost, but in history it becomes bigger by including more and more content.

This change, so precious and so fruitful, has made modern theology a vibrant activity, a real adventure of the mind. Leo was not the main or only cause of this gratifying change, but his unreflective appreciation of the work of investigation and his creative encouragement of its use by theologians has born splendid fruit in less than a century after the famous Pope's death.

Nor must we think that Leo helped theology only accidentally in his recognition of the value of investigating the historical sources of theology. In line with this general admiration for research he particularly urged the theologians to return to the Scriptures, that peculiarly proper font of Christian science and wisdom.

On October 30, 1902, Leo founded the Biblical Commission as a standing institution of pontifical government. After his death the Commission acted more as a brake than accelerator on biblical studies, but this was by reason of the rash temper of those times. As Leo conceived the Commission it was to foster and promote scientific biblical research. He had before him the example of Father Marie Joseph Lagrange, O.P., who in 1890, during Leo's reign, had organized the world-famous École Biblique of Jerusalem, which then and even more today stands in the forefront of scriptural studies. In 1892 Lagrange founded the stimulating journal *Revue Biblique,* which did so much for the enterprising solidity of biblical research in Leo's time and after.

However, the greatest stimulus Leo gave to scriptural investigation was his encyclical *Providentissimus Deus,* published on November 18, 1893. The document exudes love, esteem, and reverence for the sacred text. It is anxious to make all theologians study the Bible with passion and seriousness. From beginning to end it exhorts all Christian thinkers to a return to the Scriptures.

Leo's action manifested his awareness of the new spirit of the times. He found many theologians afraid to tackle the Scriptures according to the scientific method of the day. His letter overcame that fear. Again Leo showed himself to be of the past and the present.

He favors the new approach to the Bible, but he is quite critical of much of the work that it had done. He did not open the floodgates to irresponsible iconoclasm, but he did show what was positively good in the new studies. He did not go as far as the encyclical *Divino Afflante Spiritu* of Pius XII in 1943, but we must remember that Leo's directives were definitely path-breaking. After him Benedict XV could carry the task further in his encyclical *Spiritus Paraclitus* of 1920, to be advanced yet further by Pius XII.

The importance of the movement started by Leo XIII for the advancement of scriptural studies in theology can hardly be overestimated. The Catholic theologian must work all but exclusively on the data of revelation. As the Council of Trent taught, the Church's magisterium communicates this revelation by a double but correlated instrument; the Scriptures and the continuous Tradition of the Church. Scripture and Tradition must not be considered as two things sealed off from each other. The Scripture is in the Tradition and the Tradition is in the Scripture. They are so intertwined that they cannot be separated. The Protestant scholars of our time are seeing this truth, even though in the past they were reluctant to recognize it.

The important corollary for the theologian is that he cannot understand Tradition if he does not understand Scripture. The Scripture has a double advantage for the theologian. It is the inspired word of God and has in consequence a dignity superior to the word of man. It inspires reverence and confidence because of its source. Secondly, the Scripture is fixed in the nonchanging text, manifesting the abiding gospel message in words authorized by God. The Scripture, as Leo said, was a precious compendium of the revelation of Christ which God in his graciousness gave to the teachers of the Church as an aid in their communication of the saving action of the Lord. Like any compendium, it contained everything in a succinct, summary form. Like any compendium, it must be expanded by the teaching masters of the Church. The Church, being the Mystical Body of Christ with the Holy Spirit as its indwelling soul, always knows the full revelation of Christ, its Head. It can function without the Bible, and if by some cataclysm all the Bibles in the world were to disappear, the Church would still give the fullness and integrity of the saving word of Christ. But by God's kindly providence an inspired summary was given to the Church to help her in her task of preaching the gospel. It was not necessary, but it is a great advantage to be used with affection and awe.

The theologian will then search the Scriptures and see how the Tradition is therein contained, and he will search the Tradition to see how it expresses the biblical burden. Scripture and Tradition since they are inextricably bound together also illuminate each other. The more I know of Tradition, the more I learn about the message of the Bible; and the more I know about the Bible, the better I shall understand Tradition.

These principles are by no means new in Catholic theology. If we read the works of the Fathers of the Church, we see them practising the principle faithfully and clearly. In the Middle Age the principle works most conspicuously, perhaps most clearly, in the theology of St. Thomas Aquinas. It was the nineteenth century which raised a problem never faced by older theologians. In that century modern historical method was invented and organized, and by its rules historians went at the Bible in a way different from that pursued by the scholars of the past. The question now was: can the Catholic scriptural scholar accept the methods of the new technique? Many thought that it was impossible. The rules of lower and higher criticism were playing hob with the very postulates whereby the Catholic biblical scholar operates. The higher criticism with which Leo XIII was most concerned rejected the postulate of inspiration and deduced biblical positions which were not reconcilable with basic Catholic faith. Leo's solution was that historical method as it existed in his time could not be normative for Catholic scriptural work, but if used as a subsidiary tool, it could be useful in many ways.

This position has become basic since Leo's time. Likewise, after the encyclical of Pius XII there is no fear of the scientific philological method. It has been recognized that there are two or more dimensions to the scriptural message. One is strictly divine, and this is the proper concern of the theologian. The other is strictly human, and this is the concern of the historian of human phenomena. There is only one text, but this one text is multidimensional. Philology by its structure cannot touch the divine dimension. Moreover, because of the unity of the divine and the human dimensions the more known about the palpable human facet, the deeper will be the understanding of the divine content bound inseparably to the human expression.

After the encyclical *Divino Afflante Spiritu* Catholic scriptural scholars are acutely interested in what are called literary forms. The form dominates the human expression in which the Bible presents itself. The form is a matter of literary convention which is determined by time and place. It is not something absolute, but relative to a cultural milieu. In the light of the tastes and literary norms of the situation men will write. The form must not be identified with the substance of the writing. History for the Oriental of classical times was not conceived in the form of historiography as we understand it today. In fact, what the ancients called history would not be what we mean by history in the twentieth century. Scriptural history is theologizing about events, not a reporter's transcript of them. Historiographic process or accuracy in reporting or critical approach to traditions are no concern of the biblical writer. He does history in a different way. The Bible is not an historical source book, but when we know history from other sources we can understand the biblical writer's kind of history so much better.

In the light of these truths our present-day biblical scholars study wholeheartedly the Scriptures with all the aids of historical scholarship. They know what they are doing. They know that scientific investigation cannot give the ultimate divine truth of the Scriptures, but they also know that in mastering the merely human dimension of the word they are ready to pass easily from it into the order of the divine. The enterprise has been fruitful, and even though Leo could not see all the future developments of his initiative, he would be pleased with what has come forth.

The third contribution which Leo made to Catholic theology is also magnificent. The theologian cannot work without being deeply aware of history, but he is not formally or primarily an historical scholar. He wants to give an intelligent synthesis of reality as seen from the point of view of revelation. Intelligence has its own structure and philosophy is the discipline which investigates it. The theologian cannot escape the question of epistemology and its correlative, metaphysics. He cannot give an intelligent vision if he does not use some kind of metaphysics, and not all forms of metaphysical thinking are congenial to the theologian's task. From the days of Origen to our own time theologians have been slowly forming a metaphysics which will serve the masters of sacred doctrine. It is not the theologian's proper task to frame a metaphysics, but he will not be able to do his own work unless he has a metaphysical tool sturdy enough for the enterprise. Philosophy is a propaedeutic to theology, but it is a necessary one.

The man who saw this clearest was Thomas Aquinas. He was a theologian, but he found it necessary to work out a philosophic scheme in order to give his theology an intelligent form. He did it knowingly and reflexly. It is a mistake to think that he just borrowed the thought of Aristotle. He reconstructed it thoroughly according to the needs of theology. Aristotle wanted no eternal ideas and abandoned his teacher Plato for this reason. Thomas, on the other hand, who took so much of Aristotle, on this vital point followed Plato and insisted that it was necessary to recognize the reality of eternal ideas. Thomas was constructing a philosophy and knew that he was doing so. He had no qualms in using the insights of past thinkers, but he refused to be bound by any one of them. He had his faith and that determined the kind of philosophy he wanted. He found none ready-made, so he went about making one. His task is not yet finished, but he did the groundwork superbly.

The nineteenth century was also a philosophical age. The marks of Hegel, Feuerbach, Comte, and Spencer were heavy on it. In Catholic theological centers there was confusion. Some theologians were using a modified Hegelianism as their philosophical support. Others were still adopting the Cartesian attitude. Most were employing the Scholastic method but without any profound metaphysical insight. This was inevitable because the philosophy in use was a voluntarist eclecticism derived from various Scholastics, often in conflict with each other. It was an unsatisfactory situation, and Leo in his encyclical *Aeterni Patris* (August 4, 1879) applied a remedy to it.

In this communication he praised Thomas Aquinas and urged all directors of centers of theology to use him as a model in their work. He made Thomism official not in the sense that it was the philosophy imposed on all Catholic schools, but rather that it was the philosophy approved as adequate for the construction of Catholic theology. Pius X renewed this approval, and the Canon Law of 1918 made Thomistic method and rationale obligatory on seminaries in the undergraduate formation of future priests.

Nor was Leo satisfied with verbal praises of St. Thomas. In 1880 he also demanded a critical edition of the works of Aquinas, which the Dominican Fathers prepared. The new edition was called Leonine in honor of Leo XIII and the work is still going on.

This action was so typical of Leo. He was again in the past and in the present. He wanted the preservation of the legacy of a thirteenth-century Catholic scholar, but he also wanted that legacy alive according to the most rigorous demands of nineteenth-century scholarship.

To many at the time Leo's action seemed regressive rather than progressive. Thomas was not too well-known in the early nineteenth century, and the secular philosophers of that age looked on Aquinas as a fuzzy medieval thinker who thought the world was flat and numbered the angels dancing about a needle-point. The fact that Thomas knew and taught that the earth was round and that he would have laughed at so silly a question as angels dancing on needles was blithely unknown even by the scholars. Scholasticism was in disrepute, and many a Catholic heart fell when confronted with the papal attempt to resurrect Thomas.

But in the event the action was liberating. Men like Martin Grabmann, Pierre Mandonnet, and Maurice De Wulf went deep into the history of the thirteenth century, and their work was supplemented by a host of others. The metaphysics of Aquinas was studied from his own writings, and it was found to be brilliant. Even the non-Catholic world came to conceive a genuine respect for Thomism, thanks in great part to the work of Jacques Maritain and Étienne Gilson in our century. Theology had a sturdy tool with which to do its proper task. The Thomism which began to flourish was not narrow or antiquarian. It was wide open with a readiness to embrace whatever was good and true no matter where it came from. It was not only Catholic with a large *C* but with a small *c* as well.

The vitality of current Catholic theology and its recognized relevance to the times we live in are in large part due to the renewal of Thomism in the theological schools. The epistemological debates of the eighteenth and nineteenth centuries, the logical fencing of nineteenth-century Catholic schools were simply transcended. Ontology, the consideration of reality in its many dimensions, took over and a thorough going realism made theology energetic. Leo's intuition has been proved valid. He successfully aroused a sleeping giant.

Such were Leo's great contributions to theology in its formal being. He pushed the theologians into the science of history. He pushed them into the Scriptures. He gave them a vibrant Thomism with which they could do the constructive work needed in our time.

However, Leo did not only instruct the theologians how to work. He also gave them matter to work on. In the fulfillment of his own teaching office there were three fields of speculative theology touched. He dealt with the trinitarian nature of God; he frequently entered into the field of Mariology; more importantly, he treated the question of Church and State.

On this last subject he had much to say because most of the urgent difficulties of the Church of the nineteenth century came from governments and the political action of Catholics.

In his various pronouncements on this question Leo again showed himself to be of the past and of the present. Following in the footsteps of Pius IX, Leo would not accept the position of a Papacy without sovereignty. He could only protest against the Kingdom of Italy, which at its recent birth deprived the Pope of all temporal power and by so doing put him under the jurisdiction of Italian law, although this position was privileged. It was not temporal power which Leo sought but rather independence from the Italian state or any other state. A privileged position within a state was not enough; he had to be treated as a sovereign by Italian sovereignty in order to be what he was, a power over and above all secular governments. This could not be achieved if he did not possess sovereignty. In Leo's time the Roman Question could not be solved. Some thirty years had to go by before the outlines of solution became patent.

Pius IX had forbidden Italian Catholics to take part in Italian elections on the basis that the government was illegitimate. Leo retreated from this position, but not altogether. He modified the prohibition so that Catholics did participate in local but not national elections.

The Italian revolution itself was only part of a larger phenomenon. Republicanism was churning all over Europe, and France was in its Third Republic period. The republican spirit in Europe was definitely hostile to the Church, and Leo had to come to the Church's defense. He did not condemn the republican form of government but confirmed the ancient Catholic thesis that any of the historical political arrangements—monarchy, oligarchy, and democracy—were valid forms of governing. He merely insisted that no government could take away the liberty of the Church in her function of communicating the salvation of Christ. He also objected to the aims of republican politicians which were the elimination of religion from the concerns of a people. They were anxious to do something beyond the legitimate functions of government; they were trying to change the culture of peoples by the coercion of law.

Leo stood for the liberty of the Church, the primacy of national culture over politicians and governors, the friendly concord between secular government and ecclesiastical jurisdiction. It is along these lines that theology has been working since Leo's times.

Three factors confused the teaching of Leo, and future clarification was necessary. American democracy was different from French republicanism. Leo saw this but did not fully appreciate the reasons for it. Yet Leo was the first Pope to realize the importance of America and the American Church. He saw what its growing strength meant, and he did not look at it as something insignificant "out there." He wrote letters to the American bishops clearly showing awareness and understanding for their efforts and situation.

Secondly, Leo was of the tradition which still thought in terms of the idea of the Christian commonwealth—the *respublica christiana.* This idea existed in many Churchmen long after the Christian commonwealth had disappeared. There is little point in deciding when the Christian commonwealth did die. For our purpose it is irrelevant, because in the late nineteenth century it certainly was something of the past. Yet because of the long tradition Leo still entertained the idea, though he is well aware that as a matter of fact things were actually different. He was of the past and the present.

The third conditioning of Leo's thought was his own background and training. He was an aristocrat. He had no theoretical quarrel with democracy and was quite open to its merits. However, he could not be a democrat because his life was formed by a different vision. Leo showed love for the people, but he did not trust them. For him the people must be taken care of, but they are too immature and too undisciplined to rule. Leo by training conceived government as a paternalistic function. He definitely wanted government for the people, but it is doubtful if he wanted government by the people.

The directions and restrictions in Leo's thought gave a new starting point for the question of Church and State. The question today is much larger, as indeed it already was in Leo's time. The real question is the relation of the Church and secular society. As we all know, the theologians of our time are struggling with this problem. Not only is there much energy in the study but also no little heat. But all are agreed that the most relevant source of theology in this investigation is the body of Leonine writings, just because Leo had one foot in the past and the other in the present.

As a final summary it can be stated that Leo's deepest mark on the times which succeeded him is on Catholic theology. He had merits in many fields, but it is no exaggeration to say that his theological contributions are his most significant legacy. He renewed theology as a formal discipline by his effective call to theologians to become historically minded, to use the Scriptures with fervor and depth, to make their synthesis with the aid of Thomistic metaphysics. Not only did he aid theology by drawing attention to its formal structure but he also gave theologians matter on which to work. He dealt with many themes but perhaps the most relevant of all was his doctrine on the due relations between the Church and the secular society in which it perforce must work. Beyond any doubt today's theology bears a heavy Leonine stamp.

Selected Bibliography

COMPILED BY EDWARD T. GARGAN
AND RAYMOND H. SCHMANDT

WORKS OF POPE LEO XIII

Acta Leonis XIII. Leonis Papae XIII Allocutiones, Epistolae, Constitutiones. 7 vols. Bruges, 1887—.

Acta Leonis XIII pontificis maximi. 23 vols. Rome, 1881–1905.

Acta Sanctae Sedis. Vols. 11–25. Rome, 1878–1903.

The Church Speaks to the Modern World. The Social Teachings of Leo XIII, ed. by Etienne Gilson. New York, 1954.

L'Enciclica "Rerum Novarum," Testa authentica e redazioni preparatorie dei documenti originali, a cura di Mons. Giovanni Antonazzi. Rome, 1957.

The Great Encyclical Letters of Pope Leo XIII, ed. by John J. Wynne, New York, 1903.

La Jeunesse de Léon XIII d'après sa Correspondence Inédite, ed. by Boyer d'Agen. Tours, 1896.

Leo XIII, *The Church and Civilization*. Pastoral Letters for Lent 1877–1878. New York, 1878.

Leo XIII, *Conventiones de rebus ecclesiasticis inter S. Sedem et civilem potestatem initae sub pontificatu ssmi. d.n. Leonis pp. XIII usque ad diem 7 nov. 1893.* Rome, 1893.

Lettres Apostoliques de S.S. Léon XIII, Encycliques, Brefs, etc., Texte latin avec la traduction française, 7 vols. Paris, n.d.

Papal Documents on Mary, ed. by William J. Doheny and Joseph P. Kelly. Milwaukee, 1954.

Papal Pronouncements on the Political Order, ed. by Francis J. Powers. Westminster, Md., 1952.

Poems, Charades, Inscriptions of Pope Leo XIII, ed. and trans. by H. T. Henry. Philadelphia, 1903.

The Pope and the People; Select Letters and Addresses on Social Questions, ed. by W. H. Eyre. New York, 1895.

Principles for Peace: Selections from Papal Documents, Leo XIII to Pius XI, ed. by Harry C. Koenig. Washington, 1943.

Raccolta di Concordati su materie ecclesiastiche tra la Santa Sede et le Autorità Civili, 2 vols., ed. by Angelo Mercati. Città del Vaticano, 1954.

Scelta di Atti Episcopali del Cardinale Gioacchino Pecci, Arcivescovo Vescovo di Perugia, ora Leone XIII. Sommo Pontifice. Rome, 1879.

Social Wellsprings. Fourteen Epochal Documents by Pope Leo XIII, ed. by Joseph Husslein. Milwaukee, 1940.

BIOGRAPHIES OF POPE LEO XIII

Baumgartner, A., *Papst Leo XIII.* Freiburg, 1903.

Clarke, Richard H., *The Life of His Holiness Pope Leo XIII.* Philadelphia, 1903.

Freund, G., *Leo XIII., der soziale Papst.* Münster, 1898.

Fülöp-Miller, René, *Leo XIII and Our Times,* trans. by Conrad M. R. Bonacina. New York, 1937. (Published in England as *The Power and Secret of the Papacy.* London, 1937.)

Furey, Francis T., *Life of Leo XIII and History of His Pontificate.* New York, 1903.

Galland, J., *Papst Leo XIII.* Paderborn, 1893.

Germing, Ch. de, *La politique de Léon XIII.* Paris, 1902.

Götz, L. K., *Leo XIII, seine Weltanschauung und seine Wirksamkeit.* Gotha, 1899.

Hayward, Fernand, *Léon XIII.* Paris, 1937.

Keller, Joseph, ed., *The Life and Acts of Pope Leo XIII.* New York, 1888.

Martineau, William C., ed., *A Memento of the Death of the Holy Father Pope Leo XIII.* Albany, 1903.

McCarthy, Justin, *Pope Leo XIII.* New York, 1896.

McGovern, James, *Life and Life-Work of Pope Leo XIII.* Chicago, 1903.

Meynell, Wilfrid, *Life of Leo XIII.* New York, n.d. (Published under the pseudonym of John Oldcastle.)

Monetti, G., *Leone XIII.* 3 vols. Alba and Rome, 1936–1942.

Narfon, Julien de, *Pope Leo XIII His Life and Work,* trans. by G. A. Raper. London, 1899.

O'Malley, Charles J., ed., *The Great White Shepherd of Christendom. His Holiness Pope Leo XIII.* Chicago, 1903.

O'Reilly, Bernard, *The Life of Leo XIII.* Rev. ed. Chicago, 1903.

Schaepmann, H., *Leo XIII. Ein Charakter- und Zeitbild, Münster,* 1893.

Schneider, M., *Leo XIII., sein Leben und Wirken.* Kempten, 1903.

Schwer, W., *Papst Leo XIII.* Freiburg, 1923.

Schwerdt, F., *Papst Leo XIII. Ein Blick auf seine Jugend und seine Dichtungen.* Augsburg, 1887.

Spahn, M., *Leo XIII.* München, 1905.

Soderini, Eduardo, *Il pontificato di Leone XIII.* 3 vols. Milano, 1932–1933. (Vol. I translated by Barbara B. Carter, *The Pontificate of Leo XIII.* London, 1934. Vol. II translated by Barbara B. Carter, *Leo XIII, Italy and France.* London, 1935.)

Talbot, James. *Pope Leo XIII, His Life and Letters.* Boston, 1886.

T'Serclaes de Woomersom, Count Charles. *The Life and Labors of Pope Leo XIII,* trans. by F. Egan. Chicago, 1903.

WORKS ON LEO XIII AND HIS ERA

Acomb, Evelyn M., *The French Laic Laws, 1879–1889.* New York, 1941.

Adamow-Lambsdorff, E., *Die Diplomatie des Vatikans zur Zeit des Imperialismus.* Berlin, 1932.

Archives Diplomatiques 1876–1877, Vol. IV. Paris, n.d.

Aubert, R., *Le Pontificat de Pie IX.* Paris, 1952.

Bagnani, Gilbert, *Rome and the Papacy. An Essay on the Relations between Church and State.* New York, 1931.

Barbier, Emmanuel, *Histoire du Catholicisme Libéral et du Catholicisme Social en France du Concile à l'avènement de S.S. Benoît XV (1870–1914).* 6 vols. Bordeaux, 1924.

Bastgen, Hubert, *Die römische Frage,* 3 vols. Freiburg-i-B., 1917–1919.

Baunard, Louis, *Le Cardinal Lavigerie.* Paris, 1896.

———, *Histoire du Cardinal Pie.* 2 vols. Paris, 1886.

———, *Un siècle de l'Église de France.* Paris, 1901.

Beck, George Andrew, ed., *The English Catholics 1850–1950.* London, 1950.

Becker, I., *Relaciónes diplomáticas entre España y la S. Sede durante el siglo XIX.* Madrid, 1909.

Béhaine, Edouard Lefebvre, *Léon XIII et le Prince de Bismarck.* Paris, 1898.

Benson, A. C., *The Life of Edward White Benson.* 2 vols. London, 1899.

Billot, A., *La France et l'Italie. Histoire des années troublées, 1881–1889.* Paris, 1905.

Boudou, A., *Le Saint Siège et la Russie, leurs relations diplomatiques au XIX siècle.* Paris, 1922.

Brandi, Salvatore, *La Questione Francese e il dovere Cattolico; commentario dell' enciclica di S.S. Leone XIII a Francesi.* Rome, 1892.

Brown, Henry J., *The Catholic Church and the Knights of Labor.* Washington, 1949.

Bury, John B., *History of the Papacy in the Nineteenth Century, 1864–1878.* London, 1930.

Calvez, Jean-Yves, and Perrin, J., *Église et Société Économique.* Paris, 1959.

Candeloro, G., *Il movimento cattolico in Italia*. Rome, 1953.

Carlen, M. Claudia, *A Guide to the Encyclicals of the Roman Pontiffs, from Leo XIII to the Present Day: 1878–1907*. New York, 1939.

Castagnala, Stefano, *Da Firenze a Rome: Diario Storico-Politico del 1870–71*. Turin, 1896.

Cathrein, Viktor, *Sozialdemokratie und Christenum oder Darf ein Katholik Sozialdemokrat Sein?* Freiburg-i-B., 1919.

Cesare, R. de, *Il conclave di Leone XIII e il futuro conclave*. Città di Castello, 1888.

Cilibrizzi, Saverio, *Storia Parlamentare Politica e Diplomatica d'Italia, Da Novara a Vittorio Veneto*, Vol. II. Milan 1925–1952.

Collins, James, *The Existentialists: A Critical Study*. Chicago, 1959.

Copleston, F. C., *Contemporary Philosophy*, Westminster, Md., 1956.

Corrigan, Raymond, *The Church and the Nineteenth Century*. Milwaukee, 1938.

Crispi, Francesco, *Politica Interna*. Milan, 1924.

——, *Memoirs*, 3 vols. London, 1912–1914.

Crispolti, C., and Aureli, G., *La politica di Leone XIII da Luigi Galimberti a Mariano Rampolla*. Rome, 1912.

Cronin, F., *Social Principles and Economic Life*. Milwaukee, 1959.

Dansette, Adrien, *Histoire religieuse de la France Contemporaine*. Vol. II: *Sous la IIIème République*. Paris, 1951.

Debidour, Antonin, *L'Église catholique et l'État sous la troisième république, 1870–1906*. 2 vols. Paris, 1906–1909.

Del Guidice, V., *La questione romana e i rapporti fra Stato a Chiesa fino alla Conziliazione*. Rome, 1948.

Despagnet, Franz, *Le République et le Vatican, 1870–1906*. Paris, 1906.

Dondeyne, A., *Contemporary European Thought and Christian Faith*. Pittsburgh, 1958.

Doutreloux, V., *Lettre pastorale sur la question ouvrière*. Liége, 1894.

Duroselle, J. B., *Les Débuts du catholicisme social en France (1822–1870)*. Paris, 1951.

Eckhardt, Carl C., *The Papacy and World Affairs as Reflected in the Secularization of Politics*. Chicago, 1937.

Ellis, John Tracy, *The Life of James Cardinal Gibbons*, 2 vols. Milwaukee, 1952.

Engel-Janosi, Friedrich, *Oesterreich und der Vatikan 1846–1918*. 2 vols. Graz, 1958–1960.

Eyck, Erich, *Bismarck*. 3 vols. Erlenbach-Zurich, 1941–44.

Ferrata, Dominique Cardinal, *Mémoires*. 3 vols. Rome, 1920.

Fogarty, Michael P., *Christian Democracy in Western Europe, 1820–1953*. South Bend, 1957.

Fonzi, F., *I cattolici e la società italiana dopo l'unità*. Rome, 1953.

Foucher, L., *La philosophie catholique en France au XIXe siècle avant la renaissance thomiste et dans son rapport avec elle (1800–1880)*. Paris, 1955.

Franz, Georg, *Kulturkampf. Staat und Katholische Kirche in Mitteleuropa von der Säkularisation bis zum Abschluss des Preussischen Kulturkampfes*. München, n.d.

Giunta, Pietro Sinopoli di, *Il Cardinale Mariano Rampolla del Tindaro*. Rome, 1923.

Goyau, Georges, *Le Pape, les Catholiques et la question sociale*. Paris, 1893.

————, *Bismarck et l'église: le Kulturkampf*. 4 vols. Paris, 1911.

Gibbons, James, *Retrospect of Fifty Years*. 2 vols. Baltimore, 1916.

Guiccioli, Alexandre, *Quintino Sella*. Rovigo, 1887.

Guillemin, H. *Histoire des catholiques françaises au XIXe siècle*. Paris, 1947.

Gundlach, G., *Die sozialen Rundschreiben Leos XIII*. Paderborn, 1933.

Gurian, Waldemar, *Die politischen und sozialen Ideen des französischen Katholizismus 1789/1914*. München-Gladbach, 1928.

Gurr, J., *The Principle of Sufficient Reason in Some Scholastic Systems*. Milwaukee, 1943.

Hales, Edward E. Y,. *The Catholic Church in the Modern World*. Garden City, 1958.

————, *Pio Nono. A Study in European Politics and Religion in the Nineteenth Century*. London, 1954.

Halperin, S. William, *Italy and the Vatican at War. A Study of their Relations from the Outbreak of the Franco-Prussian War to the Death of Pius XI*. Chicago, 1939.

————, *The Separation of Church and State in Italian Thought from Cavour to Mussolini*. Chicago, 1937.

Hanus, Franciscus, *Die Preussische Vatikangesandtschaft 1747– 1920*. München, 1953.

Hayes, Carlton, J. H., *A Generation of Materialism 1871–1900*. New York, 1941.

Hocedez, E., *Histoire de la théologie au XIXe siècle*. 3 vols. Paris, 1947–52.

Hoog, Georges, *Histoire du catholicisme social en France*. Paris, 1942.

Houx, Henri de, *Souvenirs d'un journaliste français à Rome*. Paris, 1886.

Hudal, Alois, *Die Oesterreichische Vatikanbotschaft 1806–1918.* München, 1952.

Hughes, Emmet J., *The Church and Liberal Society*. Princeton, 1944.

Hughes, H. L., *The Catholic Revival in Italy, 1815–1915*. London, 1935.

Hughes, Philip, *The Pope's New Order. A Systematic Summary of the Social Encyclicals and Addresses from Leo XIII to Pius XII*. London, 1943.

Husslein, Joseph, *The Christian Social Manifesto: An Interpretative Study of the Encyclicals Rerum Novarum and Quadregesimo Anno of Pope Leo XIII and Pope Pius XI*. Milwaukee, 1931.

————, *The World Problem (Capital, Labor, and the Church)*. New York, 1919.

Italicus (pseudonym of Ernst Eduard Berger), *Italiens Dreibund- politik*. München, 1928.

Jacquin, R., *Taparelli*. Paris, 1943.

Jarlot, Georges, *Historia documentorum Ecclesiae de re sociale a Leone XIII ad Pium XIII*. Rome, 1955–6.

Jemolo, Arturo Carlo, *Chiesa e Stato in Italia negli ultimi cento anni*. Turin, 1955.

————, *Church and State in Italy 1850–1950*. Oxford, 1960. (Translation by David Moore of Jemolo's *Chiesa e Stato in Italia dal Risorgimento ad oggi*. Turin, 1955.)

Johnson, Humphrey, *The Papacy and the Kingdom of Italy*. London, 1926.

Karson, Marc, *American Labor Unions and Politics 1900–1918*. Carbondale, Ill., 1958.

King, Bolton, and Okey, Thomas, *Italy Today*. London, 1901.

Kissling, J. B., *Geschichte des Kulturkampfs im Deutschen Reich*. 3 vols. Freiburg-i-B., 1911–1913.

Kolbeck, M. O., *American Opinion on the Kulturkampf*. Washington, 1942.

Kothen, Robert, *La Pensée et l'action sociales des Catholiques, 1789–1944*. Louvain, 1945.

Langer, William L., *European Alliances and Alignments 1871–1890*. 2nd ed. New York, 1950.

————, *The Franco-Prussian Alliance 1890–1894*. Cambridge, Mass., 1929.

Latourette, Kenneth Scott, *Christianity in a Revolutionary Age*. Vol. I, *The Nineteenth Century in Europe: Background and the Roman Catholic Phase*. New York. 1958.

————, *A History of the Expansion of Christianity*. 7 vols. New York, 1937–1945.

Lecanuet, R. P., *L'Eglise de France sous la troisième République*. 4 vols. Paris, 1930–1931. I, *Les dernières années du pontificat de Pie IX (1870–1878)*; II, *Les premières années du pontificat de Léon XIII (1878–1894)*; III, *Les signes avant-coureurs de la séparation (1894–1910)*; *La Vie de L'Église sous Léon XIII*.

Lentner, L., *Die Grundlagen der modernen katholischen Soziallehre*. Vienna, 1952.

Leroy-Beaulieu, Anatole, *Les Catholiques Libéraux: l'Église et la Liberalisme de 1830 à nos jours.* Paris, 1885.

Leslie, Shane, *Cardinal Gasquet.* London, 1953.

Lorwin, Val R., *The French Labour Movement.* Cambridge, Mass., 1954.

MacCaffrey, J., *History of the Catholic Church in the Nineteenth Century (1789–1908).* 2 vols. St. Louis, 1910.

Magri, F., *L'azione cattolica in Italia (1775–1951).* 2 vols. Milan, 1953.

Manning, Henry Edward Cardinal, *The Dignity and Rights of Labour.* London, 1934.

Manfroni, Camillo, *Sulla Saglia del Vaticano.* Bologna, 1920.

Maréchal, Joseph, *Mélanges Joseph Maréchal.* 2 vols. Paris, 1950.

Maritain, Jacques, *The Social and Political Philosophy of Jacques Maritain.* Ed. by Joseph W. Evans and Leo R. Ward. New York, 1955.

————, *St. Thomas Aquinas.* Rev. ed. New York, 1958.

Massard, J., *L'Oeuvre social du Cardinal Mermillod et l'union de Fribourg.* Louvain, 1914.

Mater, André, *La Politique religieuse de la République Française.* Paris, 1903.

Matteis, Luigi de, *Non Expedit! Chiarimenti sul Non Intervento dei Cattolici Italiani alle Urne Politiche.* Naples, 1882.

Maurenbrecher, W., *Die preussische Kirchenpolitik.* Gotha, 1881.

McAvoy, Thomas T., *The Great Crisis in American Catholic History.* Chicago, 1957.

McNamara, Robert, *The American College in Rome 1855–1955.* New York, 1956.

Mollat, G., *La Question romaine de Pie VI à Pie IX.* Paris, 1932.

Moody, Joseph N., *Church and Society. Catholic Social and Political Thought and Movements 1789–1950.* New York, 1953.

Moon, Parker, *The Labor Problem and the Social Catholic Movement in France.* New York, 1921.

Mourret, Fernand, *Histoire Générale de l'Église.* 9 vols. Paris, 1918–1928.

Mun, Albert de, *Discours et Écrits divers*, ed. by Ch. Geoffroy de Grandmaison. Paris, 1893.

———, *Ma Vocation sociale*. Paris, 1909.

Neill, Thomas P., and Schmandt, Raymond H., *History of the Catholic Church*. Milwaukee, 1957.

Nell-Breuning, O., *Reorganization of Social Economy*. Milwaukee, 1937.

Nichols, James Hastings, *History of Christianity 1650–1950*. New York, 1956.

Nippold, Friedrich, *Einleitung in die Kirchengeschichte des neunzehnten Jahrhunderts*. 5 vols. Berlin, 1889–1906.

Nitti, Francesco S., *Catholic Socialism*, trans. by Mary Mackintosh from the 2nd Italian edition. New York, 1895.

Ollivier, Émile, *Solutions politique et sociale*. Paris, 1894.

Parsons, Reuben, *Studies in Church History*. 6 vols. New York, 1896–1901.

Parsons, Wilfrid, *The Pope and Italy*. New York, 1930.

Pastor, Ludwig von, *Tagebücher, Briefe, Erinnerungen*. Heidelberg, 1950.

Pietra, Angela, *Storia del Movimento Cattolico Liberale*. Milan, 1948.

Piola, A., *La questione romana nella storia e nel diretto da Cavour al trattato del Laterano*. Padua, 1931.

Piou, Jacques, *Le ralliement, son histoire*. Paris, 1928.

Pouthas, Charles, *L'Église Catholique de L'Avènement de Pie VII à l'Avènement de Pie IX*. Paris, n.d.

Procacci, V., *La questione romana. Le vicende del tentativo di conciliazione del 1887*. Florence, 1929.

Purcell, E. S., *Life of Cardinal Manning*. 2 vols. New York, 1896.

Raeymaeker, Louis de, *Le cardinal Mercier et l'Institut Supérieur de Louvain*. Louvain, 1952.

Raphaël, Paul, *La République et l'Église romaine de l'esprit nouveau à l'union sacrée*. Paris, 1948.

Reinarz, H., *Von Ketteler und Leo XIII. Der soziale Bischof und der soziale Papst des 19. Jahrhundert*. Düsseldorf, 1931.

Renard, R. P., *L'Église et la question sociale*. Paris, 1937.

Rimbault, P., *Histoire politique des congrégations religieuses, 1790–1914*. Paris, 1926.

Rivière, Jean, *Le Modernisme dans l'Église. Etude d'Historie Religieuse Contemporaine*. Paris, 1929.

Rollet, Henri, *Albert de Mun et le parti Catholique*. Paris, 1947.

——, *L'Action sociale des Catholiques en France (1871–1901)*. Paris, n.d.

Rosa, G. de, *L'Azione cattolica. Storia politica dal 1874 al 1904*. Bari, 1953.

Ruhenstroth-Bauer, Renato, *Bismarck und Falk im Kulturkampf*. Heidelberg, 1944.

Ryan, John A., and Husslein, J., *The Church and Labor*. New York, 1924.

Salata, Francesco, *Per la storia diplomatica della questione romana*. I. *De Cavour alla Triplice Alleanza*. Milan, 1929.

Salomone, A. W., *Italian Democracy in the Making*. Philadelphia, 1945.

Scaduto, F., *Guarentige pontificie e relazioni fra Stato e Chiesa*. 2nd ed. Turin, 1889.

Schilling, Otto, *Die Gesellschaftslehre Leos XIII. und seiner Nachfolger*. München, 1951.

——, *Die Staats- und Soziallehre Leos XIII*. München, 1925.

Schlözer, Kurd von, *Letzte Römische Briefe 1882–1894*. Stuttgart, 1924.

Schmidlin, Josef, *Papstgeschichte der neuesten Zeit*. 3rd ed. 3 vols. München, 1933–1936.

Schmitt, F. X., *Bismarcks Abkehr vom Kulturkampf*. Diss. Tübingen, 1930.

Schnabel, Franz, *Deutsche Geschichte im neunzehnten Jahrhundert*. Vol. 4, *Die religiösen Kräfte*. 2nd ed. Freiburg-i-B., 1951.

Simon, A., ed. *L'hypothèse libérale en Belgique. Documents inédits, 1839–1907*. Wetteren, 1956.

Snead-Cox, J. G., *The Life of Cardinal Vaughan*. 2 vols. London, 1912.

Spadolini, G., *L'opposizone cattolica*. Florence, 1954.

Stein, Edith, *Writings of Edith Stein*, trans. by H. Graef. Westminster, Md., 1956.

Stokes, Anson Phelps, *Church and State in the United States*. 3 vols. New York, 1950.

Thillet, L., *Les Doctrines politiques de Léon XIII*. Diss. Bordeaux, 1914.

Tournier, Jules, *Le cardinal Lavigerie et son action politique*. Paris, 1912.

Toutain, Edmond, *Alexandre III et la République Française*. Paris, 1929.

Turman, Max, *Le développement du Catholicisme social depuis l'encyclique Rerum Novarum*. Paris, 1909.

Van Riet, G., *L'epistémologie thomiste*. Louvain, 1946.

Vercesi, E., *Il movimento cattolico in Italia (1870–1922)*. Florence, 1923.

———, *Tre papi: Leone XIII, Pio IX, Benedetto XV*. Milan, 1929.

Vidler, Alec R., *The Modernist Movement in the Roman Church*. Cambridge, 1934.

Vigener, Fritz, *Ketteler, ein deutsches Bischofsleben des 19. Jahrhunderts*. München, 1924.

Vigo, Pietro, *Annali d'Italia; Storia degli Ultimi Trent' Anni del Secolo XIX*. Milan, 1908.

Ward, Wilfrid, *The Life of John Henry Cardinal Newman*. 2 vols. New York, 1912.

Weill, Georges J., *Histoire du catholicisme libéral en France, 1828–1908*. Paris, 1909.

———, *Histoire de la idée laïque en France au XIXe siècle*. Paris, 1929.

———, *Histoire du mouvement social en France, 1852–1924*. 3rd. ed. Paris, 1924.

Windleband, W., *Berlin, Madrid, Rom. Bismarck und die Reise des deutschen Kronprinzen 1883*. Essen, 1939.

Winter, Eduard, *Russland und die slawischen Völker in der Diplomatie des Vatikans, 1872–1903*. Berlin, 1950.

ARTICLES ON POPE LEO XIII

Abell, Aaron, "The Reception of Leo XIII's Labor Encyclical in America, 1891–1919," *The Review of Politics,* VII (1945), 464–495.

Alexander, Archibald, "Thomas Aquinas and the Encyclical Letter," *Princeton Review,* new series, V (January, 1880), 245–261.

Anon., "The Encyclicals of Pope Leo XIII," *The Atlantic Monthly,* LXXIII (May, 1894), 692–701.

Anon., "The Papal Encyclical on Labor," *The Andover Review,* XVI (1891), 175–178.

Anon., "The Pope's Encyclical," *The Andover Review,* V (1886), 75–79.

Baumgartner, A., "Bischöfliche Actenstücke des Cardinal-Erzbischofs Joachim Pecci von Perugia, jetzt Papst Leo XIII," *Stimmen aus Maria-Laach,* XVII (1879), 333–352, 479–496.

Bonansea, B., "Pioneers of the Nineteenth-century Scholastic Revival in Italy," *The New Scholasticism,* XXVIII (1954), 1–37.

Byrnes, Robert F., "The French Christian Democrats in the1890's: Their Appearance and Their Failure," *Catholic Historical Review,* XXXVI (1950), 286–306.

Calvez, Jean-Yves, "Association et corporation chez les premiers commentateurs de Rerum Novarum," *Chronique Sociale de France* (3 Dec., 1957), 647 ff.

Chabod, F., "Kulturkampf e Triplice Alleanza in discussione fra il Vaticano e il Governo Austro-Ungarico nel 1883," *Rivista Storica Italiana,* LXII (1950), 278 ff.

Claar, Maximilian, "Kardinal Rampolla als Staatssekretär und Papstwerber 1887–1903," *Europäische Gespräche,* VII (1929), 465–482.

Coleiro, Edward, "Leo XIII—A Modern Humanist," *Dublin Review,* CCV (1939), 344–360.

Collins, James, "Olgiati's Conception of Modern Philosophy," *Thought,* XVIII (1943), 478–504.

Ehrle, P. F., "Die päpstliche Encyklika vom 4. August 1879 und die Restauration der christlichen Philosophie," *Stimmen aus Maria-Laach,* XVIII (1880), 13–28, 292–317, 388–407, 485–498. Reissued by F. Pelster under the title *Zur Enzyklika "Aeterni Patris";* *Text und Kommentar.* Rome, 1954.

Engel-Janosi, Friedrich, "Aspects Politiques du Conclave de Léon XIII," *Rassegna Storica del Risorgimento* (1954), 360–365.

———, "Austria and the Conclave of 1878," *Catholic Historical Review,* XXIX (1953), 142–166.

———, "L'Autriche au Conclave de 1903," *Revue Belge de Philologie et d'Histoire* (1951), 1119–1141.

———, "L'Austria e il Vaticano durante la prima decade del pontificato di Leone XIII, 1878–1887," *Rivista Storica Italiana,* LXVI (1954), 348–376.

———, "The Resignation of Count Kálnoky as Foreign Minister of Austria-Hungary," *Journal of Central European Affairs* (1951), 259–278.

———, "Two Austrian Ambassadors Discuss the Successor of Pius IX," *Catholic Historical Review,* XXX, (1944), 1–27.

———, "Zwei Studien zur Geschichte des österreichischen Vetorechtes," *Festschrift zum 200 jährigen Bestand des Haus-, Hof- und Staatsarchivs,* II, Wien, 1951, 283–300.

Farrell, John T., "Background of the 1902 Taft Mission to Rome," *Catholic Historical Review,* XXVI (1950), 1–31, and XXVII (1951), 1–22.

Fenton, Joseph C., "The Teachings of the *Testem Benevolentiae,*" *American Ecclesiastical Review,* CXXIX (1953), 124–133.

Gargan, Edward T., "The Loyola Leo XIII Symposium," *Mid-America,* XLII (1960), 231–243.

Gaselee, Stephen, "British Diplomatic Relations with the Holy See," *Dublin Review,* CCIV (1939), 1–19.

Halperin, S. William, "Church and State in Italy during the Last Years of Pius IX," *Church History,* V (1936), 71–84.

———, "Italian Anticlericalism 1871–1914," *Journal of Modern History,* XIX (1947), 18–34.

Harnack, A., "Das Testament Leos XIII.," *Preussische Jahribücher,* LXXVII (1894), 321–342.

Heckel, J., "Die Beilegung des Kulturkampfes in Preussen," *Zeitschrift der Savigny-Stiftung für Rechtsgeschichte, Kanonistishe Abteilung,* L (1930), 215–353.

Hughes, Philip, "Leo XIII," *Dublin Review,* CCII (1938), 249–257.

Ireland, John, *et al.,* "Leo XIII, His Work and Influence," *North American Review,* DLXII (1903), 321–364.

Jansen, Bernhard, "Papsttum und Neuscholastik," *Stimmen der Zeit,* XXXVIII (1930), 321–337.

Jarlot, Georges, "Les Avant Projects de 'Rerum Novarum' et les 'Anciennes Corporations,'" *Nouvelle Revue Théologique,* LXXXI, 60–77.

Kleijntjens, J., "Paus Leo XIII en de eerste Haagse vredesconferentie, 1899," *Kultuurleven,* XVI (1949), 277–288.

Leroy-Beaulieu, Anatole, "Un Roi et un Pape—II. Pie IX et le Saint-Siège," *Revue des Deux Mondes,* 3rd ser., XXVII (1878), 388–422.

Lorenz, W., "Die Jugend Leos XIII.," *Stimmen der Zeit,* CLXV (1959/60), 415–423.

Lulvès, J., "Bismarck und die römische Frage," *Hochland,* XXVI (1929), 263–284.

Manning, Henry Edward Cardinal, "Leo XIII on the Conditions of Labour," *Dublin Review,* CIX (1891), 153–167.

Moody, Joseph N., "The Dechristianization of the French Working Class," *Review of Politics,* XX (1958), 48–69.

Murray, John Courtney, "Leo XIII; Government and the Order of Culture," *Theological Studies,* XV (1954), 1–33.

———, "Leo XIII: Separation of Church and State," *Theological Studies,* XIV (1953), 145–214.

———, "Leo XIII on Church and State: The General Structure of the Controversy," *Theological Studies,* XIV (1953), 1–30.

———, "Leo XIII: Two Concepts of Government," *Theological Studies,* XIV (1953), 551–567.

————, "The Problem of 'The Religion of the State,' " *American Ecclesiastical Review,* CCXXIV (1951), 327–352.

Novotny, Alexander, "Papst Leo XIII. und der Berliner Kongress," *Mitteilungen des Instituts für Oesterreichische Geschichtsforschung,* LXIII, 3–4, 565 ff.

Noppel, Constantin, "Rerum Novarum und Quadragesimo Anno," *Stimmen der Zeit,* CXXII (1932), 159–169.

Parker, Thomas M., "The Social Catholic Movement in France under the Third Republic," *Catholic Historical Review,* I (1921), 24–34.

Pesaro, A. A. di, "La Diplomazia Vaticana e la Questione del Potere Temporale," *Rassegna Nazionale.* (1890), 89, 114–118.

Shea, George W., "Catholic Doctrine and 'The Religion of the State,' " *American Ecclesiastical Review,* CXXIII (1950), 161–174.

Spahn, M., "Der Untergang des Kirchenstaats und Leo XIII," *Hochland,* X (1912–1913), 47–61.

Stutz, Ulrich, "Die päpstliche Diplomatie unter Leo XIII. nach den Denkwürdigkeiten des Kardinals Domenico Ferrata," *Abhandlungen der Preussischen Akademie der Wissenschaften, 1925, Phil-hist. Klasse* (1926), Nr. 2–4, 65 ff.

The Thomist, V (1943).

Ward, Wilfrid, "Leo XIII and Anglican Orders," *Dublin Review,* CLI (1912), 94–117.

Woodward, E. L., "The Diplomacy of the Vatican under Popes Pius IX and Leo XIII," *Journal of the British Institute of International Affairs* (May, 1924).

Woywod, Stanislaus, "Record of the Transfer of the Remains of Pope Leo XIII from St. Peter's to the Lateran Basilica," *Homiletic and Pastoral Review,* XXV (1924–25), 529.

Vagnozzi, Egidio, "The University and the Truth that Will Prevail," *The Catholic University of America Bulletin,* XXVII (1959), 7–8.

Viereck, Peter, "The Revolution in Values: Roots of the European Catastrophe, 1870–1952," *Political Science Quarterly,* LXVII (1952), 339–356.

Notes on Contributors

KENNETH SCOTT LATOURETTE was born in Oregon City, Oregon on August 9, 1884. He received his Ph.D. from Yale in 1909 and has subsequently been awarded 13 honorary degrees. In 1910 he became a member of the faculty of Yale-in-China at Changsa, China. Returning to the United States in 1912, he was a lecturer in history (1914–1915) and then Associate Professor of History (1915–1916) at Reed College, Oregon, followed by a professorship at Denison University. He returned to Yale as D. Willis James Professor of Missions in 1921 and retired in 1953 as Sterling Professor Emeritus in Missions and Oriental History. In 1947 he was President of the American Historical Association and has also served as President of the American Baptist Foreign Missions Society and the American (Northern) Baptist Convention. Among his many books are: *Development of China; Development of Japan; The Chinese, Their History and Culture;* the seven-volume work, *The History and Expansion of Christianity;* and most recently, the multivolumed *Christianity in a Revolutionary Age: A History of Christianity in the Nineteenth and Twentieth Centuries.*

REV. JOSEPH N. MOODY was born in New York City on April 18, 1904. He received his Ph.D. at Columbia University in 1934. He served as head of the Department of History, Cathedral College, New York City, from 1933 to 1941 and from 1945 to 1956. He was Chairman of the Department of History and Political Science, Notre Dame College, Staten Island, New York, from 1935 to 1940 and from 1945 to 1956. In 1955 he was Vice-President of the

Society for French Historical Studies. He is Pastor of Sacred Heart Church, and Professor of History at Ladycliff College in Highland Falls, New York. Among the journals he has contributed articles to are the *Commonweal* and *The Review of Politics.* Monsignor Moody has edited the volume, *Church and Society: Catholic Social and Political Thought and Movements, 1789–1950.*

ARCHBISHOP EGIDIO VAGNOZZI was born in Rome on February 2, 1906. He received doctorates in philosophy, sacred theology, and canon law from the Lateran Pontifical Seminary in the Eternal City. He received a special papal dispensation for early ordination shortly before his 23rd birthday. He served as an official in the Papal Secretariat of State at the Vatican from 1930 until 1932 when he was named a monsignor and assigned to the American Papal Delegation in Washington, D.C. Before his appointment as the seventh Apostolic Delegate to the United States in 1958, Archbishop Vagnozzi served in the Lisbon, Paris, Indian, and Philippine delegations.

S. WILLIAM HALPERIN was born in Kaunas, Lithuania, on January 11, 1905. He received his Ph.D. from the University of Chicago in 1930. Since that year he has taught at the University, where he is currently Professor of Modern History. In 1945 he served as head of the history branch of the Biarritz American University, one of the overseas universities established by the United States War Department. He is editor of *The Journal of Modern History.* Professor Halperin's publications include *Separation of Church and State in Italian Thought from Cavour to Mussolini, Italy and the Vatican at War,* and *Germany Tried Democracy.*

REV. ERIC McDERMOTT, S.J., was born in Manchester, England, on May 21, 1911. He studied at Heythrop College in Oxfordshire and did Honours work in history at the University of

London and at Oxford. Since 1950 he has been Professor of History at Georgetown University. He is the author of *The Life of Thomas Stapleton, 1535–98* and has contributed articles to the Encyclopaedia Britannica, *The Historical Bulletin, Theological Studies,* and *The Catholic Historical Review.*

REV. THOMAS T. McAVOY, C.S.C., was born in Tipton, Indiana, on September 12, 1903. He received his Ph.D. from Columbia University in 1940. In 1929 he became Archivist of the University Archives at the University of Notre Dame and is now Professor of History at the University. Father McAvoy served as head of the history department from 1939 to 1960. He is managing editor of *The Review of Politics* and the author of *The Catholic Church in Indiana 1789–1834* and *The Great Crisis in American Catholic History, 1895–1900.*

JAMES COLLINS was born in Holyoke, Massachusetts, on July 12, 1917. He received his Ph.D. at The Catholic University of America in 1944, and was a Research Fellow in Philosophy at Harvard University in the year 1944–45. Now a Professor of Philosophy at Saint Louis University, Dr. Collins was President of the American Catholic Philosophical Association in 1953. Among his writings are *The Existentialists, The Mind of Kierkegaard, A History of Modern European Philosophy,* and *God in Modern Philosophy.*

REV. GUSTAVE WEIGEL, S.J., was born in Buffalo, New York on January 15, 1906. He received his Ph.D. degree from the Gregorian in 1931 and an S.T.D. from that institution in 1938. He served as Professor of Dogmatic Theology at The Catholic University of Chile from 1937 to 1948 and was Dean of the Theology Faculty during the years 1942–48. Since 1948 Father Weigel has been Professor of Ecclesiology at Woodstock College, Maryland.

His publications include *A Survey of Protestant Theology in Our Time, A Catholic Primer on the Ecumenical Movement,* and *Faith and Understanding in America.*

EDWARD T. GARGAN was born in New York City on February 25, 1922. He received his B.A. from Brooklyn College and his Ph.D. from The Catholic University of America. He was Instructor of American History in the Graduate School of Boston College from 1949 to 1952. In 1953 he joined the Department of History at Loyola University, Chicago, where he is now Associate Professor of Modern European History. He is the author of *Alexis de Tocqueville: The Critical Years 1848–1851* and he edited the volume *The Intent of Toynbee's History: A Cooperative Appraisal.*

RAYMOND H. SCHMANDT was born in Indianapolis, Indiana on September 20, 1925. He attended Saint Louis University and received his Ph.D. from the University of Michigan. Since 1958 he has been a member of the Department of History at Loyola University in Chicago. He is co-author of *History of the Catholic Church.*

Date Due